MEMOIRS OF THE

CATHOLIC UNIVERSITY

OF AMERICA

Memoirs

OF
THE CATHOLIC UNIVERSITY
OF AMERICA
1918 - 1960

By

Roy J. Deferrari, *oseph* *1890-*

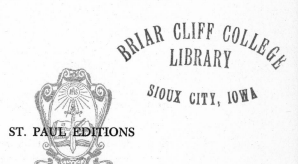
ST. PAUL EDITIONS

Library of Congress Catalog Card Number: 62-12453

Copyright, 1962, by the *Daughters of St. Paul*

Printed in U.S.A. by the *Daughters of St. Paul*
50 St. Paul's Ave., Jamaica Plain, Boston 30, Mass.

FOREWORD

When, at some future date, the historian shall assume the task of writing the biography of our National Pontifical University during the mid-twentieth century period of its life, it is well within the mark to say that the name of him, whose memoirs are herein contained, shall appear upon well nigh every page.

Doctor Roy J. Deferrari, a native of the Archdiocese of Boston, derived his academic background at Dartmouth College and Princeton University. He joined the Faculty of The Catholic University of America, as Professor of Greek and Latin, shortly after the Armistice of 1918. With this University he has been associated during forty-two of its seventy-two year life-span. He served under six of the nine Rectors, whom it has pleased the Holy See, during the course of the years, to designate as its chief administrative officer. With the passage of each succeeding decade, his ever-increasing responsibilities have kept pace with his ever-mounting contributions, as scholar, professor, and administrator.

Few among the Trustees of the University in both past and present; few among his many associates in the several Faculties of the University; few, save his most intimate friends and those closely involved in his manifold projects, have ever been aware of the tremendous scope of his academic activities and the enormous sphere of his influence.

During his early years, Doctor Deferrari's foresight and experience were beyond value, while he played a prominent part in the reorganization of the entire University. As a consequence, The Catholic University of America abandoned the European scheme of University organization in favor of a plan more suited to the needs of America. During this process, the several accrediting agencies of our nation were coming into their own. For these last three decades Doctor Deferrari has been the most influential Catholic liaison with our American system of accreditation. It is no small measure due to the freshness of his vigor and the buoyancy of his enthusiasm that The Catholic University of America remains the sole Catholic institution of higher learning within our shores retaining membership in the Association of American Universities, the group of North American institutions of higher learning, concerned with advanced instruct. in the field of Graduate Study.

Besides his important role in establishing and retaining the closest kind of contact between The Catholic University of America and her great sister Universities across our continent, Dr. Deferrari's personal efforts in developing the University's program of Affiliation, which grows wider with each academic year, have carried his influence to our Catholic Senior and Junior Colleges, to the Teacher Training Schools of our many Religious Communities, to our Schools of Nursing, and even to the Catholic secondary school system of our nation.

On the University campus, as Dean of the Graduate School of Arts and Sciences, as Director of the Summer Session, and above all, as Secretary-General, not to make mention of his sponsorship of several new schools and departments within the University, Doctor Deferrari has addressed himself to project after project, occasioned by the changing conditions of American life, during these many years. Few, indeed, are the areas of University effort which failed to become fast quickened by his dynamic determination.

The stamp of Doctor Deferrari shall long be felt by our National Pontifical University, by our American Catholic School System, and by the Church in our beloved country. His has been an unique Apostolate, realistic, competent, respectful of tradition, yet ever ready to change in the light of the successive needs of our time. In evaluating our Catholic educative effort, both on the University and on the national level, he praises those features which have borne fruit, and he criticizes those phases which he believes capable of improvement. His warnings are poignant and phrased in measured language, for after his years of educational experience, he has realized that the man, the nation or the institution, which places its privileges above its responsibilities, soon loses both. His suggestions are those of the wise man, whose days have well been spent in advancing the cause of the Faith that is so dear to his heart.

May God continue to bless with the best of His good things this great teacher, whose long life of "yeoman's service" to Catholic Education has been so clearly characterized by truly filial devotion to Christ and His Church!

+Richard Cardinal Cushing.
Archbishop of Boston

INTRODUCTION

Many people in recent years have urged me to write my recollections of the University. Before deciding to do so I asked myself a number of pertinent questions, the most important of which was: "What good will such a book do?" First and most important of all I hope that it will contribute to the completeness and accuracy of the history of the University when it was passing through a very important period of transition. Except for the actions and deliberations of the Board of Trustees, I have had first hand information on probably most of the important events of the years from 1925 to the present (1960). During this period I have been in one capacity or another a continuous member of the Academic Senate. Archbishop James Hugh Ryan was my close friend, and he confided in me greatly during his rectorship when most of the events of transition took place or got their start. In addition I hope that the reading of these recollections will give pleasure at least to the members of the University family, especially those who have lived through the more hectic days of the period of transition and whom the Lord has spared until today. All persons interested in the University will rejoice to see the tremendous advances made by our institution between 1925 and 1960.

It should be said also that it has been necessary to make a selection of the large amount of material that accumulated so rapidly as soon as the writing of these recollections was begun. It can only be hoped that my selection of this material has been wise. The basis of the selection has always been: "To what extent have I myself been connected with the event?" It may not always be clear that I am in the midst of things, but it may be assumed that if I were not, the matter would not be discussed in this book.

Every effort has been made to be honest and accurate. I have also been frank, for what would "Recollections" be without the quality of frankness? Yet at the same time serious thought has been given to being prudent and not to hurt the feelings of anyone. If these efforts have failed to any degree, I am very sorry. In a work of this kind, the temptation is great to express personal opinions. In this I have indulged to some extent. It must be remembered that these opinions are personal and not necessarily wise.

My narrative, as will be seen, follows a topical arrangement chiefly, and includes the years of 1918, the year of my first appointment, to 1960, the year of my retirement. Under each topic sub-topics are treated chronologically for the most part. On occasions other considerations have caused me to break this order.

Since writing the words above and after listening to the appraisal of my Memoirs by a number of my friends, I feel obliged to write the following supplementary remarks. Two of these readers advised me not to publish this work for reasons which I cannot accept.

First of all I must insist strongly on the value of these Memoirs for a more complete and accurate history of the University.

Words of caution have been expressed that several persons mentioned are still living and may take offense. Certainly I do not wish to offend anyone. At the same time it seems to me that all trustworthy persons should be willing to be reported or quoted provided that they are reported and quoted correctly. No society is going to prosper greatly if it does not promote frank and honest discussion. I am sure that I have been frank and I am convinced that I have been honest.

Some also have expressed displeasure at the occasional insertion of my personal views on university policies. If these opinions have no value they can easily be discarded, and no harm will be done. If they promote serious discussion and thought on the planning for the future, this will serve a good purpose. Certainly one who has lived and labored for nearly a half century within a single institution of higher education should be permitted to give his views on policies which he considers beneficial or detrimental to that institution.

The writing of this book has been a source of great pleasure. May the reading of it transmit some of this pleasure to others.

ROY J. DEFERRARI

October 20, 1960

TABLE OF CONTENTS

THE CATHOLIC UNIVERSITY

OF AMERICA, DECEMBER, 1918

The possibility of going to The Catholic University of America was first presented to me toward the end of World War I by Professor Paul van den Ven. Professor van den Ven was one of several professors of the University of Louvain who came to the United States and were received on the faculties of the leading American universities after the University of Louvain, including its priceless library, had been destroyed by the invading Germans. In addition to holding his post at Princeton as Professor of Byzantine History, he had been assigned by the Belgian government to establish and conduct a public relations office in Washington for his country, and for this purpose spent every week-end in the Capital City.

While in Washington it was quite natural that he should visit his fellow scholar and friend, Professor Henri Hyvernat, at The Catholic University of

America. While visiting Professor Hyvernat, he learned of the death of Dr. John B. O'Connor, Professor of Greek and Latin, at the University, and immediately thought of the possibility of my filling that vacancy, since I was on the point of being discharged from the 814th Aero Squadron, stationed at Princeton.

Up to this time I had heard very little about The Catholic University of America. One incident, however, regarding the University, which had been related to me, stuck in my mind and deserves repeating here. When Woodrow Wilson felt compelled to take the unprecedented step of declaring and carrying on war upon the soil of a European country, Germany, Cardinal Gibbons immediately rallied to his support, and offered him the complete plant of the University. As is fairly well known, the Federal Government did take over the newly completed Martin Maloney Chemical Laboratory where, under the direction of the Reverend Dr. J. Griffin, the deadly lewisite gas was developed. [1] President Wilson was most pleased by this immediate expression of loyalty on the part of the Cardinal, and had occasion to recall it a little later. Imprudent Americans within the District of Columbia, the seat of government, were a great problem from the first, and some of these were located at The Catholic University of America. The United States secret service discovered them and was ready to take action. When the matter came to the attention of

[1] Incidentally, the present Professor Henry Peter Ward was an assistant in the Department of Chemistry at this time.

Woodrow Wilson, he is reported to have said: "I have been president of a university for some years, and I think that I know the kind of faculty member involved here. Let me have the evidence and I will take care of it." The President did just that, and nothing more was ever heard of the matter. All this was learned from my old professor and good friend, Edward Capps, who later became Minister to Greece under his close friend, Woodrow Wilson. After I had been at the University for several years, Professor John Parker, Head of the Department of Biology, who had been in the Federal Secret Service during the war, verified the account.

Through Professor Hyvernat it was arranged that I should go to Washington for an interview with Bishop Thomas J. Shahan, then Rector of the University. I shall never forget my first impressions of the University. I arrived at the front entrance near Albert Hall, then in flaming red brick, and was directed across the campus to Caldwell Hall and the apartment and office of the Rector. It was a bleak walk indeed. All the paths across the campus were "paved" with ashes from the central heating plant and from which no one had taken the trouble even to eliminate old cans and other forms of debris. There was scarcely a tree in the entire expanse, but there were several cows tethered where our glorious Shrine is now approaching completion.

I have often wondered what Bishop Shahan thought of me when I first came into view in my buck private's khaki uniform of the United States

Army Air Corps and with all of my twenty-eight
years. At any rate the Bishop, as always, was most
kind. When we soon discovered our common interest
in the Greek and Latin Fathers we were presently
occupied in a pleasant and to me stimulating
conversation.

Just before leaving Princeton, I had been offered a renewal of my instructorship in Greek and
Latin, which would be accompanied by a light
teaching load of about nine hours a week and an
opportunity to continue research in one of the best
university libraries in the world under the continued
advice and guidance of the very learned and friendly Dr. van den Ven. Over against this I had to weigh
another instructorship in Greek and Latin, this one
accompanied not by a light undergraduate teaching
program but by the headship of the entire two-fold
department, with graduate students in both fields to
direct in dissertation work as well as to teach in
courses, and with *two* assistants, Drs. Thomas J.
McGourty and Patrick Collis, for undergraduate
teaching only. The proposed salary was certainly
not a very great inducement—$1800.00 a year! I
was however, greatly impressed by the sincere and
solid scholarship of many members of the faculty
whom I met. I believe that in all colleges and universities a certain amount of superficial and insin-
cere talk is to be found centered around the subject
of scientific scholarship; it seemed to me that there
was very little of this at The Catholic University of
America. It should be added that throughout its

history, the University has always had a significant number of genuinely sincere and outstanding scholars, who have given it at all times a truely university character. The informality of the scholarly life of the institution, although it has many times since been a source of annoyance to me, proved very attractive to me then. Furthermore, the opportunity to associate with the University's scholars, men like Dr. Romanus Butin and Monsignor Hyvernat, and the freedom which I was promised to develop the Department of Greek and Latin were also very pleasing. The job was a distinct challenge, and it was accepted almost on the spot. My contract was to run from December 9, 1918.

The following letter was discovered recently in the Archives of the University:

December 9, 1918

Dr. Joseph Dunn
Dean, School of Letters
McMahon Hall

DEAR DR. DUNN:

I have this day appointed Dr. Roy J. Deferrari of Princeton as Instructor in the Department of Greek and Latin. Doctor Deferrari will act until further notice as head of both departments, and as such will also take charge of the Latin and Greek Libraries.

Very sincerely yours in Xto.,
(Signed) THOMAS J. SHAHAN
Rector

Bishop Shahan suffered much from this appointment, as he told me later. Some members of the hierarchy on the Board of Trustees asked him: "Was it necessary to get a layman to be the head of the Department of Greek and Latin? There must be a number of the clergy available for the job." And Bishop Shahan told me that he answered them: "Show me one priest with Dr. Deferrari's training and experience(!), *who is available*, and I shall appoint him tomorrow."

Discharge from the Air Corps took place on December 22, and after spending a few days with my family, I arrived on the University campus on the day after Christmas, to take up my residence in a room in Graduate Hall. I was eager to begin my work. A few amazing experiences, however, awaited me at the very beginning, not the least of which was the enormous and numerous rats that at that time infested Graduate Hall. Then too I was met by a University professor, who in the spirit of fatherly kindness begged me for my own good to take up my career elsewhere. He said: "Deferrari, you are a young man, single and able to move about easily, don't stay and get settled here. This is no place for a layman! This is distinctly a place for the clergy. You will get nowhere here!" Another faculty member, this one a priest, said: "I want no better proof of the holiness of the Catholic Church than the fact that the authorities of this University can make so many mistakes and the University still survive!"

Although I discovered the Library in the southern corridors of the first floor of McMahon Hall, west of the Registrar's office, I sought vainly for entrance to the quarters of my department, then located as until recently, on the second floor of McMahon Hall in the extreme western end but on the south side only. I could find no one who had a key that would admit me. After three days of wasted time, Mr. Joseph Schneider, then University Librarian, found a key which fitted and which he was willing to let me have.

At last an entrance had been effected to my domain. What was discovered within it was in the main a joy. My predecessors twice removed, Dr. George M. Bolling and Dr. John D. Maguire, had bought many excellent books. There was an excellent basic collection for carrying on graduate as well as undergraduate work. In addition, across the hall from me was the departmental library of Semitic Languages and Literatures under the stimulating custodianship of Dr. Arthur A. Vaschalde and Dr. Romanus Butin. Then too, Bishop Shahan put no restriction on my purchasing of books. At least he did not for three or four years, until after I had abused this great privilege by spending between four and five thousand dollars annually. The slightly discouraging factor was the utter disarray of those valuable books. They were piled up on tables and scattered on shelves, and covered with a thick layer of dust. The next week or ten days was a period of constant cleaning and organizing, but after that all was ready for business.

GENERAL REORGANIZATION

Reorganization of the University

When Monsignor James H. Ryan assumed the rectorship of the University in 1928, one of his first considerations was to reorganize the institution along American lines. His initial move was to make the Summer Session an integral part of the University, not a part of the Sisters College migrating to the University campus for six weeks during July and August. [1] Much more important than that, however, he was thinking of a complete structural change which was put into effect in the second year of his administration.

From the beginning until the arrival of Monsignor Ryan the organization of the University was markedly of European origin, based chiefly on the plan of the University of Louvain, which took no consideration of what is known in the United States

[1] Cf. Summer Session.

as undergraduate instruction. In the leading countries of Europe there is a sharp line of demarcation between so-called university work and previous studies leading to a preparation for university work, as, for example, the gymnasium and the lycée, which are usually regarded as the equivalent of two years of college study in this country. University studies consist of work offered in professional schools and in general research. [2] Furthermore, the line of demarcation between the studies of the gymnasium and its equivalent is kept sharply defined by central government control.

In our country, with its highly desirable freedom in education, conditions are quite different. The American college is a varied thing. The only academic feature which the colleges in the United States all have consistently in common is a curriculum of four years duration. What is studied in those four years is far from standardized. Consequently, any university that has striven, as several including our own have, to be strictly devoted to graduate studies has been obliged to give undergraduate work for three chief purposes: (1) to permit students to make up undergraduate deficiencies before entering upon truly graduate work, (2) to have a means of training undergraduates from the beginning in the way in which its graduate departments wish them to be trained, and (3) at the same time

[2] The plan attempted recently at the University of Chicago is similar.

to provide a reliable source of young students for its graduate departments. This is the answer to the often repeated question and criticism of The Catholic University of America: "Why did the University ever take on undergraduate curricula when it should have confined itself strictly to truly university work?" This explains also why the University in its effort to follow a European system was obliged to add undergraduate studies, in spite of itself, to the different schools originally designed with no thought of lower studies. It explains the almost hopeless confusion that resulted. Some would like to have us believe that the sole reason for undertaking undergraduate instruction was to increase the financial income of the University. It may well have been a contributing factor. It is to be hoped that it will not become an increasingly dominating factor. The reasons given above would in any case have been compelling sooner or later.

In those early days of the University, its Schools of the Sacred Sciences, which included Sacred Theology and Canon Law, involved no problem of organization, since they were on the graduate level only. The rest of the University, however, consisted of schools with both graduate and undergraduate divisions: The School of Sciences; the School of Philosophy, including Social Work; the School of Letters; the School of Engineering, including Architecture; and the School of Law. Obviously, there was much confusion here, especially on the undergraduate side. Entrance requirements in the various undergraduate and, to some extent, graduate sections differed. Students shifted from one to another at will. Regulations pertaining to expulsion varied. Even requirements for graduation were far from uniform.

Monsignor Ryan planned chiefly along vertical lines, with a College of Arts and Sciences as an independent unit which would include all the undergraduates not in professional schools, and with a Graduate School of Arts and Sciences, closely connected with the College, independently established but cooperating with it. The professional schools were to be considered as units independent of one another and independent of the College and Graduate School of Arts and Sciences. This, of course, did not exclude one school from servicing another with courses strictly within its own province. If a professional school were to give undergraduate courses and degrees, as for example the School of Engineering and Architecture, it would have an undergraduate division. This type of vertical organization prevails in the United States today, e.g., Harvard University. Another type of arrangement, which may be called horizontal, gathers all graduate work, professional and general, into one graduate school with that simple designation rather than a graduate school of *arts and sciences*. Within this second scheme, all undergraduate work is divided into the College of Arts and Sciences and into the undergraduate divisions of the professional schools where the professions do not require a baccalaureate degree for admission. The disadvantage of this second plan is the inevitable strife that arises between faculty members devoted strictly to the liberal arts and those occupied rather with the applied arts or professional studies.

The University then began its reorganization under Monsignor Ryan according to the vertical plan, with the following schools resulting:

(1)   the School of Sacred Theology;

(2)   the School of Canon Law;

(3)   the School of Law;

(4)   the Graduate School of Arts and Sciences, which at that time included a Department of Philosophy (later to be established as a separate school), instruction in Social Work within its Department of Sociology, and several years later also work in Nursing Education as a part of its Department of Psychology and Psychiatry;

(5)   the School of Engineering and Architecture;

(6)   the National Catholic School of Social Service, established downtown and for women only; [3]

---

[3] The connection of this school with the University was always rather nebulous. It was essentially independent except for the fact that many of our teaching staff taught there, and the University granted the degrees on recommendation of the students by the faculty of the National School of Social Service to the University's Academic Senate. When I became Dean of the Graduate School of Arts and Sciences and Father Karl Alter was Director of the N.C.S.S.S., at the request of the Rector we developed a working plan which in a definite way made the School more of an integral part of the University than it had ever been before. After Father Alter left the institution, however, this plan was not completely continued.

(7)   the College of Arts and Sciences; and

(8)   the Summer Session.

The accepted procedure in forming a school was for a field of study to be set up as a part of a regularly established department or as a "division" until it was strong enough to be made a department or a school by itself, according as it was regarded as a profession or not. It will be seen that Monsignor Ryan followed this principle, believing that the university organization most prevalent in this country was also the most effective. Thus our present day Schools of Philosophy, of Social Work, and of Nursing grew out of this procedure. In this connection it should be noted that then, as well as now, the University authorities used the term "division" in a sense peculiar to themselves. In American academic circles a division is a collection of closely related departments, such as the natural sciences or the social sciences, united for the purpose of organizing courses in subject matter of common interest without undue overlapping, and also with a view to giving students comprehensive direction in programs of study that cut across two or more related departments. At The Catholic University of America, however, a division is a potential department or school not strong enough to operate independently as a department or a school and thus dependent on another department in its administrative operation.

In most instances, however, Monsignor Ryan, in his attempt to organize the University according to the prevailing American plan, endeavored to develop procedures and to employ academic terms at the University in the manner generally recognized. A survey of the practices of the member institutions of the Association of American Universities showed that the term "lecturer" was regularly used for all part-time teachers of whatever status and indicated that such appointees were not recipients of the privileges and so-called "fringe benefits" of the regular members of the teaching staff. On the other hand, the terms instructor, assistant professor, associate professor, and professor indicated full-time appointees with all the privileges pertaining to the rank. Under Monsignor Ryan, the University authorities adopted this arrangement, and subsequent administrators have followed this scheme, although an occasional variation has been allowed to creep in.

Monsignor Ryan suffered very severe criticism within Catholic circles for his interest in having the University organized along American lines. He was charged, even in some high places, with trying to *decatholicize* the University. This, of course, was quite absurd because organization of whatever sort could not very well affect the teachings and doctrines enunciated in the classrooms. In spite of such criticism, however, the new organization survived, and after three years Monsignor Ryan felt that he could write (November 16, 1931) in part as follows about the success of his reorganization:

> The increasing recognition accorded Catholic University in learned and university circles is

proof of the vitality of our institution. The Department of Latin, Psychology, and Semitic Languages are recognized as the best in America. Other departments are given equal rank with those of long established universities. We have some weak points but plans are in existence to correct them. Important departments which do not exist will be established at the earliest possible moment. As a matter of fact, the educational program for the next ten years has already been mapped out and received the approval of the Board of Trustees, and will become concrete reality, if our campaign for added endowment is a success. [4]

Monsignor Ryan was also greatly encouraged in this by the receipt of a letter from His Eminence, the Cardinal of Boston:

November 16, 1931

Right Reverend James H. Ryan, S.T.D.
Catholic University
Washington, D.C.

DEAR MONSIGNOR RYAN:

I wish to acknowledge receipt of your communication of November 13th, and hasten to assure you that I am always happy to be of service to the University.

I really feel that the University is at last on the right track and I sincerely hope that the

[4] Cf. "Aide Memoire." See School of Sacred Theology.

Board of Trustees and Officers of the University will cleave to the course of action it has outlined.

With every best wish for the success of the University, I am

Very sincerely yours,

(Signed) W. CARD. O'CONNELL

Abp. Boston

Additional evidence of the success of the reorganization was the development of the Division of Social Work of the Department of Sociology into an independent professional School of Social Work. Also during the rectorship of Bishop Ryan the program in nursing education was established as a separate school. Neither of these changes conflicted in any way with his organizational philosophy. When Monsignor Joseph M. Corrigan assumed the rectorship in 1936, the Department of Philosophy also became a separate school, and its courses of study received Pontifical approval on March 7, 1937. As far as the general plan of the University was concerned, this too was not a drastic change, since ecclesiastical authority definitely regarded the field of philosophy as a sacred science, and thus of a professional nature and worthy of independent status.

Monsignor Corrigan, however, after much wavering, made up his mind to cut off the Departments of Sociology, Economics, and Politics from the Graduate School of Arts and Science and to form them into a School of Social Science. I personally felt at that time, as I have felt ever since, that this was a mistake. The fields of sociology, economics, and politics are not the only subjects that come under the general heading of social science; nor are they necessarily the most important. Then why select these three for a special school? I thought that I had convinced Monsignor Corrigan that this move was unwise, but the pressure from other sources, the same as those which attempted to persuade Monsignor Ryan to establish such a school rather than the School of Social Work, was too great. This change was a direct violation of the principles on which the 1928 reorganization was made.

The chief reason given for establishing the School of Social Science was Pope Pius XI's then recent pronouncements on the fostering of social studies among our Catholic educational institutions. However, His Holiness said nothing about the establishment of a separate school of social science; although he did name sociology, economics, and politics as social sciences. Social studies could be fostered through departments just as well as by independent schools. Another defense of the move, which continues to be brought up occasionally, is that the establishment of such a school is a return to a carefully worked out plan in the early history of the University. A careful reading of the catalogues of the University will show, however, that the School of Social Science of that very early period was set up strictly as a temporary measure and was therefore of very brief duration.

When Monsignor Corrigan first made this change there was great confusion. Apparently, the

intent was for the new School to take over completely the already existing School of Social Work.
The distinction between the two schools was
evidently not very clear in Monsignor Corrigan's
own mind or in the minds of those who urged
him to take this step. Moreover, such a move
meant the elimination of the existing Dean of the
School of Social Work, an experienced and highly
respected social worker. This was done rather
summarily, although the injustice was largely re-
paired in the course of subsequent years. The great
difficulty arose from the Association of Professional
Schools of Social Work, so-called at that time,
which was conducting all accreditation in that field.
This group let it be known in no uncertain terms
that its accreditation of the School of Social Work
would be withdrawn if it were to be replaced by
any such school as that contemplated. Since the
School of Social Science could not in any sense of
the word be called a professional school, it was
then decided to establish a completely distinct
School of Social Science with Monsignor Francis J.
Haas as Dean and to allow the School of Social
Work to proceed as it was. By this time, however,
after all these maneuverings, Social Work was in
dire straights. It had no dean, and the powerful and
interested Advisory Board composed of the Directors of Charity of the various dioceses had lost
confidence in the direction of the School. They
were not very enthusiastic about supporting it.

Early in the rectorship of Monsignor Patrick J.
McCormick a special committee was appointed by

the Board of Trustees to consider the advisability of abolishing the School of Social Science and of returning the departments of which it was composed to the Graduate School of Arts and Sciences. I recall that Father James M. Campbell, Father James A. Magner, Monsignor Edward B. Jordan, Father Paul Hanley Furfey (representing the School of Social Science), and myself were on that committee. There may have been one or two others besides the Rector himself, who served as chairman, whom I do not recall. At any rate, the Committee voted unanimously for the abandonment of the School and the return of its departments to their original places. This report was never presented to the Board of Trustees, and nothing more was done about it.[5]

The reason why it was not presented to the Board of Trustees is clear and fairly well-known. Archbishop Ryan had not attended the meetings of the Board of Trustees for some years after he had been transferred to the Archdiocese of Omaha, but on the insistence of many of its members that they needed and wanted his help and guidance, he had again started to attend. The problem of the School of Social Science came up at that time, and Archbishop Ryan made a very elaborate report in which he too recommended the abolishment of the School and the return of its departments to the Graduate School of Arts and Sciences. It was on that

[5] It is interesting to note that this move was actually made for the academic year of 1961-62.

occasion that the Board of Trustees appointed the special committee already mentioned. But Archbishop Ryan had made the "mistake" of not consulting the Rector, Monsignor McCormick, on the problem before he made his report. The Rector, therefore, had no intention of letting the matter come up again before the Board, if he could prevent it.

Thus the University continued until the academic year 1961-1962 with the organization established by Bishop Ryan and modified by Bishop Corrigan. There seems now to be a need for the establishment of one and possibly two new schools. One is a School of Fine Arts, composed of the Departments of Art, Music, Speech and Drama, and Architecture. As regards the last department, however, there may be cogent arguments for retaining it within the School of Engineering and Architecture, depending on the specific aims of the Department. There is also a growing demand, at least within the Department of Education, for a professional school of education. In the not too distant past, I was strongly of the opinion that such an arrangement was undesirable because of the tendency that might grow of emphasizing the purely professional aspects of the field. But today it has become *necessary* for this department to stress those phases of education. Members of the hierarchy and superiors of religious groups are in increasing numbers sending men and women to the Department of Education to be trained as superintendents and supervisors of school systems and to fill other similar professional posts. Furthermore, the Department as a part of the Graduate School of Arts and Sciences is having difficulty, as is to be expected, in getting a proper understanding on the part of the faculty as a whole of the nature and importance of its professional work. This leads to what the Department of Education regards as the placing of obstructions in the way of developing its professional educational studies. In any case, if separate schools are to be established in these areas, it would seem that they should be regarded as strictly professional schools, with undergraduate and graduate divisions, thus properly fitted into the original structural organization of the University as envisioned by Bishop Ryan. [6] However, it must be added that the Department of Education has not as yet seemed strong enough to operate as an independent school.

[6] It should be noted here that it was Bishop Ryan's idea, when he reorganized the University, to stress graduate and postgraduate studies, the latter including the professional schools for which a general undergraduate training is required. He planned a College of Arts and Sciences of limited enrollment (about 500) of highly selected students who might be expected to go on for still higher studies. This would eliminate a rather common complaint that the University was duplicating the work of many good Catholic colleges and that in the annual collection for the University dioceses were contributing to the development of an institution which would be in direct competition with their own institutions of higher education. This principle, however, has not been maintained. The undergraduate portion of the University appears to be expanding without limit. This we believe to be most unfortunate, chiefly because it diverts so much of the University's resources from its first and most important aim: the development of a truly outstanding university in the best sense of the phrase. Such a task involves the gathering of a faculty of preeminent scholars. This is a never ending process and one of constantly increasing expense. Unfortunately, it cannot be said that our University has made any outstanding progress in this respect during the last generation or more.

The Office of the Secretary General
and the Registrar

The Office of the Secretary General had been in existence off and on throughout the early history of the University, but its duties had never been more definitely defined than in the very general terms of the statutes. The present description as given in the most recent and now permanent statutes represents very well the thinking of the Congregation of Seminaries and Universities on this office through the years. As will be seen, the work of the Secretary General is closely linked with that of the Registrar. The statutes of this office read as follows:

> Art. 34. The Secretary General of the University is chosen and appointed by the Rector, after consulting with the Academic Senate, from among the Professors. It is necessary, however, that his appointment be approved by the Board of Trustees.
>
> The Secretary General holds office for a period of two years and may be re-appointed.

Dr. Thomas S. Carroll, at his recent (May, 1961) inauguration exercises as President of George Washington University, remarked that he wanted to make a truly outstanding university out of his institution, one worthy of the Capital of the nation. He stated further that a university of this calibre as yet did not exist! In my opinion, this statement is essentially correct, but under proper direction, The Catholic University of America can be made such in a comparatively short time.

Art. 35. It is the duty of the Secretary General to take care of correspondence with other Universities, Colleges, and Institutions, and to attend to all matters entrusted to him by the Board of Trustees, the Rector, or the Academic Senate. Art. 36. The Secretary General shall be assisted by the Registrar, who is appointed by the Rector.

No effort was made to describe the duties of this office in any greater detail until the rectorship of Bishop Corrigan. Furthermore, no appointee was ever relieved to any significant extent of his regular professorial duties so that he could devote himself seriously on approximately a full-time basis to the Office of the Secretary General. From the wording of the statutes it might be assumed that the professor so appointed was expected to act as Secretary General over and above performing his duties as a professor. Professor Aubrey E. Landry once held the post and was given a desk in the Vice Rector's Office, at the same time sharing the clerical service of the Vice Rector's secretary, but no one was very much aware of what his responsibilities really were. Certainly the Secretary General did not make himself felt in the daily life of the University, and the office became essentially vacant most of the time.

Bishop Ryan tried to revive the post when he appointed Professor Richard J. Purcell as Secretary General. Here again the specific duties of the office were not stated, a vital necessity for the success of the holder of the post. The incumbent, furthermore, did everything possible to transfer such duties as he had been assigned to the Dean of the Graduate School of Arts and Sciences. Moreover, he succeeded in this so well that the Rector very logically asked himself: "What is the Secretary General as such doing anyway?" When he could find little or nothing, he promptly abolished the office.

The Office of Secretary General was restored in the statutes of the University which came into existence at the beginning of Monsignor Corrigan's rectorship. Determined to place it on a solid and permanent basis, the Rector consulted me on the matter. I urged strongly that he appoint Dr. Martin R. P. McGuire as Dean of the Graduate School of Arts and Sciences in my place and nominate me to the Office of Secretary General of the University. After some discussion he agreed to the proposal. There were many considerations, chiefly of a personal nature, which prompted me to put forth this suggestion. Briefly, my first years as a university administrator had been extremely arduous, especially because I was subjected to more than ordinary criticism which had been difficult both for my family and me to endure. I was anxious for a change. Although the criticism was quite unjust, it was understandable in part in universities, since university faculties in general do not like change, and condemn changes on principle.

Accordingly, on October 18th, 1937, I received the following letter from Monsignor Corrigan:

DEAR DR. DEFERRARI:

Under the new Constitution, the Secretary General of the University is obliged to assume responsibilities not previously included in the duties of this position. Searching for a member of the faculty of the required experience and capacity, I have come to the conclusion that you are the available man.

I have hesitated to offer you this position as its duties will make it impossible for you to continue as Dean of the Graduate School. It would not interfere, however, with your teaching schedule or with your supervision of the Summer Session.

I will be glad to take up with you the various duties belonging to this office, if you decide to accept. May I say that, counting on the unfailing co-operation which I have received from you since coming to Washington, I am hoping that your decision will be to accept the position?

With every best wish, I am

> Sincerely yours,
> (Signed) JOSEPH CORRIGAN

It was, of course, necessary to formulate the duties of the Secretary General in detail. The Rector finally agreed to the following tentative arrangement:

The Secretary General was to have charge of all academic records; to represent the University at important academic functions; to take part in promotional work; to have supervision of the printing of the Announcements of the University,

Commencement programs, leaflets dealing with courses offered, and other publications; to have the supervision of the making out and the distribution of diplomas; to act as Chairman of the Committee on Fellowships, Scholarships, and Student Aid; to have charge of the language examinations; to act as Director of the Summer Session; to take care of general University correspondence, especially that dealing with other institutions of higher learning; and to undertake whatever else might be assigned to him by the Rector of the University. To the Registrar was specifically assigned the task of caring for the semester registrations, and of directing the promotional work of the College of Arts and Sciences and of the School of Engineering and Architecture, also of cooperating with the Secretary General whenever possible. [1]

Over the years these duties have shifted somewhat and additional work has been taken on by both the Secretary General and the Registrar. The work of the University's program of affiliation and extension, which has become a tremendous activity, has always been associated with the Secretary General, at least since its reorganization and expansion in 1938. Under Bishop McCormick's rectorship, the chairmanship of the Senate's standing Committee on Faculty Appointments and Promotions was also given to the Secretary General, [2] and in 1946 the program of workshops

[1] Cf. Report of the Secretary General in *The Rector's Report for* 1937-38.
[2] Cf. Appointments and Promotions of the Faculty.

was initiated by the Secretary General and soon became a major operation attached to his office. [3] On the other hand, the immediate responsibility of academic records, the supervision of the printing of most of the Announcements of the University, and the making out and distribution of diplomas have been given over to the Registrar. In addition, the enormous task of the chairmanship of the Committee on Undergraduate Admissions, involving the College of Arts and Sciences, the School of Engineering and Architecture, and the School of Nursing, was given to the Registrar. While the Registrar has very properly refused to accept the responsibility of directing the promotional work of these undergraduate schools, the Registrar continues to contribute to this work very extensively. Other numerous details of the two offices might also be mentioned, but I believe that those already given set forth the main lines of demarcation between the two parts of the Secretary General's province.

Originally, all the work of the two offices was included in the one office of the Secretary General, with an office-manager acting as the Assistant Secretary General or Registrar. This so-called office-manager was Miss Catherine Rich. By right of the duties she was performing, I felt that she should have been named Registrar of the University. However, when I so presented her case to the Rector, Bishop Corrigan, early in his administration,

[3] Cf. Workshops.

for some reason or other he became terribly incensed and emphatically stated: "I shall never appoint a woman to any position of importance in the University!" This seemed rather absurd, since many of the institutions of higher education in the land at that time had women registrars, among them St. Louis and Fordham Universities.

Instead, the Rector appointed a male member of the teaching staff as the official Registrar, but failed to relieve him of any of his professorial duties. Obviously, he could not devote full time to both jobs, and each of the two jobs really required the full attention of a competent person. The result was that Miss Rich continued to do the work of the Registrar, including the answering of all correspondence addressed to that office. The official Registrar showed up in the office irregularly for a few minutes to sign the letters which she had composed. This absurd situation, however, did not last long. The Registrar in name only resigned from that post, and the Secretary General's office reverted to its previous state. The Secretary General with the aid of Miss Rich took care of the business of both offices, and all correspondence and documents requiring an official signature were signed by the Secretary General. When Monsignor Patrick J. McCormick became Rector and the facts were presented to him, he immediately appointed Miss Rich as Registrar of the University. This was one of the very first acts of his administration.

Thus far no mention has been made of the Registrar of the University whose duties I took over as part of the first responsibilities of the Secretary General; nor has anything been said about the Registrar who preceded him and was officially the second Registrar [1] of the University. It may very well be conceded that they both in their manner served the University as well as they could, but it must be maintained that neither was a representative university registrar. Many stories are still in circulation regarding the second Registrar. I recall that when I was making every effort to procure a chapter of Phi Beta Kappa for the University, a representative of that organization visited us to make the required evaluation. He asked to be brought to the Registrar's quarters for an examination of the records. When I brought him there and explained his mission, the Registrar turned his back on us and said gruffly: "No one is going to examine my records!"

Also while I was Dean of the Graduate School, I was in despair over the incomplete and at times entirely missing academic records. I asked permission of the Rector to keep my own records, which request Monsignor Ryan readily granted. Upon my making this known to the Registrar, he remarked: "Take them over, but you will never be able to get the members of the faculty to turn in any grades!"

[1] The first Registrar of the University was Dick Robinson, the son of Judge Robinson, the first dean of the University Law School.

Stories about the other Registrar are not so numerous and of quite a different character. It is worthy of note, however, that in his regime the Registrar's office took on the appearance of a swanky receptionist's parlor, with fine carpets and vases of flowers properly placed here and there, hardly a place where the extensive business of a university registrar would be expected to be carried on.

The present incumbent, Miss Catherine Rich, entered upon her responsibility with good training. She not only has regularly attended the meetings of the American Association of Collegiate Registrars and those of the Registrar's Section of the Middle States Association of Schools and Colleges, but she has also taken an active part in their deliberations, having been appointed to the top-most positions in the two groups. She has also published extensively in this field of university administration. In short, Miss Rich has given the University the representation in the outside academic world which it deserves and needs and which it had never enjoyed before.

In the academic year 1948-49, a complete renovation of the Secretary General's office was accomplished, making a sharp distinction between the quarters of the Registrar and those of the Secretary General. The duties of both have continued to be carried on very much as if in one office, and the same cooperation exists. There is, however, the additional advantage of a more definite establishment of responsibilities.

At the same time, Miss Rita Watrin became Assistant to the Secretary General and manager of the Secretary General's part of the office. Miss Watrin, as my assistant and in charge of my immediate duties, has been indispensable. It would be most ungracious on my part did I not mention her devoted work in carrying on the work of affliliation and extension, especially the testing program for secondary schools. Furthermore, she has an exceptional genius for organization. As irrefutable proof of this, I point to the arrangement of the Secretary General's office in all its ramifications.

The chart in Appendix 1 will give a clear picture of the Secretary General's Office and its activities as evolved from the time when it was first definitely established by Monsignor Corrigan, until the time of my retirement, the academic year 1960-1961.

Here again great changes have taken place. With my retirement (1961), the duties and quarters of the Registrar were distinctly separated from those of the Secretary General. The work of the Summer Session and the Workshops were placed under a Director, Dr. Robert Paul Mohan S.S. The activities of Affiliation by an exception to the regular practice with respect to retirements were continued under my direction, although I am officially in retirement. Most of the remaining duties of the Secretary General as defined above were given over to my successor in that office, Dr. George Rock. Each of us three has been provided with a separate office and staff.

SCHOOLS

The Summer Session

The Summer Session was first established in 1911. The following is taken from the minutes of the first faculty meeting of the Summer Session:

> July 23, 1911. The Faculty of the Summer Session of the Catholic University held its first meeting on Sunday, July 23, at 10:30 A.M. in the Senate Room, McMahon Hall, the Very Rev. Dean, Thomas E. Shields, presiding. There were present: the Rt. Rev. Rector; Doctors Pace, McCarthy, Turner, Landry, Weber, Moore, Furger, Francis Schneider, and McCormick, Fathers Gabert, O'Connor, Wagner, Hoey, Marcetteau, Messers Doolittle, Crook, Teillard, Hemelt, Parker, Joseph Schneider, and Miss Maguire.

I quote also from a Summer Session faculty meeting held in 1912:

> July 9, 1912. A meeting of the faculty of the Second Summer Session of the Sisters College

was held today, the Very Rev. Dean, Dr. Shields,
presiding . . . .

Upon motion of Dr. Lennox it was voted that
the Administration be respectfully requested to in-
stall at least two noiseless electric fans in every
classroom and it was further noted that the
Administration be respectfully requested to furnish window screens for all of the classrooms.

I could not resist quoting this last paragraph. It is
just about as applicable today as it was then! As of
1961 the classrooms have no screens, but a limited
number of fans were provided in certain cases for
the first time in 1957.

My real purpose, however, in quoting these
minutes is to show that the Summer Session started
off as an operation of the University proper, and in
its second year became an activity of the Sisters
College, as Mr. Charles Fox Borden, the second
Registrar of the University, had always insisted.
The Summer Session continued through the year
of 1928 as a part of the Sisters College, primarily
for Sisters doing undergraduate work. A few laywomen were admitted each summer, almost never
as candidates for degrees but as special students
seeking instruction in a few specific courses.

In 1929 Monsignor Ryan, Rector of the University, established the Summer Session as an
integral part of the University and appointed me as
its Director. Monsignor McCormick, who had been
the Director following the first Director, Dr.
Shields, had resigned as he wished to use the summer periods for purposes of rest. Needless to say,

there was strenuous opposition on many sides to this new appointment. First of all, Monsignor McCormick had expected to be asked to suggest his successor. His choice probably would have been Monsignor Jordan; thus the tradition of the Department of Education conducting the Sisters College and the Summer Session would have been maintained. All the members of the Department of Education therefore naturally disliked Bishop Ryan's choice. Others objected professedly on the ground that I was a layman, and that the Sisters, who at that time essentially made up the entire student body, would not only protest but would even stay away en masse.

I immediately restudied the objectives of the Summer Session and reestablished them as follows:

(1) to supplement the work of the regular year whenever desired by the University authorities:

> (a) to facilitate the completion of work by graduate and undergraduate students in accelerated time (Catholic teachers throughout the country constitute a large number of this group), and
>
> (b) to enable students to meet requirements which they could not meet or should have met in the preceding academic sessions here or elsewhere, e.g., fulfillment of prerequisite courses, taking care of previous conflicts in courses in students' schedules, removing grades of incomplete and failure;

(2) to offer refresher courses to persons long engaged in particular academic or professional activities;

(3) to offer persons not interested in degrees or credits but in their own self-improvement alone an opportunity to achieve this at the national center of Catholic culture; [1]

(4) to act as the University's experimental station for new courses and programs, for the purpose of enriching the course offerings of the regular academic year and of ascertaining the desirability of new schools and departments;

(5) to test possible faculty members (experienced persons) who might be added to the regular faculty; and

(6) to bring distinguished teachers and scholars from other institutions of higher education to teach here during the summer.

Two administrative changes were also made which had a great effect on the character of the Summer Session and did much to stimulate its growth:

(1) all persons, men or women, religious or lay, on meeting the academic requirements would be admitted to the Summer Session; and

(2) the Master's degree, which hitherto, like all other degrees granted at the University, required at least one full academic year of residence at the University, could now be earned in a minimum of five summer sessions of residence.

The second of these changes was indeed a great concession. The authorities of The Catholic

[1] There has been and is some local opposition to this objective, but I regard it as unjustifiable. A former director of the Summer Session at Harvard University, Dr. Cotton Mather, regularly boasted about the emphasis which his summer session placed on this aim. Furthermore, the Association of Deans and Directors of Summer Sessions has always accepted this as a very proper objective.

University of America had always been unyielding
in their requirement of an actual regular year (two
semesters) minimum residence for every degree in
spite of the prevailing practice nationally of permitting the equivalence in summer sessions or even
a certain total of semester hours of credit, however
earned. No additional changes have ever been
made in this policy.[2] Only a terrific struggle
in the Academic Senate, supported by the Rector,
was able to bring this about.

From time to time special curricular features,
not as yet adopted in the regular semesters, were
added: e.g., the program of the Confraternity of
Christian Doctrine, the training of teachers for the
visually handicapped and the hard of hearing, a
Workshop on Intergroup Education, and a Family
Life Institute. Non-credit courses also have been
offered to fill specific needs: e.g., the Preachers
Institute, the Institute of Catholic Social Action,
the Journalism Institute for High School Students,
the Yearbook Short Course, Speech and Drama

[2] An apparent change should be mentioned here. In 1958 the
degree S.T.B. was granted to students in affiliated theological seminaries
who had passed an examination as presented by the School of Theology
of the University. This is distinctly an un-American practice, granting
a degree to a student on the basis of an examination and without
spending any time in residence at the University, and it is being continued. This was done, however, with the approval of the Commission
on Institutions of Higher Education of the Middle States Association of
Colleges and Secondary Schools. As a matter of fact, this was a revival of an old practice begun early in the history of the University
but discontinued in the first years of the rectorship of Archbishop Ryan.
It should be also stated that this approval was granted verbally to me
by the then chairman of the Commission on Institutions of Higher
Education of the Middle States Association of Colleges and Secondary
Schools, Dr. Ewald Nyquist.

Laboratory for High School Students, and the Music Laboratory for Elementary and High School Students.

It should also be recorded at this point that the present departments and divisions of Library Science, Art, Music, and Speech and Drama were first established and carried on in summer sessions only. A Master's degree program in business education and courses in special education are still given only in the Summer Session.

As a result largely of these innovations and changes in policies and programs, the growth of the Summer Session has been most remarkable. By November 16, 1931, when the Summer Session was about to enter upon its second year under my direction, Monsignor Ryan saw fit to write as follows regarding it in his "Aide Memoir." [3]

In 1929 the Summer School had 350 students. In 1930 I placed the Summer School in charge of Professor Roy J. Deferrari. That year the attendance was 755. In 1931, 891 students attended and 80 additional courses were offered. The prospects for 1932 ensure an attendance of at least 1,100. The increase in attendance and the popularity of our Summer School are due almost exclusively to the energetic promotion of Professor Deferrari, who, by letter and personal visit, urges it upon Religious Communities of Men and Women. It is scarcely necessary to add that the Summer School has increased the prestige of the University, both in and outside the Church.

[3] Cf. School of Sacred Theology.

Attention should also be called to the steady growth of the Summer Session from a small body of approximately 350 women undergraduate students to a large session more characteristic of the regular semesters of the University, both as to number and as to the predominance of graduate students. It has become more like a regular session of the University also in that its enrollment is made up of men and women, religious and lay, not of women alone and these chiefly Sisters. The chart in Appendix 2 shows these enrollment trends very clearly.

The comparatively large number of special students is composed of the following: (1) those undergraduate students, whose homes are for the most part in the local area and who during the regular academic year are candidates for degrees in other institutions, wishing during the summer session to make up deficiencies or to gain additional knowledge and training, especially in Catholic doctrine; and (2) those undergraduates and graduate students, who are not interested in degrees and usually not in academic credit, wishing either to refresh and bring their knowledge up-to-date or simply to have the benefit of new information for its own sake. These latter are for the greater part religious from various parts of the country. All these students represent an activity characteristic chiefly of a summer session rather than of a regular semester. This activity, moreover, is almost universally recognized by directors and deans of summer sessions as very important and quite proper for a summer session of a university.

The Summer Session Branches

A distinctive feature of the reorganized Summer Session was the development of the so-called branches of the Summer Session. These branches represent an attempt to project the work of the Summer Session into areas which lack such facilities and whose people could come to the University proper only at great trouble and expense. In other words, this is an attempt on the part of the University to fulfill better its obligations as The Catholic University of *America*. Thus far the work has been restricted to a limited number of departments, usually three or four, and to the program of the Master's degree. The departments selected are determined by the needs of the locality as expressed by the administrators of the housing institution, after consultation with the Director of the Summer Session.

The application for a branch summer session is initiated by the Ordinary of the diocese in which the host institution is located and proceeds in the name of the host institution to the Rector of the University. Moreover, the host institution must have been accredited by its regional association of schools and colleges. In each case, the institution has also been affiliated with the University. All this is to guarantee the necessary basic equipment, especially library facilities, for the operation of the branch.

These branches represent an honest attempt on the part of the University to operate on the campuses of other institutions which have invited them there. They are not mere paper arrangements, unfortunately rather common of late, whereby the local institutions may operate on a level or in a sphere for which they are not properly fitted or for which they may not even have legal sanction. Some educators have difficulty in understanding this, and on occasions completely misunderstand it. Moreover, the plan is entirely original with us and has been worked out after much deliberation and experience. Also, it has received the approval of all educators who really have understood it. It has even been imitated in a very superficial way and thus without success.

The regular students in the branches are working toward Master's degrees. The requirements for admission are the same as for the University as a whole. While the Master's degree may be earned in as few as five summer sessions, the tendency toward a longer period grows. In each branch summer session, as in the main session in Washington, the modern language examinations, the Graduate Record Examination, qualifying examinations for students entering the Department of Education, and comprehensive examinations are administered

through the close cooperation of the branch directors, the office of the Director of the Summer Session, the Registrar's office, and the Deans' offices
in Washington.

During the course of the Summer Session the
branch directors forward to the Director of the
Summer Session in Washington all admission forms
and academic credentials, the applications for
admission to candidacy for the Master's degree,
applications for approval of dissertation topics, the
dissertations to be read and approved, and final
copies of dissertations with their summaries. All
this material is transmitted to the proper graduate
school with a letter of transmittal, a carbon of which
is kept as a record in the Summer Session office.
These are acted on by the respective deans and
department heads, and the response of these officers
with regard to each item is sent to the branch director concerned, a copy of which is given to the
Director of the Summer Session for his files. Summer programs and course offerings are regularly
planned through joint consultation of the branch
director and the Director of the Summer Session
with the heads of the University departments involved. It should be noted also that whenever
possible members of our regular faculty teach at the
branches and that visiting teachers are invited to
do so only as the need arises and qualifications
permit. At the end of the session, each branch
director submits a final general report to the Director of the Summer Session. All student grades and

records of the branches are kept in the Registrar's office in Washington. Only these are official, and accordingly official transcripts of students' records may be issued only by the Registrar of the University in Washington.

The following are the branches of the Summer Session with the dates of their establishment and, in three cases, the dates of closing. All others are still in operation.

BRANCH	LOCATION	FOUNDED	CLOSED
Pacific Coast Branch	Dominican College of San Rafael, San Rafael California	1932	
Midwest Branch	Loras College, Dubuque, Iowa	1934	
Southern Branch	Incarnate Word College and Our Lady of the Lake College, San Antonio, Texas	1935	Our Lady of the Lake College withdrew in 1951
Memphis Branch	Siena College, Memphis, Tenessee	1941	1946
Chicago Area Branch	Rosary College, River Forest, Illinois	1945	1954
Tulsa, Oklahoma City Branch	Benedictine Heights College, Tulsa, Oklahoma	1956	1958
Toledo Branch	Mary Manse College, Toledo, Ohio	1959	

It should be noted that when the Southern Branch was founded it was bilocated. While it was administered from Our Lady of the Lake College in San Antonio, only several of the departments were located there. The others were operated at Incarnate Word College a short distance away in the same city. In 1951, the authorities of Our Lady of the Lake College saw fit to withdraw, and those of Incarnate Word College requested permission to carry on the entire Branch within their own institution. This permission was granted by the administration of the University.

The authorities of Rosary College, after the Chicago Area Branch had operated there for ten years, requested permission to withdraw from their agreement with the University, on the ground that their region seemed sufficiently well supplied with opportunities to do graduate work under Catholic auspices. Because there seemed to be no need in their area for such a branch, the agreement was terminated.

The Memphis Branch was quite different from all the others. First of all, it offered only undergraduate courses and was devoted to the improvement of the training of elementary school teachers. The Catholic Committee of the South, consisting in part of the diocesan school superintendents of the South, carried on a survey of their elementary Catholic schools and felt that they should do something to strengthen them. They called upon the University to carry on a branch of its summer session somewhere in an institution of higher education in the South in order to offer the necessary courses for this purpose. Siena College in Memphis, conducted by the Dominican Sisters who have their motherhouse in Springfield, Kentucky, was chosen as the host institution. The relations of the University with Siena College were always most cordial and cooperative. The controlling members of the Catholic Committee of the South, however, were never quite satisfied with their place in the triangle. The authorities of the University felt that the Committee made the request for the branch but that the University granted the request by completing arrangements for it with Siena College. The form of agreement was entered into by the University and Siena College alone. Both the University and Siena College, however, expected the Catholic Committee of the South, since they had requested that the branch be set up, to cooperate by directing students to the branch and by any other helpful means in their power. Unfortunately, the Director of the Branch, while he was appointed by the University authorities and was paid by them, felt that he owed his allegiance and cooperation to the Catholic Committee of the South. To be sure, he had been recommended to the University for the position by the Committee and was himself the superintendent of Catholic schools in a large eastern diocese. Academically, I believe much good was done, but naturally troubles arose over jurisdictional questions.

Finally early in the spring of 1946, I became alarmed since I had heard nothing about the approaching summer session from either the Catholic Committee of the South or the authorities of Siena College. I wrote to Sister Raymunda, Dean of Siena College, to see what the cause of the silence was. Her answer explained all. It seems that the Catholic Committee of the South with the cooperation of the Director of the Branch and without any communication of any kind with the authorities of the University, least of all with myself, the Director of the University's Summer Session, and ignoring the agreement between the University and Siena College, had withdrawn the branch from Siena College and had located it at Loyola University in New Orleans. Very naturally, Sister Raymunda was at first very much hurt by the affair, since she had thought that the University authorities were fully aware of the entire transaction and had given it their approval. Actually, they were entirely in the dark about the whole matter. It seems also that the Committee had not even consulted their episcopal chairman on the change of location. The position of the University was quite clear. Being responsible, as it was, for the quality of the courses and for the granting of college credits under its own name, it could not very well share this responsibility with any such group as the Catholic Committee of the South. At any rate, the work did not prosper even in its new location and has long since come to an end.

When the project of a branch of the Summer Session, to be located at Dominican College of San

Rafael and to be devoted exclusively to graduate work, was first proposed (in the early 1930's) and I was asked to think the matter through and work out the details, the thought immediately came to me that such a project, if confined to summer sessions alone, would not be sufficiently worthwhile. If graduate studies under the direction of The Catholic University of America were sufficiently important to Catholic educators on the Pacific Coast to be brought all the way across the Continent for summer sessions, they must certainly be doubly needed during the regular year as well. Accordingly, I began to speak and write about the possibility of establishing branches of graduate studies under the auspices of the University, both in San Francisco and St. Louis, during the regular year also. My thought was that the University would find it increasingly difficult, as the country developed and its population increased, to serve as The Catholic University of America while located completely in the far East.

Certain difficulties, however, soon appeared to put an end to this thinking. The plan was taken seriously in the Archdiocese of San Francisco, especially by the late Bishop O'Dowd, but the first and most formidable stumbling block was the tremendous initial expense involved, to say nothing of the substantial endowment necessary to take care of the unavoidable deficit incumbent on any graduate program properly executed. Then too, even with the availability of the needed funds, it would be difficult indeed to obtain both adequate faculty and administrative personnel. Finally, Monsignor James H. Ryan, Rector at the time, told me to make no further mention of the idea, but to stick to the summer branch plan. The Sacred Congregation of Seminaries and Universities, he said, was still impressed by the difficulty which the University had had in getting financial support in its early days and also by the failure in other parts of the world of attempts to establish more than one national papal university in a single country. Furthermore, because of this feeling, the Congregation had recently refused Cardinal Mundelein's request to establish a papal university at Our Lady of the Lake Seminary.

Through my efforts over the years to spread the work of the University and Catholic education throughout the land, I have come to the conclusion that branches and extension centers are only temporary measures, and that it is a mistake to think of them in terms of permanent establishments. By far of greater and more lasting value is the work of affiliation. As will be seen from my description of this activity, [4] institutions are aided to stand on their own feet and to be independent. In this way strong Catholic schools and colleges are established on a truly firm basis and may expand and grow freely. By a branch or extension center, if the need increases to any great extent, necessary growth and expansion are hindered and curtailed. Moreover,

[4] Cf. page 131.

the rise and development of important institutions are checked. The Catholic University of America cannot serve in its national capacity by attempting to function directly as the University for all Catholics of the nation. This is impossible for many reasons, financial and otherwise. It will perform its national function best, in my opinion, by developing on its present site the best possible Catholic university within its resources, and, in the manner exemplified by "Affiliation," by assisting in the setting up and encouragement of all kinds of independent Catholic educational institutions throughout the land. Thus, if in any region the need of a Catholic university is paramount, a beginning may be made through the extension or the branch, but the Catholic authorities of that region should take steps to found their own university, and the Catholic University should give all assistance possible out of its long experience by advice and leadership.

Before closing this section something should be said about the relationship of the University with the Catholic Summer School of America located at Cliff Haven on Lake Champlain in the State of New York, long since departed. To restrict myself to the academic phase of this project, it cannot be said that this institution ever strictly enjoyed any administrative connection with the University at any time. It will be recalled that the Catholic Summer School of America was primarily a summer resort where lectures of a popular nature were given, at times by eminent speakers. It was always clear, moreover, that people went to Cliff Haven primarily for rest and relaxation, not to hear the lectures. When first established this summer school enjoyed great prosperity. This kind of intellectual summer resort, however, soon lost its popularity throughout the country. With this trend the Catholic Summer School of America faced very hard times.

From time to time members of the University teaching staff gave lecture series at this resort. I myself on two different occasions spoke on the Fathers of the Church. I cannot say that my lectures were very well attended. In fact, I recall very vividly one summer being scheduled to speak immediately following his Excellency, Bishop Fulton Sheen, and seeing a packed hall quickly divest itself of its audience except for possibly twenty-five hardy souls. On occasions some one of the University administration was elected a member of the Board of Trustees of the Catholic Summer School of America, but, of course, all this did not officially tie the two institutions together.

In 1940, shortly after Monsignor Corrigan became Rector of the University, Monsignor Michael J. Splaine, who was at that time a member of the University's Board of Trustees and also Director of the Cliff Haven Summer School, approached him with a plan whereby the University would offer college courses at Cliff Haven for academic credit. On Monsignor Splaine's part this was an effort to bolster the sagging fortunes of the Catholic Summer School of America. Monsignor Corrigan, on the other hand, as he told me himself, was attracted by the thought that many persons of great wealth were frequenting the Cliff Haven resort, and some of them might be interested in the University sufficiently to give it money. Accordingly, I was summoned to the Rector's Office and told to plan and proceed with the project. My opinion was not asked regarding it. Indeed, neither of the two prime movers had a very definite idea of what he wanted, other than that the one wanted more vacationers at Cliff Haven and the other was looking for more contributions for the support of the University.

I had a faint recollection that the Catholic Summer School of America had been chartered by the New York State Board of Regents and was entitled by law to grant academic credit and even degrees. Obviously, my first task was to ascertain exactly what this status was. An appointment was soon made to meet with a representative of the Regents, Mr. Conroe, in a hotel in New York City. Incidentally, I waited in the hotel nearly a whole day. Mr. Conroe had nearly forgotten his appointment. He did not care to talk at any length about the academic powers and privileges of the Cliff Haven Summer School. Apparently, strictly under the law the early founders had obtained such but these had never been exercised. It was obviously farcical to attempt to revive them and use them now, at least with the resources at hand. Mr. Conroe, however, had no objection to the University's moving in there and giving courses for academic credit on its own, if it saw fit to do so.

The next step was to inform Bishop Francis J. Monaghan, the Ordinary of the Diocese of Ogdensburg, within which the Summer School was located, of what was being planned. At the same time it was hoped that the Bishop would encourage students, both religious and lay, to attend the classes. I spent a very pleasant day and night with Bishop Monaghan discussing the matter. While he pledged his full support, I cannot say that either of us was very sanguine about the possibility of the success of the project.

We made every possible effort to establish at least the beginning of a good program. An attempt was made to set up a working library out of the books in storage at the Summer School itself. It was not, of course, exactly an up-to-date library, and no money was available to make it such, but a librarian was appointed to service the books. A group of teachers was also recruited from the University staff. But in spite of the support of the Bishop of Ogdensburg and others, very few students appeared for instruction. The entire project was a dismal failure from every point of view, and it succumbed at the end of the first summer. As a matter of fact, it very obviously should not have been started at all, as I told Bishop Corrigan at the very beginning.

The Catholic Sisters College

When the Very Reverend Dr. Thomas Shields inaugurated the Catholic Sisters College in 1911, he started a kind of educational institution very novel indeed for the time. It was to be a four-year college for Sisters only. A least one year of this period, and this the last, had to be spent in residence on the campus of the Sisters College. The most shocking feature of the curriculum at the time was just that: the candidate for the bachelor's degree, a Sister, had to spend a full academic year away from her convent!

It should be said that the Sisters College was actually started in the chapel of the Benedictine Convent on Monroe St. between 9th and 10th Streets, Northeast. It was not until two years later that the present site of the Sisters College, at Eighth and Varnum Streets, Northeast, was purchased and the first building, Brady Hall, was built.

Two conditions of the time prompted Dr. Shields to take this apparently revolutionary step. First, there were exceedingly few Catholic colleges for women, which nuns might attend, located near the convents of the Sisters ready for college work and in which they might study while living at the home convent. These were the only conditions then conceivable under which a Sister could do her college work in residence. Secondly, the training of religious for teaching in Catholic primary and secondary schools was so urgent that some procedure had to be devised to speed up the process. I am, of course, using never failing hind-sight when I say that Dr. Shields' approach to the problem seemed logical and feasible, but few people thought so at the time, even on the University campus. As a matter of fact, Dr. Shields' first resident college for Sisters started a long series of such institutions, the end of which is not yet; at this moment the succession of Catholic colleges for women and colleges restricted to Sisters is at its highest, thanks to the Sister Formation Conference.

When I arrived at the University, the Catholic Sisters College had been incorporated independently but with the permission to grant degrees only through the powers granted to the University proper. The arrangement was very unusual, to say the least. The Sisters College was quite independent in all financial and business affairs, and also in all academic affairs such as curricula and standards, but it could not actually grant degrees except by the authority of the Academic Senate of The Catholic University of America. Interestingly enough, the diplomas granted to students featured the Catholic Sisters College in large letters and The Catholic University of America in small letters directly underneath. All this caused the University much embarrassment at times with the accrediting agencies. Did the Sisters College enjoy the same approval for its work as did the University? Obviously, because of its independent academic and financial status it did not under the law, but actually for all practical purposes it did for the most part. The accrediting agencies with some reluctance were willing to accept the word of the University officials that the Catholic Sisters College was an integral part of the University itself. It must be said, however, that Dr. Shields could probably never have launched the Catholic Sisters College, which started the fast pace of present-day Sister-education, had he not enjoyed this freedom of movement. Of course, within comparatively recent times the Catholic Sisters College has fulfilled its great mission. Colleges and universities open to Sisters are now numbered in the hundreds. This includes The Catholic University of America itself, which has now placed all of its educational opportunities at the service of the Sisters. The need of the Catholic Sisters College as an independent academic institution for Sisters only seems to have passed. It has quite naturally become at the present time very important and valuable as the purely residential section for the Sister students of the University.

I do not wish to chronicle the early history of the Catholic Sisters College in detail, but merely to peg the story of my experiences there at a definite point. At the time of my arrival on the campus, the Catholic Sisters College was just passing through its heyday as an undergraduate institution for Sisters only and was even taking up such programs as circumstances permitted in the way of graduate work, both for the Master's and Doctor's degrees. I entered into the midst of this movement, and I withdrew just as all the graduate students were permitted to take up their studies in the regular classes of the University. Furthermore, by this time the undergraduates were becoming steadily fewer and fewer, so much so that the obvious question of admitting them to the College proper of the University and closing the classes at the Sisters College was beginning seriously to be considered. All this was taking place about the time of the inauguration of the then Monsignor James Hugh Ryan as Rector of the University.

In the fall of 1919, I was asked to teach several courses at the Sisters College in undergraduate Greek and Latin, and in the Summer Session of 1920 likewise. There is little to record about these courses. I was edified by my students and experienced the most delightful and stimulating teaching of my career. The Sisters worked very hard and intelligently and were most appreciative of any effort made to speed the progress of their studies. One day it appeared to me that the millennium had been reached, when, in an effort to cover more ground which I felt was important, I offered very cautiously to hold several extra classes, some even on holidays, and my suggestion was received with applause!

My great disillusionment, however, came from the authorities of the Sisters College in connection with graduate studies, and this indeed deserves chronicling. Dr. Shields was still living. He told me that there were several Sisters who wished to do graduate work in Latin both for the Master's and Doctor's degrees, and one or two who wanted to do Master's work in Greek. This was in the very earliest years of my work at the University, and I had not as yet received the assistance of Dr. Campbell and Dr. McGuire. I was still alone at the University proper with a growing number of graduate students in need of dissertation guidance and with all the basic graduate courses to give these students as preparation for dissertation work. I did not see how I could give all the basic courses over again each week at the Sisters College, to say nothing about directing more dissertations. Then too there was the problem of an inadequate library at the Sisters College. I was told, however, that I could take them into my undergraduate courses at the Sisters College, assign them a dissertation topic, give them a few instructions on how to proceed, and all would be well. My amazement would be difficult to gauge, but it was greater still when I learned that this was the general procedure at the Sisters College in all departments. I was not quite able to submit to this condition of things, and so I asked to give two courses of graduate caliber without compensation of any kind. This permission was readily granted! Such an arrangement, however, did not prove very satisfactory, since the undergraduate Sister students with their great thirst for knowledge crowded into the classroom, and I did not have the courage to put them out! Then too the library was barely equipped to serve undergraduate courses in Greek and Latin to say nothing about advanced instruction in these fields. Under the circumstances the courses could be little other than of an advanced (?) translation character.

Finally, in desperation a conference on the problem was arranged with the Rector, Bishop

Shahan. With youthful brashness and little knowledge of the strict regulations against the integration of the sexes in the classroom and with no knowledge of the traditions of the institution, I asked for permission to bring my Sister students over to my University classes. I received a shocked "No!" for my answer. Then I asked if I might continue my segregated classes but transfer the Sisters to my seminar library in McMahon Hall where we could work with the books necesary for graduate instruction, provided I held the classes at a time when the seminar library would not be used by others. The reply was that I would be permitted to do this, if I promised to keep the Sisters on the first floor! "But, Bishop, my seminar library is on the second floor!" The good bishop finally agreed with great reluctance that the Sisters might be brought to my seminar library on Sundays.

I do not wish to give a wrong impression of Bishop Shahan's attitude toward women. He was a most kindly man in every respect, and he also had a very keen sense of the importance of high standards of scholarship. On the other hand, he was Rector of an institution being conducted for men only, which for more than a generation had kept women out of the confines of the University. This was true not only of women students but also of women members of the clerical force, the latter with one exception, Miss Brawner, the Vice Rector's secretary. What I was asking for was indeed quite revolutionary, much more than I realized at that moment, and I later regretted the embarrassment which I had caused His Excellency. Indeed, after the word got out that I was working with the Sisters in McMahon Hall on Sunday, one gentleman of the faculty, a venerable professor of English and a layman, Professor P. J. Lennox, met me in the hallway. He approached me very sadly and whispered: "Be very careful about arranging classes for women at the University. The first thing you know, we shall be having women on the faculty!" What the Professor feared has indeed become true, but I do not believe that anyone resents or regrets it.

With my little band of Sister graduate students of the Classics, we began work immediately on the Sunday following the granting of the necessary permission by Bishop Shahan. Then was inaugurated one of the most gratifying and rewarding periods of my teaching career. Sunday after Sunday until women were regularly admitted to the University proper for graduate studies, our group met in the Seminar room of the Department of Greek and Latin on the second floor of McMahon Hall at 7 A.M., after an early Mass at the Sisters College for the Sisters and the six o'clock Mass at the Franciscan Monastery for me. It was often cold, when the heat in McMahon Hall was cut off, but the enthusiasm of the group over the opportunity to study in the midst of the superb collection of Classical books was always high. All Sunday morning and sometimes through the early hours of the afternoon I went from student to student for consultation on individual dissertations, and before they left to return to the Sisters College they each had an armful of books for study during the week. The quality of the dissertations as well as the accomplishment of these Sisters after leaving the University are proof of the high achievement of that training. In fact, I often think that the difficulties which we all had to overcome in connection with our work were largely responsible for the highly satisfactory results. Of course, there were complaints about all these Sisters being in McMahon Hall the greater part of Sunday. So much so that I asked Monsignor Pace whether or not I should continue with the work. A strong "By all means" was the answer. I shall always remember also when I presented Bishop Shahan with one of the dissertations which came from this group. It was on St. Ambrose, one of the Bishop's favorite Fathers of the Church. He looked it over carefully and said: "This is as good as a priest could do!" I took this occasion to tell the Bishop that I knew that there were many religious communities eager to send some of their Sisters to the Catholic University, if only they could be assured of receiving proper attention at the University proper; furthermore, with the establishment of so many colleges by religious communities of women, it was imperative that facilities for good university training be make available to them, otherwise they would be obliged to resort to non-Catholic institutions. At that time few or no satisfactory opportunities for graduate women were available

in other Catholic universities. This seemed to be a
new idea to the Bishop.

Word about our Sunday seminar soon passed
throughout the world of the Sisters of the country,
and my group became rather large and extremely
burdensome on top of my regular heavy load in the
program of the University itself. An interesting side
issue was an increasing volume of mail from graduate students of the Classics in other Catholic
institutions asking me to suggest topics for both
Master's and Doctor's dissertations for them to develop there. I was very soon obliged, however, to
put an end to this practice.

At about this time also the authorities of
Trinity College invited me to give graduate work
leading to the degree of Doctor of Philosophy to
three of their nuns: Sister Albania (Burns), Sister
Julia (Stokes), and Sister Wilfrid (Parsons). The
first two have long since passed to their eternal
reward, but Sister Wilfrid is still active as Professor
of Latin at Emmanuel College. She just recently
completed most adequately a translation of the
letters of St. Augustine for my series, "The Fathers
of the Church." A very well trained and promising
little group of scholars they indeed were, and it was
well that they were such. Although conditions have
changed much since, at that time the Sisters at
Trinity were not permitted to come to the University except for most compelling reasons, and scholarship was not regarded as one of these. I was
obliged to bring the University to them. I did

succeed, however, once a year in holding my Trinity class at the University in the Greek and Latin library for a whole Saturday afternoon! Yet they also did excellent graduate work largely on their own initiative with a little regular guidance from myself. But the sum total of graduate work with the Sisters at Trinity, the Sisters at the Sisters College, and my regular schedule of graduate courses and dissertation guidance at the University itself was getting to be too much even for the strong constitution with which the Lord had blessed me.

My desperate situation was not relieved any by a conference which I had one day with Dr. P. J. McCormick, who was then Dean of the Catholic Sisters College. Briefly, I presented what I thought was an impossible situation as far as graduate work at the Sisters College was concerned and asked if there was any likelihood in the foreseeable future that the Sisters would be permitted to attend at least the graduate courses at the University. I pointed out the impracticability of the Sisters College attempting to duplicate even a significant part of the University's graduate program. With some enthusiasm I depicted the tremendous need on the part of our Sisters of having the graduate departments of the University open to them, now that so many religious communities were building colleges and were training faculties for them. The answer was direct, certain, and final: "No, never."

At just that time the authorities of Cornell University made me an offer to go to their institution as

Professor of Classics. They also suggested that I teach in their summer session that year so as to become acquainted with that university before making my final decision. I agreed to go there for the summer, reserving my decision with respect to the regular year until the end of the summer. I was seeking escape from the avalanche of work that had piled upon me. Incidentally, my absence from the University to teach at Cornell that summer was the only interruption of my forty odd years of teaching and administration at The Catholic University of America, covering both the regular semesters and the summer periods.

After I had been at the Cornell Summer Session for several weeks I received a very pleasing letter from the then Monsignor James Hugh Ryan. He informed me that he had just been appointed Rector of the University to succeed Bishop Shahan, and that he expected me back at the University, stating further that he had some special work for me to do. Needless to say, I was most pleased to give up the furtive inclination to leave The Catholic University of America and to return to it with renewed vigor.

The College of Arts and Sciences

When Monsignor James H. Ryan was planning the reorganization of the University as a whole, except for the Sacred Sciences, he had as many undergraduate schools or colleges as he had graduate schools. One was the counterpart of the other. All undergraduate admissions, however, were in the hands of one person, the Registrar, Mr. Charles Fox Borden. Speaking strictly from the academic point of view, Mr. Borden had no aptitude or training for an administrative position of this kind, and we need not dwell on the matter further. Bishop Shahan, the Rector, expected him to get as large an enrollment as possible, and neither seemed to care much about how the students were obtained. I honestly do not think that either the Rector or the Registrar had any great realization of the many problems involved in the admission of students. Furthermore, the vicious but not uncommon policy was followed that in the early years of an institution essentially every one who applied should be admitted and that selectivity of students should be introduced later when the enrollment became large. There was evidently little realization that if the entrance requirements remain low the enrollment also usually remains low, since even mediocre students, to say nothing of good students, are not going to rush to get into a college which accepts essentially everyone who applies.

Thus the scholastic reputation of the undergraduate studies at this time sank very low. It became common talk and knowledge that essentially anyone could get into one or another of our undergraduate groups. At this time also there was no full-time dean. A dean was a regular member of the teaching staff, who assumed the administrative functions over and above his professional duties, a practice taken over from European higher educational institutions. Naturally the deans had little time to devote to the problems of the undergraduate, and they frankly neglected him.

All the deans of the schools which had undergraduate students formed a Board of Deans served by a single secretary. This secretary alone gave some unity to the undergraduate body by being always on the job and having no other distracting duties. Actually, he performed most of the duties of the deans, although he had no special training or experience for the post. He simply did the best he could. One of the unfortunate results of all this was that the undergraduates very naturally felt that they were neglected and that they were an unwanted appendage of the University, except for their tuition fees. This attitude was confirmed by many of the clergy and of the teaching staff, who stuck stubbornly to the European idea that a university should have no undergraduate body and openly proclaimed it. This attitude of mind still persists to some extent despite the outstanding organization and administration of the College today, and is being perpetuated by persons who should know better.

Such was the condition of things when Monsignor Ryan took over his work as Rector. He thought that with the establishment of the College of Arts and Sciences, amalgamating all the non-professional undergraduate work of the University, conditions would improve for the undergraduate students. They did to some extent socially, but there was no change in the plan of admissions and essentially no change in the curriculum, notwithstanding the efforts of a curriculum committee appointed by the Rector to improve the program of studies. The reasons for the lack of improvement are clear. The same person as Registrar was still in charge of admissions, and the proper leadership was lacking in the College of Arts and Sciences. The enrollment meanwhile, in spite or because of the low admission requirements, was growing less annually.

In 1934 Monsignor Ryan discussed the woes of the College with me. We came to the conclusion that a proper dean was needed for the present crisis, one who would take care of the admission process, the curriculum, and other matters of less importance also in need of attention. I recommended my colleague and former student in the Department of Greek and Latin, the Reverend James M. Campbell. Shortly thereafter he received the appointment and took over the formidable task of pulling the College of Arts and Sciences out of its doldrums in November, 1934.

The first problem was that of getting a student body of a much higher intellectual caliber. This meant a great deal more than merely raising the entrance requirements. It was a job which required much patience and skill in making the College such that students of high quality would want to enter it. A system of selection such as would sift out the students that we ourselves really wanted for the College but at the same time would not exclude any that could do satisfactory work in the College had, of course, to be devised. As usual, Father Campbell went at his task slowly and very painstakingly by making a number of studies in order to obtain reliable data on all that pertained to his problem. For example, he studied the achievement of the students in our college who came from the various ranks of their graduating high school class. Among other things he discovered that those who came from the lower half of their class were a distinct liability to the University in every way. The disciplinary problems came from them almost exclusively; the time and attention given to them for such difficulties as well as for scholastic troubles were prohibitive; if they graduated, they did not represent the product which we professed to develop. He also visited the deans of some of the leading institutions of the land, both to discuss outstanding questions with them and especially to study the curricula of the general college.

Father Campbell's description of the aims of the College as presented in the Announcement of the College of Arts and Sciences, in which he discusses "A Liberal Arts College" and "A Catholic Liberal Arts College," was probably the first result of his preliminary studies. It is, moreover, a masterpiece of its kind. I will quote only the first two paragraphs:

The College aims to give a training which is both liberal and Catholic. In these adjectives—which are not mutually exclusive terms—it recognizes certain prescriptions as to the content of courses, but it sees in them chiefly an attitude of mind and a way of life determined by that attitude. These larger results, it believes, depend upon the organization of college life in all its phases. They cannot be fully realized by a mandate of specific courses. In imposing certain definite prescriptions the College does not assume for a moment that all students will profit from them equally or that every student can do better than acceptable work in them. Nor does it deny the possibility that a particular student might derive more academic benefit from some other course denied him because of the primacy of a certain prescription in a program of studies already exacting. These prescriptions are simply indispensable minima required of all students because of the College's specific objectives. In discharging them, each student secures as much of them as he can.

As a liberal arts institution, the College believes that the student is an individual who must always be regarded as such and that his welfare, and not the dignity of a subject nor the convenience of the department which professes it nor the good order of the curriculum which includes it, comes first. His academic well-being demands that he be placed among associates with whom he can work to the limit of his capacity and in an environment where the formalities of instruction will yield at the earliest feasible moment to the enterprise of self-education.

This is only a part of what may be called a masterful essay both in style and content. I sometimes feel that it is a pity that such a literary product is lost in a catalogue, which is a notorious document for not being read by the very people for whom it is intended as a guide! But it is important to note that after his having written this many years ago, Father Campbell has never seen fit to revise it in any way. This is characteristic of the finality with which Father Campbell does everything.

Criteria for admission, in which Father Campbell had confidence, were soon set up. While changes of a minor nature have been made as experiences dictated, these too have remained very much the same as when first established. They have, indeed, formed the very basis of the present admission process adopted by all the undergraduate groups of the University and executed by an admissions committee made up of all the deans concerned, with the Registrar as chairman.

I do not intend to go into all the details of the long and laborious task which rehabilitated the College, but I must mention the curriculum which Father Campbell devised and which has no equal in the colleges of the country. He has called it "The Program of Concentration." While the title may perhaps give the impression of a narrow intellectual experience, it is far from that. It is broad and deep, paradoxical as that may appear at first sight. Because it is impossible to give an adequate description of it within the limited space available here, let it suffice for me to refer to several outstanding articles on the curriculum which Father Campbell himself has written:

(1) *The Curriculum of the Catholic College,* edited by Roy J. Deferrari. Washington, D.C.: The Catholic University of America Press, 1952. All the articles in this volume are of value for an understanding of the Program of Concentration, but the following three by Father Campbell are of special importance.

"General Problems of the Curriculum in the Modern College. Part I: Preliminary Problems."

"General Problems of the Curriculum in the Modern College. Part II: Some Attempts to Construct a Curriculum."

"The Program of Concentration."

(2) *Theology, Philosophy, and History as Integrating Disciplines in the Catholic College of Liberal Arts,* edited by Roy J. Deferrari. Washington, D. C.: The Catholic University of America Press, 1953. Again all the essays here presented will be helpful but the first in the volume by Father Campbell deserves special note.

"Preface on the Program of Concentration."

While Father Campbell was steadfastly proceeding with his labors, for some years the enrollment was steadily going downward. Poor students still continued to apply for admission but none was accepted. Moreover, the new College was not as yet well known enough to the most promising high school graduates to be an attraction to them. The enrollment went down to below a hundred students, a condition which, I am sure, taxed the patience of the several Rectors, Bishop Ryan and his successors. One or two of them did ask a few pertinent questions, but it must be said that not one of them raised any serious objection to Father Campbell's plans and procedures. The upward trend finally came, and has been in progress ever since. The ideal enrollment was set at about 500 students, but this number has already been slightly surpassed. What measures, if any, will be taken to keep the enrollment at that figure, I cannot say. The fact is that few truly poor students apply for admission to the College anymore. More and more students of exceptional ability seek to be admitted. Furthermore, the program of studies devised by Father Campbell is being followed in many colleges throughout the land; Father Campbell himself is being sought out for visits to institutions of higher education to present and delineate his program of studies. But even so, the College of Arts and Sciences of The Catholic University of America is not sufficiently well known for what it is: an outstanding college of liberal arts, one of the very best in the land.

One of the older professors of the University has often made the following statement both in private and in public:

> When I came to the Catholic University, the College had the reputation of being one of the poorest colleges in the United States, and in many respects it was. Dr. Campbell has transformed it into the best college under Catholic auspices in this country.

In closing this chapter I wish to register my pleasure and my pride in having been permitted by

Father Campbell to look in on his work and to make an occasional suggestion as it progressed. This is one of my most pleasant recollections.

The Graduate School of Arts and Sciences

Monsignor J. H. Ryan appointed me Acting Dean of the Graduate School of Arts and Sciences early in the academic year of 1930-31. My task was to carry out the reorganization of the University insofar as it pertained to the Graduate School of Arts and Sciences. [1]

Few, if any, members of the various faculties of the University realized that the reorganization in question had been under consideration by the University authorities many years before. For the most part they regarded it as a revolutionary and undesirable innovation. As a matter of fact, however, as early as on November 22, 1916, the Academic Senate appointed the following committee to consider the possible organization of a Graduate School, which also involved the establishment of a College: Dr. Thomas Carrigan, Dr. Joseph Dunn, Dr. Aubry Landry, Dr. Charles H. McCarthy, and Dr. Edward A. Pace. In this connection, the Faculty of the School of Letters at its meeting of January 15, 1918, went on record as follows:

[1] Cf. also Reorganization of the University.

Resolved that the Faculty of Letters endorses so far as it goes the Report of the Committee on the Graduate School presented to the Senate on March 1, 1917 and referred for discussion by that body to the Faculty of Letters.

And resolved that in consequence thereof the Faculty of Letters respectfully recommends to the Senate and through the Senate to the Board of Trustees:

1. to establish as soon as possible, in the University, one College of Arts and Sciences, leading to the A.B. degree, to take charge of all collegiate work at this University,

2. likewise to establish as soon as possible one Graduate School for all graduate work now being done or to be done in the future in any of the Departments, present or future, of this University.

Evidently there was strong support for such an organization twelve years previously, although nothing was done finally about it at that time, nor can I discover precisely what was the exact fate of this initial move.

When I, in the academic year 1930-31, took up the job of establishing the Graduate School of Arts and Sciences, one member of the teaching staff in particular chose to object very strenuously to the proposed reorganization of the University as a whole and especially as it affected the Graduate School of Arts and Sciences. The following letter addressed by me to the Executive Committee of the Board of Trustees on February 18, 1931 depicts the opposition effectively enough.

MOST REVEREND, RIGHT REVEREND, AND DEAR SIRS:

I beg to submit for your consideration my version of what happened at the preliminary meeting of the Faculty of the Graduate School of Arts and Sciences Tuesday, May 27, 1930 insofar as it concerns the case of Dr. . . . . .

Some weeks before the Spring meeting of the Board of Trustees in 1930, the Right Reverend Rector, at a joint meeting of all the Faculties, had announced the approved reorganization of the then three schools of Philosophy, Letters, and Sciences into the divisions which now obtain and had announced my appointment as Acting Dean of the Graduate School to be erected. The Rector had stated at the time that the new school would not function officially until the day after the close of the Academic Year, 1929-30, but that it was necessary that many inevitable and routine matters incidental to the launching of the School be disposed of before that date and the long vacation to follow. Among other things, therefore, a preliminary meeting of those who were to constitute the Faculty of the new Graduate School was called on Tuesday, May 27, 1930—15 days before the temporary officers of the new Schools could function officially. It is obvious from this chronology that determined opponents of the approved reorganization could have embarrassed its program merely by insisting that no meeting could be held until the assembled body was *de facto* the Faculty of the Graduate School—an objection actually suggested by several of those present. Dr. . . . chose to concentrate upon another point.

At the very moment the meeting was opened and before I, as acting Dean, had an opportunity to make the first of several general announcements, Dr. ... took the floor and demanded, in an obviously challenging tone, by what authority the changes in the organization of the University were being made. I thereupon asked Dr. ... to postpone his question until I had made certain preliminary remarks which I thought would answer a number of questions in the minds of those present.

As soon as my preliminary remarks were completed, Dr. ... again put his question in accents as challenging as before. I thereupon informed him that to the best of my knowledge the changes had been made, or at least sanctioned, by the Executive Committee of the Board of Trustees. He then declared that neither the Executive Committee of the Board of Trustees nor the Board of Trustees itself had the power to make such changes without the approval of the Holy See, and he demanded to know whether or not the approval of the Holy See had been obtained in this instance. I then replied that I could not answer from personal knowledge, but I thought that all present could reasonably assume that the Rector and the Executive Committee would not effect any changes without proper authority. This answer seemed to provoke Dr. ... and he demanded that I cease to be evasive but answer his question specifically. Futhermore, much to my embarrassment, he refused to yield the floor until I would answer "yes" or "no" to his question. Meanwhile he quoted in Latin, without the aid of notes, what he claimed were passages in the Constitution which were being violated. Before he finally yielded the floor he presented a motion, which was not seconded, that the meeting be not adjourned until I gave a definite answer to his question.

In the discussion which followed, Dr. ...'s remarks were interpreted to imply that the Rector and the Executive Committee had overreached their power, and this not by accident but by design. Dr. ... vigorously protested this interpretation. At length he succeeded in securing a seconder to the following motion:

"That the Chairman of the present meeting be directed to procure information, first as to whether the Holy See has approved of the recent radical changes in organization, and secondly as to whether the Board of Trustees judged it not necessary to secure such approval of the Holy See in view of the wording of paragraphs 79, 108, and 109."

The purpose of the motion, as explained by its proponents, was to secure official information upon the exact legal status under the constitutions of the faculty of the Graduate School as at present constituted. The calm and dispassionate tone which characterizes this motion was achieved only after several speakers had objected to the implications mentioned above which were evident in the original form of the motion.

Before the motion was put, a number of those present expressed themselves as opposed to it, not in itself, but because of the spirit and attitude toward the authorities of the University manifested on the floor by the mover. The motion was lost 31-20.

What I wish especially to bring to your attention is the fact that as it stands the motion is very reasonable, and, if there were no unfavorable attendant circumstances, would certainly receive a large majority vote from any body of honest-minded men. To my mind, the reasonableness of the motion *per se* accounts for most of the votes which the motion did receive. The circumstances attending the motion account for the votes which the motion did not receive. I may add that several men who voted for the motion came to me later and apologized for so voting, declaring that they were unaware of the real motives of the mover.

In private conversations, after the meeting, some of those who had been present told me that they had been opposed to the motion on the ground that Dr. ... was acting as the spokesman of a group of men who had been consistently opposing every change in the existing state of things sponsored by the Rector; that the arguments put forth by Dr. ... were the same as those being circulated by members of this group among the University Faculties.

Respectfully yours,
(Signed) ROY J. DEFERRARI
Dean of the Graduate School

Early in October of 1930, Monsignor Ryan made plans to call, on the 16th of the month, a meeting of the Faculty of the Graduate School, at which he would preside. On the 15th I received a letter sent by campus mail, "receipt requested," which deserves to be quoted in full.

Dr. Roy Deferrari
Acting Dean, Graduate School

DEAR DR. DEFERRARI:

A meeting of the Graduate School to be held Oct. 16, 1930, has been called for the purpose of electing Faculty Officers.

Before officers can legally be elected, the status of the School as to its constitutionality must be clearly established. This applies especially to the following points:

A) Suppression (or submersion) of the School of Philosophy as such. The School of Philosophy is expressly mentioned, and its existence thereby approved, in Gen. Const. 24 and 79; as its suppression (or submersion) clearly supposes a change in said Constitution, it requires, in order to be valid, the express approval of the Holy See, i.e. the Congregation of Seminaries and Universities (Const. Gen. 108).

B) Erection of the Graduate School. The erection of a new School is reserved by the General Constitution 11 and 100, i.e., exclusively to the Hierarchy as a body; not to the Board of Trustees or an Executive Committee.

C) Suppression of the Schools of Philosophy, Letters and Sciences. As the erection of these Schools is reserved by the Constitution exclusively to the Hierarchy as a body, so, consequently, their suppression cannot but be exclusively reserved to the same body.

D) Appointment of a Council of the Graduate School. According to Gen. Const. 56, all administrative power in a School is vested in the Faculty of the School as a body. Although a Faculty has, in a special case, the right to appoint a Committee with power to act, its right of administration is per se not transferable in generalitate causarum. Such a transfer, clearly involving a change against the Constitution, must, in order to be valid, be

made, or at least be approved, by the Holy See
(Gen. Const. 108).

E) Stated meetings of the Faculty. The right
of administration of a School must be exercised in
Faculty meetings to be called, according to Gen.
Const. 55, regularly at least once a month. Any
change in this mode of administration as established by the Constitution, must at least be approved by the Holy See. (Gen. Const. 108).

In order to expedite business and to prevent
discussions that may become undesirable, you are
kindly requested to see to it that the Faculty in
said meeting be clearly informed of the following
facts:

1) That the Holy See has approved, in writing or in any other canonically demonstrable way,
the suppression of the School of Philosophy.

2) that the Hierarchy as a body, not the
Board of Trustees or an Executive Committee,
has (a) suppressed the Schools of Philosophy,
Letters and Sciences, and (b) erected a new
Graduate School in their stead.

3) that the Holy See has (a) transferred in a
canonically demonstrable way the administrative
powers of the whole Faculty of the Graduate
School in their entirety or in part to another body
as v.g. an advisory Council, and (b) withdrawn,
either by abrogation or dispensation, the obligation of the Faculty to conduct their business in
regular monthly meetings.

The additional information as to when and
how in each case the legalizing action has been

effected by the respective authority, is by no means unimportant.

It may not be amiss to remind you of the fact:

a) that A) and #1 were mentioned first by Dr. Motry in the Senate and then by Dr. Rolbiecki in the meeting of May 27, who also, at your suggestion, as you well remember, made them the object of a motion which was supported by 29 or more Professors as v.g. Dr. Hyvernat, Dr. Lennox, Dr. Purcell, Dr. McCormick and others; and

b) that E and #3 were emphasized by Mons. McCormick in the same meeting of May 27.

Other features and aspects in the organization of the new Graduate School, apparently impractical and undesirable, seem not to be of such a basic nature as are the points mentioned above, and thus they may well be left for a later consideration.

Be so kind as to inform the Rector of this letter; it is only fair to inform him of what is expected and to give him an opportunity to prepare his statements.

And kindly assure the Rector that this letter has been written not in a spirit of criticism or obstruction, but in a spirit of helpfulness and assistance, so that the new Graduate School, having been placed on the only safe basis possible, may develop and succeed.

Sincerely yours,
(Signed) JOHN A. RYAN
FRANZ J. COLN

This letter contains at least two valid criticisms. The Sacred Congregation of Seminaries and Universities regards philosophy as a sacred science and thus a professional field. Naturally, as in the case of sacred theology and canon law, a separate and independent school is required and desirable. This defect was soon remedied. The other is the validity of the Graduate Council as an independent body. I personally feel responsible for this defect. I had suggested the establishment of this group in order to meet the problem of conducting important and complex business with a large faculty body, but I did not emphasize sufficiently its dependence on the faculty for whatever powers it might have. At any rate, this difficulty was soon met by specifically naming the Graduate Council as a Committee of the Faculty, strictly responsible to it for all decisions reached. Much of the criticism in the letter, however, I do not hold as valid or even accurate, but I do not wish to present a detailed discussion of the letter here.

At any rate, Monsignor Ryan was apparently quite unperturbed by the letter, when it was shown to him, and said: "Say nothing to anyone. We shall proceed with the Faculty meeting as planned." He must have been quite sure of his ground to have gone ahead as he did. Furthermore, when the famous meeting was held, none of the difficulties mentioned in Dr. John A. Ryan's letter were even mentioned by anyone. The meeting went on to the business at hand without any incident. Dr. P. J. Lennox and myself were nominated as candidates for the office of Dean, and I was elected by receiving the votes of all the members of the Senate except four.

The task before me was formidable to say the least. Frankly, there was little or nothing by way of administrative procedures already in existence that could be retained. Before discussing the reforms which were needed, however, it would be well to quote from a letter which was written to the Rector on October 30, 1933, and which will indicate some of the fringe problems with which we had to contend, and also the serious concern which was felt for the Graduate School of Arts and Sciences. Monsignor James H. Ryan had shortly before been elevated to the episcopacy.

YOUR EXCELLENCY:

I returned late last Saturday from the conferences of the Association of American Universities held at Princeton, New Jersey. They were as usual most interesting and profitable, much of the discussion touching problems of immediate concern to the Catholic University.

I was impressed for one thing with the fact that many of our longstanding departments are utterly unknown for any special work. This may be due in part to my ignorance of the activity of certain departments, but I do not think so. At any rate I shall discuss this matter at our next faculty meeting. I also believe, however, that a very negligible number of members of our faculty attend the meetings of their learned society, least of all read papers at those meetings. I think that it would be decidedly worthwhile for the University to do something to stir them up. I suggest that you offer to have the University pay all or part of the expenses of all members of the faculty who attend these meetings and *take an active part by reading a paper.* You could well consider money so spent as a most worthy contribution to the advertising of the University.

There was some discussion of comprehensive examinations in the graduate school, and I obtained some interesting information on how they are carried on elsewhere, which I shall offer to the consideration of our faculty. There is a tendency to offer a special type of comprehensive examination at the end of the first semester of a student's attendance at the University, with a view to the early elimination of the unfit.

This leads to another very important matter. What are we doing to eliminate the unfit in the Graduate School of C.U.A.? While we are doing more than we ever did, we are by no means doing enough. With your approval, I would like to request that the head of every department report to the Dean at the end of every academic year on every graduate student in his department—whether or not he should be permitted to enroll in the Graduate School again as a candidate for a higher degree. Also, the preliminary requirements to do graduate work in some of our departments are practically *nil.* I have reference particularly to the Departments of Education and Sociology. I find that in the other members of the Association no one is accepted as a graduate student in any department unless he has had at least three years of study in that subject while an undergraduate. We certainly should have some similar plan here.

Of very great importance for the development of our College of Arts and Sciences was a consideration of the type of college that could best be developed in connection with the Graduate School. I would like very much to go into this now, but I do not wish to make this report too long.

Brief thought was also given to the importance of coordinating departments. Dean Seashore, of the University of Iowa, presented an interesting experience in this connection at his graduate school. A student of the Department of English presented a dissertation entitled "The Imagery in Milton." The student, however, had not the slightest idea of the modern pyschological concept of imagery. There had been no contact in this study between the Department of English and the Department of Psychology.

There are other minor matters which I feel will be rectified in the course of the execution of our present plans. In presenting the following major considerations, I fear that I shall cause Your Excellency much displeasure.

The first point has reference to the work of the Registrar in connection with the Graduate School. While I have taken over for my own convenience much of the keeping of the records, it does not have the official stamp of the University. The method now employed in the Registrar's office of keeping the records of the Graduate School will not pass muster.

The second point has to do with the Library. Our graduate students do not have admission to the stacks. Our students, moreover, cannot use the Library after dark. Most of our graduate departments can spend little or no money for books. What we took upon ourselves as a measure of economy, I fear has remained, or will remain, with us long enough to affect vitally the work of our graduate departments. Dr. Bishop of the University of Michigan read a paper on "The

Present Status of Schools of Librarianship." You will recall that we wrote to him about having an inspector from the American Library Association examine our work in Library Service in the Summer Session with a view to its approval by that body. I had a short talk with him and he told me very frankly that unless we have a trained librarian in charge of our library, at least in the process of reorganizing it as it should be, we will never receive the recognition we seek. Someone has evidently given Dr. Bishop some inside information. This library situation will never be accepted by the Association of American Universities.

The third point and the one which I dislike most to discuss pertains to the form of discipline now exercised over our graduate students. The members of the Association hold as a fundamental principle that graduate students should be made to associate with one another as much as possible in their lives outside the classroom. I have reference to their living in dormitories reserved for graduate students only, and dining at least at tables reserved for them alone. They hold also that any discipline to which graduate students may be subjected should be entirely distinct from that imposed on undergraduates, just as much as the classes they attend should be conducted decidedly differently from those attended by undergraduates. The members of the Association regard these matters as very important in rounding out the training of graduate students. Incidentally, this entire matter is under the control of the Dean of the Graduate School. The Dean of Men is concerned only with undergraduates. As far as the Catholic University is concerned, a large number of our graduate students, namely, the religious, are out of consideration. They are properly cared for. A graduate dormitory for nuns [2] however, might well be considered for the future. As far as the laywomen are concerned, I believe that as soon as possible a Dean of Women should be appointed who should cooperate with the Dean of the Graduate School, and with him be responsible to Your Excellency. I suggest this, not because anything unpleasant has as yet happened among the female lay students of the Graduate School, but because I believe that they are so numerous now that we ought to show some practical interest in their lives outside the classroom. I believe that the Association of American Universities will expect that of us. But the most serious phase of this problem has to do with the laymen. The present scheme of interspersing graduate laymen among the undergraduates and making them submit to the discipline of the undergraduates will never be countenanced by A.A.U. Moreover, we may never expect any graduate laymen to live on the campus under these conditions unless they have to in order to hold a fellowship or scholarship,—a most deplorable situation. The graduate laymen should be put back in Graduate Hall by themselves. They should eat at special tables in the dining hall. A priest (and I could suggest anyone of several young instructors now with us who would do the job well) should be put in charge of Graduate Hall to cooperate with the Dean of the Graduate School and with him be responsible to your Excellency. The form of discipline would be simple. The priest in charge by living among the men and taking an intelligent interest in their work, and by comparing notes with the Dean and the records

[2] It is interesting to note that in September of 1960 St. John's Hall on the University campus was given over as a resident hall to graduate Sister students.

of the Graduate Office, would soon find out those graduate laymen who were not attending to business. Those would be put off the campus, deprived of their scholarship or fellowship, or expelled according to the circumstances. Life on the campus should be so pleasant that the graduate laymen will prefer to live there than elsewhere. It is far from that now. I have many other practical ideas in accordance with which the priest in charge could cooperate with the Dean of the Graduate School to give our graduate laymen the well rounded training that they ought to have and to put some mark of distinction on the holders of graduate degrees whom we send forth. But I have already dragged out this letter too far.

I am enclosing the new recommendations (of the A.A.U.) for handling scholarships and fellowships. Needless to say the Catholic University should carry them out faithfully.

I would greatly appreciate Your Excellency's careful consideration of the important matters of this letter, and I assure you of my eagerness to discuss them further with you.

Respectfully yours,
ROY J. DEFERRARI
Dean

The following features of the new Graduate School of Arts and Sciences deserve special consideration.

(1) oral examinations,
(2) comprehensive written examinations,
(3) language examinations for a reading knowledge,
(4) dissertations for the Master's degree,

(5) selection and approval of dissertation subjects, and

(6) publication of dissertations.

The oral examinations for the degree of Ph.D. had descended to an extremely disgraceful state. Some departments kept up acceptable standards, to be sure, but others seemed to take pleasure in making the entire procedure a farce. Certain departments held this important examination in the home of the major professor who, in at least one instance, relieved the strain and nervous tension of all concerned by serving snacks and refreshments. Anyone failing the final examination for the doctorate was an unheard of thing. Of course, there was no appropriate supervision of the requirement, and there was nothing definitely expressed as to exactly how it should be conducted. Some examiners spent about an hour questioning the candidate about his dissertation only and excluded any general questions on the field as a whole. This was farcical, especially because this final oral examination in many instances was the only test which the candidate had been obliged to take during all his years of study for the degree. Then too, infrequently completely extraneous questions were introduced. In the late period of World War I a student of German extraction, who was a candidate for the doctorate in Latin and Greek, was asked by a Professor of German, himself a native German and serving as an examiner, if he thought the destruction of the University of Louvain by the German forces was justified. To make the situation worse, the Professor in charge of the proceedings was Monsignor H. Hyvernat, the distinguished Semitic scholar. The fireworks which ensued need not be recorded here.

Obviously, much systematic legislation touching on all the problems involved was necessary. The following plan was promptly expedited and has been in successful operation ever since:

The Oral Examination for the Doctorate

After the dissertation has been approved, but ordinarily not before April 1 of the last year of graduate work, the candidate must undergo an oral examination upon the whole of his graduate work in the presence of the major and minor professors and representatives of the Council.

1. The oral examination for the degree of Ph.D. shall be a searching test of the candidate's knowledge and understanding of the field of his major and minor studies.

2. The examining board shall be appointed by the Dean and the Council after consultation with the Head (s) of Department (s) concerned and shall consist of

   a. Two members of the Council, as representing the Council and Faculty.

   b. The major and minor professors, or instructors, as representing the respective Departments involved.

3. The examinations may not be held unless all members of the board appointed are present.

4. The two members of the Council shall have each one full vote, and one full vote shall

be cast for each of the three (one major, and two minor) subjects, thus totaling five full votes, it being understood that, if the candidate is examined in a given major or minor subject by two or three professors or instructors, each of these examiners will have a half or third vote, respectively.

5. The candidate, to pass the oral examination, must receive at least four out of five full votes, it being understood:

a. That in the case of a three to two vote in favor of the candidate, the majority may, if notice be given before the close of the deliberations of the board immediately following the examination proper, appeal to the Council.

b. That unsatisfactory results in the major subject, or notably unsatisfactory results in either minor subject, shall entail retaking of the whole oral examination.

6. If a candidate fails in the final oral examination, he must obtain permission from the Council before he can become eligible to retake this examination. A candidate shall not be permitted to retake the final oral examination until at least one semester, or an equivalent period of time, has elapsed from the date of his failure. If he fails a second time in the final oral examination, he shall cease to be a candidate for the Ph.D. degree.

7. The Dean is de jure Chairman of the the Examining Board, but he may appoint a member of the Council to act in his place. The Chairman shall be in charge of the examination. He shall see that the examination begins punctually on the minute, shall maintain the proper time schedule, and shall require orderly procedure in all other

respects. The second representative of the Council and Faculty shall act as Secretary of the Examining Board.

8. The final oral examination for the doctorate shall be a minimum of one hour in length and a maximum of two hours. The Council would suggest that ordinarily the preliminary questioning during the first hour be divided as follows: thirty minutes for the major subject, twenty for the first minor, and ten minutes for the second minor subject.

9. A leaflet, containing the name of the candidate who is about to take his final oral examination for the doctorate, the names of those constituting the Examining Board, the time and place of the examination, the candidate's major and minor subjects and the courses completed in these subjects, the title and an abstract of the candidate's dissertation, and sufficient biographical data to indicate the candidate's academic career, shall be printed or lithographed, and a copy of this leaflet shall be posted on the Bulletin Board of the School at least three days before the date scheduled for the examination. The data for this leaflet, to be furnished at the Office of the Dean by the candidate, must be submitted at least ten days before the date of the examination. Copies of the leaflet will be distributed to other institutions.

10. The final oral examination shall be held in the Office of the Dean or other published place, and shall be considered a public examination. To avoid possible confusion, however, permission to audit the final oral examination should be obtained from the Dean.

11. Ordinarily, no oral examination for the doctorate will be held during the summer session.

I do not intend to go into such detail in describing other reforms, but this particular procedure was so pivotal for the up-building of the Graduate School and had such beneficial effect that it seems worthy of full presentation. Incidentally, this procedure has continued to the present day.

In the very first year of the operation of the new plan, six candidates for the doctor's degree failed their oral examinations. All, however, in the minds of their fellow students, had been notorious loafers, and no question of any injustice was involved. Many, however, foretold the doom of the Graduate School of Arts and Sciences by reason of the ill-will supposedly thus engendered among the religious communities. But all proceeded with remarkable precision and smoothness.

Merely taking courses, for most of which final examinations were not given, and presenting a worthy dissertation, climaxed by an oral examination based essentially or entirely on the doctoral dissertation, seemed scant preparation indeed for the degree, Doctor of Philosophy. So after establishing the routine of the final oral examination, as described above, I turned to the task of assuring myself of the student's general knowledge of his field. The passing of a comprehensive examination was demanded at least one academic year before the oral examination was taken. This gave the departments an opportunity to sift out very poor students before they came up for the oral examination and even before they had proceeded far with the dissertation. This was a completely new procedure for our campus, but one fairly common in the leading universities of the land. Of course, careful provision had to be made so that these comprehensive examinations would be taken seriously by both student and department. Furthermore, similar comprehensive examinations were demanded in the minor fields for the doctorate and in the major field for the Master's degree.

The language examinations required for advanced degrees had, as in most graduate schools of the country, become ludicrous. I felt that either they should be made worthy of their purpose or abandoned entirely. Some kind of examination adequate for determining a student's ability to read a modern foreign language easily enough for scholarly purposes not only had to be devised but the requirement also had to be enforced. The latter was the more difficult problem, but, after several test cases had been satisfactorily carried through, all again went smoothly.

The question of the composition required for the Master's degree, then called the essay, presented still another problem. There was no difficulty about the standards of the doctoral dissertations. These always were of high quality on the whole. But the Master's essay had reached a very low state indeed. The faculty had no definite idea of what should be required in the Master's essay, and the saying, "Not very good, but good enough for a Master's essay" became almost a by-word in faculty meetings. It was finally decided that, as far as it went, the Master's essay should exhibit in every respect the correct principles of scholarship just as vigorously as for the doctoral dissertation. To emphasize this conclusion the name was changed from "essay" to "dissertation." "The candidate for the M.A., M.S., or M.S. in L.S. must write such a dissertation on an approved subject as will demonstrate his ability to proceed further in scientific research. This dissertation should consist, for example, of a thorough history of a problem or some phase of it, or some minor piece of research such as the standardization of a single test, the analysis of a part of an author's vocabulary, etc."

The matter of the approval of topics of dissertations also needed careful thought and legislation. Within the sphere of the Master's degree this gave little trouble, especially since the publication of the work was the exception. The following legislation, again quite new, took care of matters very effectively: "The topic of the dissertation must be approved by the major department and by the Dean and the Council before the close of the second week of the semester at the end of which the candidate expects to receive the degree. A brief description of the topic and an indication of the method of investigation to be employed must accompany each Master's dissertation topic presented to the Dean and the Council for approval."

In the case of the doctoral dissertation, much confusion arose at times. Since no approval of the topic was required other than that of the major professor and the department, overlapping of fields, inappropriate topics, and inadequate direction of investigations sometimes took place. To illustrate, the Department of English once approved the topic "The Essence of Poetry in Dante," to be investigated within its own confines and with no contact with the Department of Romance Languages. Furthermore, the student in question and the major professor himself knew no Italian. The absurdity of this situation was obvious. Accordingly, legislation was enacted requiring the approval of the topic not only by the major professor and the head of the department and the Graduate Council, but also by the Rector himself, as was required in the Schools of the Sacred Sciences.

Many a disagreeable and frustrating struggle took place over the final approval of a doctoral dissertation, chiefly because the two readers other than the major professor rarely saw the dissertation until it was completed and frequently misunderstood its purpose and plan of investigation. To end all this, the following legislation was enacted: "A Committee, usually consisting of three readers, is appointed for each Ph.D. dissertation by the Council as soon as the subject of the dissertation has been approved. No student should proceed beyond the preliminary stage in the investigation of his topic until it has been approved by the Council and the Rector. All members of the committee are to keep in frequent and close touch through the major professor with the student's dissertation during its progress, it being understood that the final direction of the candidate's work on the dissertation remains under his major professor and that all directions and suggestions given to the candidate shall be given by the major professor alone." This bit of legislation, I fear, has not been carried out as carefully as it should be.

Another major problem was the establishment of an official format for the doctoral dissertation. Thus far they had been published in all sizes and colors. This was a matter that had to be worked out in great detail. But it was done, and the directions have all in all been followed closely ever since.

Many other details of administration in the Graduate School of Arts and Sciences were evolved and put into practice. Indeed, so much by way of reform was done in a comparatively short time that complaints arose on all sides to the effect that neither students nor members of the faculty could keep up with the new regulations. They could not remember them all, to say nothing about carrying them all out. It was imperative that some means be discovered whereby all new legislation be systematically promulgated and enforced. As a means toward this end there was founded the "Bulletin of the Graduate School of Arts and Sciences," which appeared accordingly as new material was ready for publication and dissemination. The Bulletin, distributed without charge, was continued as long as major reforms were being carried through, and the demand for the Bulletin from other institutions and individuals outside the University became rather great. All the members of the Association of American Universities received copies; their reaction was most favorable and flattering. Needless to say, this did the University much good in academic circles.

Just before the so-called "shakeup"[3] under Monsignor Corrigan, I was working on the construction of a "Handbook of Information" for students of the Graduate School of Arts and Sciences. I completed and published it shortly before I left the Graduate School and became Secretary General. This Handbook contained all the important legislation, carefully organized, which had been enacted during my deanship. This publication has since become, essentially without change, "Handbook of Information for Graduate Students" with the following notice in the front: "N.B. This Handbook is intended for graduate students in all schools of the University. The content has been prepared for the graduate schools of Arts and Sciences, Social Science, and Engineering principally. Particular requirements of these schools and other schools should be studied by the student in the Announcements of the School."

---

[3] When Monsignor Corrigan first came to the University, it became painfully evident that he was anxious to make changes, although it was not at all clear to him just what changes should be made. He grasped at every suggestion that came his way, and in the fall of the first year of his rectorship carried out a good many "reforms," all of them quite minor. They did, however, cause much excitement around the University, and the student paper, the Tower, got out a special "shakeup" edition announcing the changes.

My narrative should be interrupted long enough to say that during the strenuous days of the early reforms within the Graduate School of Arts and Sciences, Monsignor John Cooper and Dr. Thomas Verner Moore were towers of strength for me. Not only were they loyal, but they were forthright priests, ready to express an honest opinion, however distasteful to others, when the occasion called for it. I badly needed such support, and these priests gave it to me without stint.

In 1933 and 1934, a joint committee of the Association of American Universities and of the American Council of Learned Societies set out to evaluate the graduate work of such graduate schools as pretended to offer worthy programs for the degree, Doctor of Philosophy, and to list them, department by department, as "excellent" or "satisfactory" or "inferior." The results, as published late in 1934, created a great furor, especially in Catholic circles. Moreover, the ratings as given for graduate departments in Catholic graduate schools were a distinct shock. Only seven departments in all the graduate schools conducted under Catholic auspices received any classification above "inferior," and none was rated as "excellent." Of the seven departments rated as "satisfactory," one (Chemistry) was from the University of Notre Dame, and the remaining six from the Catholic University of America.

I do not wish to go into the details of the method employed in the making of this survey, but

I do wish to say that all in all it seemed to me to be as accurate as such studies may be expected to be. One thing is certain: it blasted Catholic graduate schools out of a heavy lethargy, and the progress made by these institutions in the last generation, and still going on, as a result of this criticism has been nothing less than phenomenal. After all, at that time the history of the Catholic college for men, to say nothing of the Catholic college for women, was very brief, and its accomplishments were very great. But the Catholic graduate school of arts and sciences, except at The Catholic University of America, was just getting its start and seemed to be dawdling along. This investigation was just the impetus needed. If a similar study were to be made today, the results with reference to Catholic graduate schools would be very satisfactory, I am sure.

Dr. George Johnson, then Secretary General of the National Catholic Educational Association and the only Catholic educator who was invited to take an active part in the direction of the survey of departments of graduate study, asked me if I would be willing to speak at a closed session of deans and directors of graduate study on the significance of this recent investigation to Catholic graduate schools. He admitted that this was a very delicate subject for Catholic educators, and his plan was to avoid as much embarrassment as possible while getting as much good out of the report as could be gained. His plan, of course, was quite agreeable to me.

Several cross currents were operating at this time which resulted in a most interesting occasion. At the annual meeting of the N.C.E.A. of the year before an attempt had been made to separate the women's institutions from the main body of the N.C.E.A. This resulted in a terrific ordeal and was fortunately quite unsuccessful. The women, or perhaps I should say the Sisters, were smarting under this apparent slight, and were very alert to any similar attempt to shut them off from the center of things. Furthermore, the Jesuits were extremely offended by the results of the investigation of the quality of graduate study in our American graduate schools and were very sensitive to the possibility of someone making capital out of this devastating information to their detriment. Bishop Francis W. Howard of Covington, the first episcopal president of the N.C.E.A., had always lived in fear that the Catholic University of America would dominate the N.C.E.A. and on every possible occasion acted, as he thought, to prevent this. Actually, through Bishop Shahan and Monsignor Pace, the University had been the real founder of the N.C.E.A., but as a result of this attitude, principally of Bishop Howard, Bishop Shahan and Monsignor Pace withdrew completely from active participation in the activities of that organization. Bishop Ryan was inclined to follow in their footsteps, as were succeeding Rectors, up to Bishop McEntegart. I convinced the latter that it was time to break this long line of retirement from N.C.E.A. participation, and he created quite a sensation when he attended

SCHOOLS

the first annual meeting (1954) of the N.C.E.A.
within his administration of the University. But I
could not convince Bishop Ryan completely that
he should participate in these meetings. He did,
however, say to me: "All right, Deferrari, you go
and represent the University, if you want to."

Still another wave of ill feeling existed at the
time. In Bishop Ryan's campaign for funds for the
University, much irritation was caused within certain Catholic circles by the constant reference to
the University as the papal university of the United
States and the capstone of Catholic education in
the country, as well as the only Catholic member of
the Association of American Universities. All these
cross currents are evident in the following letter
which I shall quote essentially in full, describing
what took place at the annual meeting of the
N.C.E.A. in Chicago in 1935, when I attempted
to carry out Dr. Johnson's wishes with reference
to the report on graduate studies.

April 27, 1935

Most Reverend James H. Ryan
The Catholic University of America

YOUR EXCELLENCY:

I am presenting a brief report of my trip to
Chicago for the annual meetings of the N.C.E.A.

As you will recall the meeting of deans and
officers of graduate schools was scheduled as an
informal meeting, not open to the public, on Wednesday afternoon at 2:30. At the general meeting
on Wednesday morning, to my great surprise,

Father Hogan [4] of Fordham University and
Father Wilson [5] of Loyola University, Chicago,
very openly declared that the meeting on graduate
affairs scheduled for the afternoon was irregular
and should be abolished. This was a signal for the
nuns, led by Mother Antonia [6] and Sister Aloysius, [7] who demanded in a body not only that
the meeting on graduate problems be retained but
that it be opened to the public and be made a part
of their meeting. They consulted me and asked if
I would be willing so to conduct it. My reply was
that, in my opinion, in the future there should be
both a public informational session and a private
conference of deans and officers of graduate
schools, but as a matter of fact for the present occasion only a private conference had been arranged. However, if the majority of those present
wished me to conduct the meeting as a public affair, I would do my best. A motion was so passed,
with the exception that we should hold a private
session in the evening to make plans for the future.

In the afternoon, Father Cunningham [8]
turned over one hour and three quarters of the
time to me. First I presented a report on the work
thus far accomplished by the joint committee of
the A.A.U. and A.C.L.S. That was easy. Then I
took up the problems of the graduate school as indicated in the enclosed paper. Before I presented
these problems, however, I announced that in my

[4] Father Aloysius Hogan, President of Fordham University.
[5] Father Samuel Knox Wilson, President of Loyola University,
Chicago.
[6] Mother M. Antonia McHugh, President of the College of
St. Catherine, St. Paul, Minnesota.
[7] Sister M. Aloysius Molloy, President of the College of
St. Teresa, Winona, Minnesota.
[8] Father Cunningham, C.S.C., of the Department of Education of
the University of Notre Dame.

opinion these problems were facing all Catholic graduate schools to a greater or less degree, and nothing said by me was to be construed as referring in any special way to any particular institution. Furthermore, since my plans had been made, as directed, for a private meeting, I requested that no name of any institution should be mentioned by anyone. We must confine our proceedings to general principles.

I had just started to present the first problem, our relations with standardizing agencies, and Dr. Edward Fitzpatrick of Marquette at the rear of the hall interrupted and asked me to name the one Catholic institution that was a member of the A.A.U. I recalled my recent request and the reasons therefor and insisted on refusing to mention any names. After I had finished the first topic, Dr. Fitzpatrick walked to the front of the hall and faced the audience, and said essentially this:

"That great Catholic University of America in Washington! Well, we are all pretty tired of its "holier than thou" attitude. The papal university of the United States—ridiculous! etc. etc."

I was sorely tempted to say much but I said nothing, and proceeded to the end of my program with much interesting discussion from the floor and no more open hostility. In closing I spoke essentially as follows:

"Ladies and gentlemen. If I have said anything which has given any of you any offense, I humbly beg your pardon. If I could have detached my identity for the period of this meeting from the name of my university, I would gladly have done so. At any rate, if by my talk this afternoon I have been able to renew to greater activity among you the discussion of problems of Catholic graduate schools I shall be very happy." The effect was almost emotional. All the nuns and many of the clergy came around me with congratulations, etc. In fact, it was an additional hour before I could get back to the hotel.

Most interesting were Bishop Howard's comments later. He told me himself, and I heard indirectly from others, including Dr. Johnson, [9] that he was greatly impressed and hoped that I would continue to carry on the movement on graduate matters within the N.C.E.A. Of one thing I am definitely certain: The nuns and many of the priests look to the representatives of the University for leadership at these meetings. They feel that we are definitely "letting them down" by not sending active representatives to these meetings. Mother Antonia and Sister Aloysius are particularly anxious about this. I would take the liberty to suggest that both Dr. Campbell and I attend these meetings as official representatives of the Catholic University in the future.

But the end was not yet. On Thursday noon, Dr. McElwane of St. Louis University and Father Daniel O'Connell, Director of Studies of all Jesuit institutions in the United States, asked me to have dinner with them in a private dining room to discuss graduate school problems. It was a most interesting meeting. In parting they begged me not to take any remarks by Fitzpatrick very seriously.

Incidentally, I had many conferences with Sisters Superior about work in the summer session and graduate school for their subjects.

I almost forgot to say that Bishop Howard said that you should decide whether or not the

[9] Dr. George Johnson of The Catholic University of America, then Secretary General of the N.C.E.A.

discussion of graduate studies should be in a separate organization. I took the liberty to say that I
was sure you wanted it to continue where it was!

Yours very sincerely,

(Signed) ROY J. DEFERRARI

Dean

P.S. I almost forgot to say that Father O'Connell
discussed with me the plan of the Jesuits to send us
a number of their men this summer and at least
three for the next academic year to do graduate
work.

ROY J. DEFERRARI

Before closing this chapter another incident,
which resembles the proverbial fish story, "The Big
Fish That Got Away," deserves to be recorded. It
was in the very early days of the Rectorship of Monsignor Ryan; I was still in the office of the Department of Greek and Latin. I was correcting the test
papers of the affiliated schools, when I received a
visit from several gentlemen sent to my office by
the Rector. I recall Mr. McManus, Mr. Ward, and
Mr. Graham, but I do not remember the names of
one or two others who were in the group. Mr. Mc-
Manus seemed to be the leader. They were all dedi-
cated Catholic laymen from Detroit and connected
in one way or another with the automobile industry
in that city. When Mr.McManus saw me correcting
papers of high school students, he remarked that
this was rather an unfitting occupation for the future Dean of the Graduate School of Arts and Sciences of The Catholic University of America. I

quite agreed with him but remarked that a man with even a small family needed enough money to live on. His answer gave me the cue to the purpose of their visit: "Perhaps you will soon be able to devote all your time to the Graduate School."

This group had for many years been thinking of endowing heavily a graduate school of arts and sciences under Catholic auspices. As one of the group put it, "We have been very fortunate in our business affairs, and we feel that we are morally obligated to use at least some of our money for charitable purposes." They had, moreover, made a careful investigation of Catholic graduate schools, and had selected our Graduate School of Arts and Sciences as the institution to be endowed by their funds. They were especially impressed by the fact that The Catholic University of America was (and still is) the only Catholic institution which is a member of the Association of American Universities.

A short while later, on a Sunday morning, I received a telephone call from the Rector asking me if I could go to his office for an important conference, which, of course, I was glad to do. As I stepped into the room, I found the Rector with the same group of men who had visited me in my office. They had drawn up a contract according to which they would give the University a fabulous sum of money to endow a strong faculty for the Graduate School of Arts and Sciences. This money was to be used only to strengthen the faculty. I wish that I could remember the exact amount of money involved, but after figures reach a certain point, they do not mean much to me and I forget them. We discussed the various departments of the School and possible new and strengthening personnel for for these departments. We also planned for certain entirely new departments. The Rector, after the meeting was over, remarked to me joyfully: "Well, Deferrari, you are going to have plenty of 'jack' for your graduate school!"

After the meeting I took the contract home, at the request of Monsignor Ryan, to study it once more with a view to putting it into final shape. I was also to give further consideration to plans for the expansion and strengthening of the faculty of the Graduate School of Arts and Sciences. Shortly thereafter, the famous stock market crash came. We had one more rather saddened meeting of our group. The general feeling was: "We had planned our endowment chiefly on the sale of stocks. With this drop in the stock market we cannot proceed as we had planned. Furthermore, this recession is only temporary (!) and we will wait until there has been some significant recovery." We are still waiting!

The Beginning of Instruction in Nursing at The Catholic University of America

Early in the academic year of 1930, Sister M. Thérèse Flatley of the Sisters of Mercy, of Mercy Hospital in Chicago, wrote to me essentially as follows:

Nursing education as a professional and cultural training for nurses is making great strides forward, and is spearheaded by a group of nursing educators who will give force to their movement by the formation of a group of nursing schools to be known as the Association of Collegiate Schools of Nursing. This group through its schools seeks to establish nursing as a branch of education in the same relationship to the hospital, as the medical profession has been set up for the study of medicine. Since Catholic hospitals are almost exclusively owned and controlled by religious communities, which at the same time operate the nursing schools, while facing the difficulties of hospital finance, it is extremely difficult for them to view nursing as a profession and education. They have difficulty in submitting to the general axiom of nursing educators that the actual training received by the nurses in a hospital should be confined to the matters and to the extent that contribute to the development of students as nurses. They cannot break away from the traditional idea that nurses in training are in the nature of charwomen without pay, to be used in the general up-keep of the hospital. The Catholic University of America

> should take the lead in this movement, first of all because it is The Catholic University of America, and secondly because it is free to make working agreements with hospitals of all kinds and can thus give its students a varied and educational hospital experience. Furthermore, no other Catholic institution of higher education seems likely to make any positive effort to solve the problem.

This statement condenses greatly the correspondence carried on between Sister M. Thérèse and myself on this subject, which indeed introduced me to the problems of this interesting and important phase of professional education. Sister Thérèse also, it should be added, urged the importance of an active and effective scheme of affiliation of Catholic schools of nursing with The Catholic University of America. While this latter suggestion of affiliation has been carried out and has been in operation for some years, much still remains to be done before it can be called a genuine success. However, the development of the School of Nursing has been definitely successful, and we all are justly proud of it.

The earliest years of the School of Nursing Education were rough indeed. First of all, it was discovered that the Sisters College on our own campus was inviting nurses to come here to further their education through a program which, paradoxically enough, except for the title had nothing whatsoever about nursing in it! The Sisters College was following a program which had been set up in a college of the mid-west, whose president was quoted to me by Bishop Ryan as saying: "I have never met a nurse yet who had anything more than the equivalent of an eighth grade education. What nurses need is some fundamental general studies." This may seem ridiculous now but it was something which arose again and again for several years to plague us at the University and had to be counteracted.

My first step, naturally enough, was to confer with the Rector of the University, Bishop James H. Ryan, to see how far I could go in the matter. The first problem that confronted me was to pry the work for nurses, poor as it was, away from the Sisters College, so that it could grow and develop under the combined direction of professional nursing educators working together with sympathetic general educators. The following letter, sent by me to the Rector and dated December 9, 1930, sets forth the initial difficulties.

> Some time ago I talked to you about the urgent need existing for Sister Nurses obtaining the B.S. degree, and the possibility of the University offering a fitting program for such students leading to that degree. At that time you asked me to consult with Monsignor McCormick on the matter to ascertain what plans, if any, he was making to offer such a program of studies at the Sisters College. I have since had several brief conversations with him on the subject, and find that he has had the matter under consideration for a number of years and as yet has not reached any definite decision. He may possibly be ready at the end of this year to offer such a program for nurses, but I am not sure.

This entire problem of offering a suitable program leading to the B.S. for Sister Nurses I consider to be so pressing that the University should make some provision to meet the same as soon as possible. I would suggest that we accept Sister Nurses in the Summer Session and after giving them proper credit for their Nurses diploma offer such courses as are necessary in addition to that, in the Summer Session, and in due time grant the B.S. degree for Nurses without the usual required year of residence at the University—that is, for Summer Session residence alone. I suggest this merely as a temporary measure until the University in one way or another shall be able to require one full academic year in residence leading to that degree. I am at present seeking information on this whole matter from other universities doing this kind of work, and after a short time shall be able to offer you a definite program.

I am very anxious to have my Announcement for the coming Summer Session published as soon as possible and I am particularly anxious to have this prospective program for Nurses announced in it. I shall, accordingly, be very anxious to have your decision on this question as soon as possible.

When I spoke as I did in this letter about the then Monsignor McCormick, I knew that Bishop Ryan would understand the situation. Judging from past performances by Monsignor McCormick, who disliked intensely to embark on anything new and was always the champion of the *status quo*, it was clear that he had neither a plan nor any intention of doing something about a program of studies in nursing.

Since at the time I was both Director of the Summer Session and Dean of the Graduate School of Arts and Sciences, I could always ask for permission to try out something new in the Summer Session, and, if it were successful there, to suggest with some confidence that it could be carried on successfully during the regular semesters. There was always much less hesitancy about giving permission to try something out in a six-weeks term than over assenting to a two-semester proposition. Furthermore, there was little possibility of any entanglement with the Sisters College in the Summer Session.

Finally, an unenthusiastic permission was given to try out several courses in nursing education in the Summer Session of 1932. These were to be for nurses already in possession of the Nurses Certificate and might lead to the degree Bachelor of Science in Nursing Education. No permission, however, was given to grant the Bachelors degree to nurses with only summer session residence.

My next step was to confer with Dr. Thomas Verner Moore. I hoped first of all that he would be willing to shelter the new-born field of study within the well-established confines of his Department of Psychology and Psychiatry. It was necessary to anchor it somewhere before it could begin to offer courses. I also hoped to get from him some suggestions as to staffing the proposed section or division of Nursing Education. It really had no name at all at that time and was responsible directly to me as Dean of the Graduate School of Arts and Sciences. I found him most encouraging from the very beginning and always helpful. At the suggestion of the Rector we both called on the Chancellor of the University, Archbishop Michael J. Curley of Baltimore, who professed to be in favor of the work. The purpose of our visit, of course, was to make sure that the Chancellor would support the new program when it was presented to the Board of Trustees of the University. It would have little chance of success otherwise.

Dr. Moore suggested that I procure the services of one Sister M. Olivia Gowan, of the Sisters of St. Benedict of Duluth, Minnesota, who was then directing his St. Gertrude's School of Arts and Crafts. This was toward the end of the first semester, and, when I discussed the matter with her, she expressed herself as very happy to undertake the work, but very dutifully added: "provided my Superior consents." She also said: "I shall suggest to her that I be permitted to go to Teachers College, Columbia, to finish my work for the Master's degree, which I think I can do shortly, and be ready for the Summer Session." Sister also suggested that I invite Mrs. Eugenia Spalding [1] to serve as a second teacher that summer. All proceeded very smoothly for the moment, and the courses in the Summer Session were reasonably well attended. But all our troubles were by no means over; we were not even well started on our way.

[1] A friend of Sister Olivia's from her days at Columbia University.

Because all went very well during the first summer session of 1932, a strong demand arose for continuing the program through the regular semester. The Rector agreed, and literature was composed to make the historical event known wherever we might expect to find a source of students. At the same time another event helped us greatly. Several local hospitals had suddenly found themselves without any instruction in the sciences for their student nurses. They asked us if we could do the work provided they took the responsibility of transporting the students to our laboratories. This was in the summer, and the Rector and Vice Rector were absent from the campus. I hesitated to make a decision, but, as usual, I took the chance and concluded the arrangements in the name of the University. This work continued for some years, although I often heard much grumbling on the part of those at the University who had to participate in it. But it was the financial income from this arrangement which subsidized the nursing program in its earliest years, and I doubt very much that we would have been allowed to go ahead with it, if these funds had not been available.

Sister Olivia was, of course, to continue in general charge during the regular year, and she was to have an assistant. Since Mrs. Spalding found it impossible to continue during that academic year, Sister Berenice Beck, O.S.F., was engaged to fill the post. The student response that first year was very small and a little discouraging, all of which was made worse by the reluctance on the part of many of the University personnel, including some members of the regular faculty, to accept both women students and women teachers. Indeed, I was unable to find a room for one of Sister Olivia's classes scheduled for five o'clock in the afternoon, and had to resort to turning my office over to her for the purpose. This was about the time when Dr. Lennox, Head of the Department of English, made his classic remark: "Now be careful, De-ferrari, the first thing you know we will be having women on the faculty!" But with the steady increase of the student body, a fixed curriculum was devised and approved by the Academic Senate, and all went smoothly for a number of years. During this period Dr. Moore with his Department of Psychology and Psychiatry proved the ideal host. He left the work in nursing severely alone to the Director and the Dean of the Graduate School of Arts and Sciences, but was always ready with helpful advice when called upon.

Almost from the beginning applications were received from students who wished to follow a program leading to the Master's degree. At that very point I urged Sister Olivia to require a dissertation, however small, that was worthy of being printed. Most members of the University faculty were very dubious about even the possibility of there being worthy material for graduate study in the field of nursing. I myself was doubtful about our being able to draw a sharp line of distinction between graduate and undergraduate courses in the academic, not the professional, sense of the terms. I felt strongly that excellent Master's dissertations would put an end to the general criticism. Dr. Gladys Sellew helped greatly by supplying a fund to meet the expense of publication. It was hoped that the income from the sales of these dissertations would keep the fund intact, but this has not been the case. Gradually, the fund has been depleted, but the practice of publishing at least those for which there may be a demand has continued.

Finally in 1935, the news broke that Bishop Ryan was being transferred to the Diocese of Omaha. Furthermore, opponents of our nursing education movement outside the University, who had discovered that they could not alienate Bishop Ryan from his support of the new program, had been trying different tactics. They reported to Mother Agnes, Sister Olivia's Superior at the time, and also to the Bishop of Duluth, that Sister Olivia was attending faculty meetings on the campus in the evening and was even going to New York to attend the meetings of the Association of Collegiate Schools of Nursing, when she should have been safely tucked away in her convent. Mother Agnes consulted with me because it really was a serious matter for her, since the Bishop had been brought in on the problem. It was also extremely serious for me, or perhaps I should say for the University. As I told Mother Agnes, "If you pull Sister Olivia out of here, this nursing education movement will collapse." Now, with Bishop Ryan leaving us, it was almost a foregone conclusion that our opponents, both on and off the campus, would move in on the attack and bombard the new Rector with petitions for the abolishment of the nursing program.

Two things saved us. Bishop Ryan through a committee appointed for the purpose had recently sent a new set of statutes, or constitution, for the University to the Sacred Congregation of Seminaries and Universities for approval. At a farewell gathering tendered him by the faculty, he took me aside and said: "The statutes are approved, and they include the setting up of the work in nursing as a separate and independent school." What His Excellency did not tell me was that the new school was called the School of Nursing Education, whereas we had definitely agreed that it was to be the School of Nursing. There was a slip somewhere. [2] But this was comparatively of little importance. The official papal recognition of the School was the important thing. This relieved us of a great deal of anxiety. Surely with the Sacred Congregation of Seminaries and Universities placing its blessing on the work in nursing, it would behoove our critics to proceed cautiously against us. At first Sister Olivia and her faculty were a little nonplussed with the realization that they would now be on their own and would have to fight their own

[2] This has been corrected. The School is now known as the School of Nursing.

battles in official circles, but I assured them that it was all for the best. I was always puzzled why the leaders in nursing did not insist more on an independent status for their studies just as all the other professions did. On making inquiries I found that they regarded this as of no great consequence. In this I disagreed with them strongly. I do not wish to go into the details of the matter here, but I would simply point to the history of nursing studies at our University from this date on as a conclusive argument in favor of such a status.

Now it happened that at just about this time, at Sister Olivia's request, I had constructed a letter to be sent to the various Superiors of the country in an effort to stimulate the enrollment of the School of Nursing. The famous outside opponent of our School of Nursing procured a copy and hastened with it to Bishop Corrigan, the new Rector. With much disgust he pointed out the absurdities and the abysmal ignorance of nursing displayed throughout the letter, assuming that I had written the letter. He was right in that the phraseology was mine with most of the content furnished by Sister Olivia, but he had failed to note that Bishop Corrigan had signed the letter. The Bishop himself reported the incident to me. He said with much indignation: "I asked him when he had finished his tirade, 'Who do you suppose wrote this letter anyhow?' And he replied: 'Deferrari, of course,' and then I showed him my signature!"

There is one more incident to record before I
close my narrative, namely, Father Schwitalla's [3]
attempt to set up an independent Catholic accrediting agency for nursing schools. This took place
simultaneously with the incident which I have just
described. He presented his plan at the first meeting of the Hierarchy of the United States on our
campus in the Rectorship of Bishop Corrigan. He
argued that if we Catholics set up our own accrediting group and scrupulously refused to join the
Association of Collegiate Schools of Nursing or any
similar organization, we could maintain our freedom and not be constantly annoyed as Catholic
general education was by the demands of outside
associations. He said further that if Catholic general educators had acted in this fashion in the
beginning, they would today be entirely free of
any outside influence. Again this is an old question,
and I do not intend to argue it here. Suffice it to say
that Catholic nurses throughout the country, especially those holding positions in the state and Federal government, wrote to a number of us on the
campus, begging us not to stand idly by and let the
bishops of the land agree to demand that all Catholic
nursing schools accredit themselves only with the
Catholic organization to the exclusion of all others.
The great argument was that, if they did so, graduates of Catholic schools of nursing would not be
eligible for state or Federal positions in nursing.

[3] Father Alphonse Schwitalla, S.J., Professor of Biology at St.
Louis University, and for many years President of the Catholic Hospital Association, the position now held by Father John J. Flanagan, S.J.

The Hierarchy very wisely appointed a committee to study the question and to report back at the next annual meeting on the University campus. Bishop John B. Peterson, then Bishop of Manchester, New Hampshire, was made chairman of the committee. I was very pleased to receive an invitation from him in Manchester to visit him to discuss the problem in some detail. This I readily accepted, and about a month or so later I was Bishop Peterson's guest at dinner. We spent a good part of the evening going over the pros and cons of the exclusive Catholic accrediting agency for Catholic schools of nursing. Briefly, at the next meeting of the Hierarchy it was voted that the Catholic accrediting agency be regarded as *one* of the accrediting groups whose approval might be sought by Catholic schools of nursing, if they so desired.

The following throws more light on the problem from the University's point of view. It represents an effort on my part to inform the Rector as completely as possible on the entire matter of accreditation of schools of nursing and also the relation of the University's plan of affiliation to it.

April 12, 1939

RT. REV. MONSIGNOR JOSEPH M. CORRIGAN:

I shall try to present briefly the nursing situation with reference to Father Schwitalla, at least as I see it.

The only accrediting of nursing schools undertaken by non-sectarian and national groups thus far has been carried on by the Association of

Collegiate Schools of Nursing. Incidentally, Father Schwitalla's own School of Nursing at St. Louis University holds membership in this Association. This Association, however, is not attempting to act as a general accrediting association for the entire country. It plans rather to be an association for the very best nursing schools of the country. It has left to the American League of Nursing Education the task of placing the stamp of approval on such nursing schools in general throughout the country as deserve it. It should be said here that the problem of accrediting nursing schools has been taken seriously only comparatively recently because the teaching of nursing has always been regarded as part of the activity of the hospital and not an educational matter. Nursing schools are now regarded as educational institutions just as are medical schools, and the hospital serves the nursing school as it does the medical school.

The American League of Nursing Education has been on the point of launching its program of accreditation for the last five years. It will in all probability succeed in doing so this month at its annual meeting in New Orleans. The examining boards of the various states stand ready to take over their standards.

Father Schwitalla has set up an accrediting agency for nursing schools under the auspices of the Catholic Hospital Association. This is unfortunate at the start as it appears to make a hospital group the dominating influence over schools of nursing, which to educators is no more tolerable than to have a hospital group dominate medical schools. Father Schwitalla believes that if Catholic schools of nursing are accredited by his organization, the non-sectarian agencies will recognize them without requiring anything further. This both the Association of Collegiate Schools of Nursing and the American League of Nursing Education have said that they cannot do. It is to be noted that unless they do, the graduates of Catholic schools of nursing accredited only by Father Schwitalla's organization will not be eligible for the best jobs in the states and country. This eventually, as it becomes known, will mean a very inferior type of student in our Catholic schools of nursing, chiefly those who cannot get into nationally accredited schools.

Father Schwitalla insists that the Association of Collegiate Schools of Nursing and the League will not recognize Catholic philosophy. The presidents of both organizations have signed a statement composed by Dr. Ignatius Smith to the effect that they will recognize Catholic ethics and philosophy generally as taught in the Catholic schools of nursing. Father Schwitalla says that this is not sufficient; that they should sign a statement that they recognize Catholic philosophy as the only true philosophy. This, of course, they will not do.

Personally, I see no reason why the Catholic schools of nursing, if they wish, should not strive to be accredited both by the Catholic Hospital Association and by the non-sectarian groups. Father Schwitalla insists that they be accredited by his organization alone. It should also be said in this connection that Father Schwitalla has already largely discredited his accreditation program in the eyes, of educators by reason of the fact that he has been accrediting practically all, if not all, the nursing schools which have applied to him. Lack of accrediting standards is already evident.

The program of affiliating Catholic schools of nursing with the Catholic University is not another attempt at accreditation. It is an effort to carry out several articles of the Statutes of the University (especially the first part of Article 71, Section 2) as approved by the Sacred Congregation of Seminaries and Universities. The aim of affiliation is to bring the affiliate closer to the University in order that it may benefit most from the facilities of the University. The two conditions necessary for affiliation are first, that the institution seeking affiliation wish to improve itself, and second, that the University feel that it can assist the institution to achieve its aim.

The process through which an institution must pass when seeking affiliation is admittedly similar to the procedure required by the accrediting agencies. It is so, however, only because by such a process the University seeks to know an institution, especially its problems, thoroughly, so that it may be in a better position to assist its affiliate. It should be stated also that the University is on the constant lookout to improve the Catholic element in such institutions. For example, five Catholic junior colleges were examined recently by the Committee on Affiliation, in every one of which no provision whatsoever was made in the curriculum for the teaching of philosophy. The proper treatment of philosophy in the curriculum was insisted upon before these institutions were affiliated.

Affiliation with the Catholic University, then, represents a systematic effort on the part of the University to assist Catholic academic institutions of all kinds to achieve the objectives which they have set up for themselves, without in any way interfering with their autonomy.

(Signed) Roy J. Deferrari
Secretary General

We had no more trouble from outside sources thereafter. All our troubles from that time on had to do with matters of finance and enrollment, and these were comparatively minor. Before long I was able to tell Sister Olivia that she would have to go on alone with her nursing education colleagues; that she could no longer send me to all these nursing education meetings as she had been doing in an effort to educate me in the field of nursing. I would, of course, always be interested in her school, but I was sure that she and her co-workers could now take good care of themselves. The truth of this statement has been proven by the accomplishments of Sister and her group: the educational organization within the School, the cooperation of the School in national educational movements; the leadership of the School especially within Catholic circles; and the very building to house the School long since outgrown for present day needs.

The School of Sacred Theology

I had not intended to devote a special section of my *Memoirs* to the School of Sacred Theology but to speak of it incidentally in connection with matters with which I was directly concerned. Thus I have spoken of it under the "General Organization of the University" and also when appraising Archbishop Ryan as a Rector under whom I had served. But several persons who have been aware of my writing these recollections have suggested that I cannot very well pass it by so easily. In addition it has been my good fortune to be able to view two very important documents, written by Monsignor Ryan and now located in the archives of the Archdiocese of Omaha, which deal at length with this subject. One of these sources is a communication dated November 16, 1931, and inscribed as follows: "Sent to Msgr. Bernardini in Rome to assist him in discussing the affairs of the University with the Sacred Congregation—not to be left there." The other is a copy of a letter addressed to His Eminence Cardinal Bisletti, Prefect of the Sacred Congregation of Seminaries and Universities and dated May 11, 1931. Both of these communications, which are rather lengthy, will be indispensable to any historian who wishes to give a serious appraisal of Archbishop Ryan's rectorship.

The letter to Monsignor Bernadini, entitled "Aide Memoire," gives a general description of the University as a whole, including the School of Theology, as of that date and the progress which had been made in its improvement since 1928 when Monsignor Ryan assumed the Rectorship. In my humble estimation it is an excellent account, complete and accurate, without any display of spleen. I have quoted parts of this elsewhere. The letter to Cardinal Bisletti was very difficult for Bishop Ryan to write. It was written at the request of Archbishop Curley "to clear up some of the allegations" made in a so-called "statement" submitted to the Board of Trustees by the Faculty of Theology. In spite of the emotional stress under which the Bishop wrote this letter, it too, insofar as I am able to judge, is calm and honest, all in all most edifying.

> To understand the present condition of the Faculty of Theology a history of this Faculty is necessary. Since 1920, and even somewhat earlier, the Faculty began to lose influence. This was due, in part, to their traditional attitude of opposition to the Administration of the University, to the factions existing in the Faculty itself, and to the character of some of the members of the Faculty. Dr. Shanahan, an esteemed Professor of Dogmatic Theology, resigned in 1918. No successor was appointed up to 1939. Again, the Faculty was not productive, many of the members engaging in work outside the University. The direct result of the above cited facts was that students refused to frequent the theological courses. Bishops, aware of the controversies existing in the Faculty and the inferior kind of work offered and done, did not support the School of Theology, preferring to send their students to Europe. The prestige of the faculty which was high until the end of the World War, diminished and, in the last ten years, the attendance never exceeded twenty, and the number of Doctor's Degrees given anually was reduced to one or two. The Faculty *deliberately* cut itself off from the general life of the University and spent most of its time criticizing the Administration of Bishop Shahan and other officials, and schools of the University, and fighting among themselves. [1]

[1] Communication to Monsignor Bernadini.

It would be difficult to improve on this description of the status of the School of Theology when Monsignor Ryan first became Rector. In fact, it might well be considered very restrained. For example, I remember well that students in this school in some years numbered as few as four! The conditions in this school continued for several years as just described. While I do not intend to go into the details of the bitter struggle that followed when the Rector attempted to bring this School in line with all the other schools of the University, one thing more must be said. The Faculty of Theology clung stubbornly to the contention that as a faculty of theology it was independent of the rest of the University in every phase of its existence and was entitled to separate statutes to protect this independence. [2]

The following quotation from the Rector's letter to Cardinal Bisletti illustrates the impasse which was reached.

In order to save, at least, the appearance of things, a Seminary for members of Religious Communities was started. This Seminary has been anything but a success. Its intellectual atmosphere is not vigorous; classes are conducted in English instead of Latin, and from all information I can obtain, there is little or no Seminary discipline of the type required to produce first-rate priests. The activities of this Seminary, as well as those of the Graduate School, are practically unknown both to

[2] This has been referred to under other sections.

the Vice-Rector and myself. In spite of all efforts, no information regarding the regular conduct of the School of Theology is available. It may seem astounding to your Eminence to learn, but it is a provable fact that neither Monsignor Pace nor I know any more about the functioning of the School of Theology here than we do of an institution situated in China. The Faculty has excluded us deliberately from all its acts, in open violation of the Constitution of the University. The acts and attitude of the Faculty in these respects are easy to understand. It is their method of covering up deficiencies which are many and grave, as well as a starting point for criticizing the administration of the University and accusing us of not cooperating in their work.

The Sacred Congregation can be of great assistance in the reorganization of the Faculty of Theology if it should expressly declare in the new Constitution of the University that all so-called "Propriae Constitutiones" are abrogated and that each and every school of the University must be governed by the general Constitution of the University, after it is revised to meet the demands of the Constitution *Deus Scientiarum Dominus*. Only in this way can the unity of the University be preserved as we have pointed out, on previous occasions, to the Sacred Congregation. Moreover, there is no need, as exists in some European countries, of a *Propria Constitutio* for the Theological Faculty. Every faculty of the Catholic University is made up exclusively of Catholics, priests and laymen. The State does not interfere in the slightest in our educational policies, and not even *indirectly* does the State or accrediting agencies interfere in the curriculum or work of a School of Theology. Why, given these circum-

stances, the Faculty of Theology should be cut off
from the general life of the University and ac-
corded a Constitution which no other school
possesses is difficult to understand.

Bishop Ryan won his particular struggle, and
the School of Sacred Theology was at least cleared
of the serious obstructing elements. His successors
in the rectorship carried on and developed the
present flourishing School of Sacred Theology as
planned by the present Archbishop Francesco
Lardone.

In closing I would like to quote from this letter
to Cardinal Bisletti particularly to give further in-
sight into Archbishop Ryan's character. The person
who spearheaded the war of the School of Sacred
Theology was the Dean, Dr. Coeln.

> To have surrendered to this man under the
> circumstances would have wrecked my whole
> administration and would have left my successor
> to face the self-same problem which I encoun-
> tered on entering upon office.
>
> I bear no ill will to these gentlemen for
> their vicious attack upon my probity, honesty, and
> good name. If what I have had to suffer per-
> sonally helps even in a small way to solve the
> problems of Catholic University and opens up for
> it a new day in its development, I am more than
> repaid. The most Reverend Chancellor of the
> University, who is in intimate daily touch with
> the happenings at the University, has made plain
> what issues are involved in this sad controversy,
> and has always accorded me the support of his
> high authority.

DEPARTMENTS
AND DIVISIONS

The Department of Greek and Latin

Originally, the University had at least in theory two separate departments, one of Greek directed by Dr. George M. Bolling and one of Latin headed by Father John D. Maguire. When Dr. Bolling moved to Ohio State University, Dr. John B. O'Connor was brought in from Adelphi College to succeed him as Head of the Department of Greek. But when Father Maguire died, no successor was employed in his place. Dr. O'Connor took over both departments which were then officially made one, the Department of Greek and Latin, when I took over in December of 1918. The Department has so continued until the present.

When my appointment was made in 1918, I found myself faced with a most difficult task, but the work while arduous was most pleasing. To begin with, the entire department had to be reorganized. The undergraduate division presented little difficulty. The traditional undergraduate courses continued to be offered with little or no change, except that courses in beginning and intermediate Latin were given for the first time for college credit, a practice accepted almost everywhere because of the growing trend of the secondary school to offer either no Latin at all or only two units of it. Dr. Thomas J. McGourty and Dr. Patrick A. Collis took care of these courses for a number of years.

The task of reorganizing or rather organizing the graduate division presented a real problem. The University in its early years, because of both lack of funds and lack of students, had in its graduate divisions one-man departments for the most part. This one person took complete charge of the training of students for masters and doctors degrees. Of necessity little and insufficient preliminary training was possible through fundamental courses. The main attention was given to the essay, now called dissertation, for the master's degree and the dissertation for the doctorate. A remarkably high standard of achievement for doctoral dissertations was maintained then and always has been through the years, probably as a result of the rigidly maintained requirement that all doctoral dissertations had to be published in full and had to be circulated where they would be appreciated and critically appraised. In any case, the general plan of training for graduate degrees as then carried on would not be

accepted as satisfactory by serious university educators. Some plan had to be devised whereby
graduate students would receive a thorough preliminary training in research before they were
actually required to attempt a work of scholarship
by themselves.

Before proceeding with my narrative an incident must be related which, momentarily at least,
interrupted my plans for reorganizing the Department of Greek and Latin. I had by no means
become well settled, when I received word from
Bishop Shahan asking that I visit him. His words
were essentially these: "I have always wanted to
bring the Jesuits into close relationship with The
Catholic University of America, as they should be.
It appears that the opportunity has come, if I can
only offer them two or three important professorships. I would like to propose to them one each in
English, History, and Latin? Would you be willing
to give up the Latin and confine yourself to Greek?"
I could only assent, but I did not like it. My chief
objection was that it meant a return to the old arrangement of two separate and distinct departments
for Latin and Greek, which had been tried in several of the leading universities of the land, notably,
the University of Chicago, with very poor results.
Latin and Greek civilization is a compact unit, and
cannot be studied primarily on its Latin or on its
Greek side without a distorted result. However, I
heard nothing more about this matter. The bringing
of the Society of Jesus into the University family
was left for a later date.

In the meantime, plans for the reorganization of the Department went forward. The following general plan was devised and still persists. The first year, ordinarily leading to the degree of Master of Arts, would consist of a basic general training in the field of the Classics, sufficient to enable students to develop increasing knowledge and efficiency in this area by themselves, even if they should cease to continue their formal training in it. Some have called this training "in and for research," which is satisfactory enough, if at the same time it is understood to be the most desirable training for teaching or general culture as well. A fundamental principle was established that the two languages and civilizations were not to be separated into individual compartments with little or no integration of the two. A student could emphasize one or the other, especially by his choice of dissertation subject, but he must have an interest in both and must consider himself as working in the fields of the Greek and Latin languages and literatures, and not in only one or the other.

Thus, during the first or master's year of graduate work all students regardless of their field of special interest are obliged to take the so-called pro-seminar, in which the fundamental principles and tools of research are learned and an introduction to their use is received; the history of classical scholarship, so as to gain an accurate perspective of their area of study and of the chief figures responsible for its development; Greek and Latin composition, chiefly to acquire a good basic knowledge of the two languages in the periods of their best literatures; comparative Greek and Latin grammar, in order to procure some understanding of the two languages from the historical point of view, regardless of the literature of the various periods; the history of Greek and Roman civilization, both political and social, as a general background for both teaching and research; and as much reading as possible of the Greek and Latin authors themselves, either through formal courses or by directed private reading, preferably by both. After all, the most accurate knowledge of a people's life and civilization is obtained through first-hand contact with the literature of that people. In addition the usual master's essay was required, but now a definite concept of this task was evolved. It was no longer to be a mere rehash of what others had written, perhaps even many times over, but, as far as it went, it was to require and exhibit the strict and scientific principles of research. Thus, very appropriately its name was changed from "Master's essay" to "Master's dissertation." Later, when I became Dean of the Graduate School of Arts and Sciences, this change was effected for the entire School. Naturally, because of the time factor, the Master's dissertation could not be as extensive as that required for the doctorate, but as far as it went, it was to be just as meticulously and accurately done. Because of the restricted area of investigation, the conclusions might well be of only slight importance, but it was to be none the less scientifically executed.

With the introduction of such well regulated directing and caring for students, the enrollment in the graduate division began to soar. I was soon overwhelmed with the burden of the work. Bishop Shahan was most appreciative of the condition of things, and was most pleased with it. At that time I had among my students James Marshall Campbell, whom I had had as a graduate student at Princeton University just before the outbreak of World War I and whom I had induced to come to the University when I first went there; also Martin Patrick Rawson McGuire, who after World War I had taken up teaching at Georgetown Preparatory School and who, through Dr. James Geary,[1] I had persuaded to enter our graduate division. With Dr. Campbell assisting with the Greek courses and dissertations, and Dr. McGuire with the Latin, we were able to give at least adequate attention to the many students who were now coming to the University for advanced instruction in Greek and Latin. It must be noted, however, that I was obliged to call upon them for assistance even before they had completed their own training for the doctorate, but the success of their work is ample evidence of the wisdom of our planning.

It has already been said that the first or Master's year of graduate study was arranged to be the same for all students, the thought being that the general background training of Classical students

[1] Professor and Head of the Department of Celtic Languages and Literature.

should have a due proportion of study in appropriate phases of both Greek and Latin languages and civilizations. A proper understanding of one cannot be obtained without at least a certain minimum training in the other. After the first year, however, strong emphasis must be laid on one with only comparatively slight attention to the other. This emphasis would include the satisfactory completion of a dissertation of doctoral quality in the field of the student's choice. After the first year, moreover, the student could specialize even more. He might select any one of three periods within either the Latin or the Greek area: thus, the Classical Period, roughly through the early period of the Empire, exclusive of Christian writers; the Patristic Period, that is, all of the Fathers of the Church in the broad sense, including certain heretics of worthy literary achievement, through about the first five centuries of our era; and lastly, the Medieval Period.

    To correspond with these three great fields of study culminating in an outstanding piece of research, three series were established to receive the doctoral dissertations as they were printed and published: The Catholic University of America Classical Studies, The Catholic University of America Patristic Studies, and The Catholic University of America Studies in Medieval and Renaissance Latin Language and Literature. The first of these three series has not prospered, although this does not indicate any lack of interest in or appreciation of the Classical field on the part of the members of the Department. In fact, it is a basic principle within the Department that in order to achieve any real success as a scholar in either the Patristic or the Medieval fields, one must have a solid basic training in the Classical. Hence the arrangement of the program of studies in the first year as described above. The growth of each series is an indication of the preferred special interest of the students who have come to us for training. Thus the Classical Series has but two volumes accomplished as dissertations under my direction in the very early part of my career. The Patristic Series has now reached well over a hundred volumes, of which the first portions were done under my own direction, those of the years of my deanship chiefly through the guidance of Drs. McGuire and Campbell, and the last under the care of the three of us. I should record here that very little was done on the Fathers of the Church in the Department of Greek and Latin before my arrival, since all my predecessors were traditional classicists with little or no interest in the later periods. My own personal interest in the Patristic languages and literatures was fostered at Princeton University and especially by Professor Paul van den Van, visiting professor from the University of Louvain. Thus it may be said that I brought the germ of this extensive activity in the Fathers to The Catholic University of America from Princeton University. However, the volumes in the Mediaeval Latin Studies were guided primarily by Dr. McGuire and Dr. Aloysius Ziegler, [2] and in recent years by Dr. Bernard Peebles. I have done little more here than get the series under way.

We must point out that after my appointment as Dean of the Graduate School of Arts and Sciences, Dr. Campbell was appointed Dean of the College of Arts and Sciences in 1934. When I was appointed Secretary General in 1936, Dr. McGuire succeeded me as Dean of the Graduate School of Arts and Sciences, and retained that post until 1948, when he returned to the Department of Greek and Latin. He also, a little later, assumed the leadership of the Department, which I had held from the time of my first appearance on the campus in 1918, and which he still holds. Dr. Campbell has retained his deanship of the College of Arts and Sciences to this day. In spite of these serious interruptions occasioned by administrative duties, we all have maintained the same interest in Greek and Latin studies as is evidenced through our teaching, research, and publications. Dr. Bernard Peebles was added to the departmental staff in Bishop McCormick's rectorship primarily to assist in the graduate courses and in the guidance of dissertations. We have all been grateful for his assistance, as we have been for the help given us through the years by those who have taken care of undergraduate instruction.

Mention should be given of the nearly ideal conditions under which the graduate work of the

[2] Professor and Head of the Department of History.

Department of Greek and Latin had been conducted from 1918 to 1958. All the books of the Department were carefully arranged in appropriately assigned rooms, and all classes, as well as the personal direction of the students' research projects, were conducted in the very midst of the necessary bibliographical tools. At the very mention of a work of any importance in the field, one had but to rise and take a few steps to obtain the book itself. The value to all of us and especially to the students of being in such close propinquity to the tools themselves can hardly be gauged. The original quarters of the early years were nearly doubled when the first part of the Mullen Library was completed. The Semitic Libary across the hall was then moved into the new building, and the rooms thus vacated were turned over to us by Bishop Ryan. Visiting scholars, such as Dr. Jean Malyé, founder of the Association Guillaume Budé, and Dr. Christine Mohrman, the well known Dutch Latinist, spoke of this wonderful advantage in carrying on graduate work.

The greatest number of our years were spent in those ideal surroundings. During the summer of 1958 we moved to the newly completed Mullen Library building, and took our place with the other members of the University family. Considering the welfare of the University as a whole, this will undoubtedly be for the best. We hope and pray, however, that the old spirit of comeraderie and of *pares inter pares*, which has existed in the Depart-

ment of Greek and Latin thus far and which has
been such an important factor in establishing and
maintaining the high quality of scholarship so
widely recognized up to this moment, will not
wane. [3]

The Department of Library Science

I recall very clearly one day in the spring of
1929, while teaching at the Sisters College, receiving a telephone call from Mother Agatha, O.S.U.,
of Wilmington, New Jersey, telling me that she
was on the University campus and would like to
talk to me before she returned to her convent. Arrangements were made for us to meet in my office
at the University as soon as my class was over.

Mother Agatha proposed that she give two
courses in library science in the Summer Session of
1929. She explained that not only was there no instruction in library science in this area, approved
by the American Library Association, but that
there were several important problems in this field
of serious concern to Catholic institutions of higher
education. If the University would develop work
in library science acceptable to the A.L.A., it would
be performing another valuable service to Catholic

[3] See also "Greek and Latin" under "Sisters College" and under
"Trinity College."

education. Her plan was readily approved. Mother Agatha was a person of good professional training and of intelligent foresight. It was clear that she was looking forward to the eventual establishment of a Department or School of Library Science to meet the needs not only of the local area but also of all Catholic educational institutions.

Mother Agatha worked hard and very success-fully on her summer session project. The students respected her greatly, and their number grew steadily. In 1936, shortly after Bishop Corrigan was appointed Rector, the time appeared opportune to begin work in library science during the regular academic year. The demand for it was strong. Furthermore, several attempts were made to obtain the approval of the American Library Association for our Summer Session program, but without suc-cess. It was clear that this group was not inclined to approve programs in the field which were confined to summer sessions only, and official approval by the professional organization (A.L.A.) engaged in the work was quite necessary for our program if it was to have any local or national appeal.

Father Francis A. Mullin, [1] in the meantime, had taken over the position of University Librarian and was very much interested in the establishment of organized instruction in library science during the regular academic year. One of the most difficult

[1] Formerly Professor of History at Loras College, Dubuque, Iowa. See V, 1, The Library.

decisions that I have ever been required to make now loomed on the horizon. Mother Agatha had looked forward to being placed in charge of this work, and this reward for pioneering in library science at the University was certainly due her. Furthermore, our relations had always been of the friendliest. It could well be said of her that she had an active and vigorous mind in spite of her age. But there were several considerations that would have made it very unwise to have given her this responsibility. Accordingly, I recommended and Bishop Corrigan appointed Father Francis Mullin in charge of the incipient Department of Library Science at the University. Later the Bishop gave heed to Mother Agatha's first reaction of disappointment and when the new activity got underway in Father Mullin's hands, he proceeded to call me on the carpet about it. However, he soon changed his mind, when he had examined the problem thoroughly. I must add that Mother Agatha quickly rose above her first feeling of disappointment, and our friendship continued without change. She herself later declared that she felt that the final decision was wise.

Father Mullin reorganized the Library as a collection of books, a herculean task in itself, and also developed the Department of Library Science to the point where it was able to receive the approval of the American Library Association. Father James J. Kortendick, S.S.,[2] shortly before Father Mullin's death, became Head of the Department

[2] A friend and early student of Father Mullin.

and has directed it ever since. This is another example of an experiment of the Summer Session successfuly meeting the test and becoming an integral part of the University's academic family.

The Division of Art

Although undergraduate courses in art had been given for many years in the Summer Sessions of the Catholic Sisters College, which were held on the University campus, no formal department had been organized, and no courses were offered during the regular year. Indeed, even in the Summer Sessions no permanent teachers were employed. Whoever happened to be available did the teaching.

Shortly after the Summer Session had been organized as an integral part of the University, my attention was called to the availability of Sister M. Jeannette Blair, O.S.U., of Cleveland, Ohio, as a good person to establish and develop a university department of art. I succeeded in engaging her services for the Summer Session, and each year she performed a near miracle in setting up quarters of dignity befitting work in art. In the beginning, the only space available for the new department was the basement of Albert Hall. If there ever was a forbidding spot for academic work on the campus, it was this place at the end of an academic year, after several student activities had been housed there during the regular semesters and the place had been left without any attempt to clean it. Sister Jeannette was never daunted. Summer after summer she would take over, and within two or three days she would make very respectable quarters out of the dismal location, even for work in art.

Finally in 1939 I succeeded in getting the University authorities to establish a regular department of art in part of the quarters of the Salve Regina building which had just been relinquished by the post-card and other sales activities up to that time associated with the National Shrine of the Immaculate Conception. This division was in the beginning to serve the students of the Sisters College and the Graduate School of Arts and Sciences, since no program in the College at that time required such courses. Later when the undergraduate program at the Sisters College was abandoned, an undergraduate sequence was established in the College of Arts and Sciences at the University. Meanwhile the special graduate program leading to the degree of Master of Fine Arts was introduced.

In the beginning, the Division did not attract the number of students expected, but Sister Jeannette, with the aid of Sister Killian of the same community, struggled on. The Division was always very busy in the Summer Session, but lacked what was regarded as a satisfactory minimum number of students during the regular year. In 1947 Sister

Jeannette resigned for reasons of health, and returned to her community in Cleveland, as did her companion, Sister Killian. Miss Clare Fontanini, who at the time was teaching in the public schools of Washington, succeeded Sister Jeannette.

The Division of Art has been growing steadily in recent years. In fact the present quarters are very inadequate and, in my opinion, are actually hindering the growth and development of the Division. It is high time, it seems to me, that this flourishing activity be recognized officially as a department of the University organization.

The Department of Speech and Drama

Just before the Summer Session of 1935, Father Thomas Fabian Carey, O.P., who was an instructor in the Department of Psychology and Psychiatry, suggested that courses in drama be offered in the next Summer Session. At that time there were no extensive offerings in this field either among the summer sessions or the regular semesters of Catholic institutions. In view of the extensive use of the drama in the extracurricular life of our schools and colleges, such a program seemed likely to succeed. The University authorities readily agreed; and in 1935 the Summer Session offered the suggested courses with Father Carey and Father Urban Nagel of the Order of Preachers as instructors. The program was enthusiastically received, judging in part from the large numbers that came to us for this work. Although these numbers did fall off slightly as summer session after summer session in other Catholic institutions hastened to offer similar programs, nevertheless, the enrollment of this department in our Summer Session has held up well through the years.

In the summer of 1936, shortly after Bishop Corrigan had been made Rector, the time seemed opportune to continue the work throughout the regular semesters. Father Gilbert Hartke, O.P., had joined the original group of Dominican Fathers carrying on the summer work that year, and he was especially enthusiastic about such an expansion. When a plan was presented to the Rector, he was quite willing to permit the work to start in the following academic year. When I made the first announcement of the project in the University gymnasium, before a gathering of the teaching staff and of all the students at that time taking courses in the drama, I realized that I was guilty of an inexcusable oversight. I had failed to consult Father Carey and Father Nagle, assuming that Father Hartke was speaking for them also and that they were all of one mind on the plan. At any rate, they were most tolerant of my blunder, and it was agreed that Father Hartke would take over during the academic year.

This was the first time that formal courses in the drama, both graduate and undergraduate, were offered during the regular year. The undergraduates had been putting on an occasional play under the direction of various persons, some engaged to do the work and others volunteering to do so without compensation. Certain members of the faculty feared that the undergraduates would for the most part be ousted from their regular dramatic performances by the more experienced graduate students in the field. But Father Hartke handled the problem most tactfully, and all went forward smoothly.

Soon the work in speech, including speech therapy, was added, and the Department became that of Speech and Drama or "Screech and Clamor," as some campus wits called it. The work in speech therapy has been of great value to the University family. The various religious communities centered around the University have made abundant use of its facilities for their members who are afflicted with speech defects. The reports from these quarters as well as from others have always been most favorable to those carrying on this work.

Mention must be made of the skillful way in which a very talented teaching staff was brought together by Father Hartke. In some cases, he would recognize talented teaching material in a youngster and train him in his department for future service on the departmental staff. Mr. Leo Brady is a notable example of this. In other instances, he would select them from outside sources, invariably choosing wisely. Examples of this are

Mrs. Josephine Callan and Mr. Walter Kerr. In a period of two or three years only, the play-production of the Department become nationally known, and leaders in the field were drawing material for professional purposes from our campus. Both acting personnel and scripts were going from the campus to Broadway. During all this time, demands for teachers of speech and drama were coming in at a rate far beyond our ability to meet them. Of course, the training of teachers has always been the first objective of the Department, although it is difficult to make a sharp distinction between this aim and the development of good script writers and actors. The two to a great extent overlap.

Again, the Department of Speech and Drama is another example of a try-out of the Summer Session becoming a fixture in the offerings of the regular year.

The Department of Music

The Department of Music came into being in a manner very similar to that of the Department just described. However, although it was most in demand, it was the most difficult to get established. From the earliest days of the Summer Session, while it was still being conducted by the authorities of the Sisters College, courses in Music were offered and continued to be offered at the Sisters,

College during the regular year. Although all the musical affairs of the University were under the control of a person solely concerned with directing its musical functions, no formal courses in music were offered at the University until the authorities of the University officially took over the Summer Session as one of the regular terms of the University calendar. Even then no attempt was made to offer a program in music during the regular year.

While the work in music was given at the Sisters College, Mrs. Justine Ward supported it strongly and generously. When Bishop Ryan became Rector, Mrs. Ward indicated to him that she would be interested in helping to establish music at the University proper. If her conditions were met, she agreed to erect a building at her own expense and to help pay the salaries of the teachers. Her conditions were: that the work in music be set up as a separate and autonomous school; that a priest named by her be made an ordinary professor and also Dean of the School; and that the Ward method of teaching Gregorian chant be featured in the program of the School. The establishment of an independent School of Music had nothing wrong about it in itself, and might well have been accepted in the light of the contingent possibility of the gift of a new building and perhaps other financial benefits. But both the appointment of the priest in question as ordinary professor and as Dean and the presentation of the Ward method of teaching Gregorian chant as the chief activity of the

School were objectionable in the extreme. The priest, a fairly young person, had been at the University but a few years; to raise him to the dignity of both an ordinary professor and a dean with a single stroke of a pen was at least not good university procedure! The Ward method of teaching Gregorian chant may have many excellent features, as far as I know. I am not prepared to argue that. But for a university to commit itself to one method to the essential exclusion of all others, and even more surprising to make a method of teaching music the central and focal point of the activity of a university school of music are academic practices of doubtful wisdom, to say the least.

Bishop Ryan, however, agreed and explained his reasons to me which I need not go into here. Moreover, he signed all the papers binding himself to these agreements.

It is a generally accepted principle that it is never good for university authorities to accept gifts with strings attached which violate basic university policies. However, up to this time the University had not worked out a careful scheme for promoting the members of its faculty, such as it has today. The general outlines of such a scheme have always been in the University statutes, but they were never until recently worked out in detail. Promotions were made very much according to the decisions of the individual Rectors themselves and to a great extent with reference to the funds available for faculty salaries. Furthermore, Bishop Ryan was extremely anxious to develop the University in every possible way. He felt that there was much money to be received by the University, if its needs were properly presented to people of wealth. Thus it was evident enough why the Bishop made the great mistake that he did. It must be said also that he learned a good lesson, for in years to come several temptations arose to make similar mistakes, all of which he successfully resisted.

The plans for the Music Building were drawn up, and work on it was begun. The academic organization of the School was set up and some teaching got under way, but suddenly all came to a halt. The building was approximately half finished, and the teaching had not gone on long enough to make many of us realize that a new school was functioning on our campus. Not to go into the details of this rather shocking affair, I shall give what appears to have been the crucial point in the matter, as described by His Excellency Bishop Ryan. Mrs. Ward and the priest came to the parting of ways and she insisted that the priest be replaced. This was too much for the Bishop to endure. He could now see the absurdity and unwisdom of having a school on the campus, in which one person, an academic outsider even though a very generous benefactor, could make striking and far-reaching decisions by herself. Mrs. Ward then escaped from her contract, leaving the building far from completed. While withdrawing, she called the Bishop's attention to the fact that the priest had no doctorate, although he professed to have one and was using one publicly. The Rector felt that he could not ignore this charge, and, when he faced the priest with it, the priest frankly admitted that the charge was true. He explained his action by saying that his European training was easily the equivalent of the various doctorates given in the institutions of the United States, and he felt that he was justified in appropriating the formal doctorate.

Here again we have the deplorable results coming from malpractices current on the campus for years. First of all, members of the faculty were engaged without being required to show credentials of any kind. I myself was never obliged to show irrefutable evidence that I had a Ph.D. degree from Princeton University. Just before me an acquaintance of mine from Princeton was hired to teach English and his name appears in several annual catalogues with Ph.D. degree after it, a degree which he has not received to this day. Bishop Ryan established a new policy in this respect immediately. Secondly, the priest in question should not, of course, have taken unto himself a degree which had not been formally conferred upon him by a reputable institution of higher education. But it had been done not infrequently on the University campus. When I became Dean of the Graduate School of Arts and Sciences, I took it upon myself to investigate a number of such suspicious cases and verified my suspicions. Indeed, in later years a Dean of one of the Schools of the University used a doctoral degree publicly, which might accurately be described as having been received from a diploma mill.

At any rate, the building was finally completed with University funds, and the structure, although still called the Music Building, was put, temporarily, at least, to other purposes than those of music. The teaching of music reverted to its former state as an activity of the Sisters College during the regular academic year and of the University in its Summer Session only.

Dr. Leo Behrendt, out of his love for music, carried on a remarkably successful student glee club. However, it seemed completely incongruous to me and others that the University proper should have an official to take charge of functions involving music but have no regularly organized department of music and offer no formal courses in the subject of such a truly university nature.

I should mention also the names of Mr. Alexander Henneman and Mr. Malton Boyce who respectively carried on work in music at the Sisters College and in the Summer Session; also that of Sister M. Agnesine, S.S.N.D., who followed them and tried so hard, but to no avail, to patch up the breech between the University and Mrs. Ward. For several summer sessions also I added Mother Georgia Stevens of the Religious of the Sacred Heart to our music teaching staff, between whom and Mrs. Ward the most friendly feelings did not exist. Moreover, in one Summer Session, I introduced the teaching of the method of Archbishop Schrembs in addition to the systems of Mother Stevens and Mrs. Ward, with the hope of breaking up the widely spread notion that the University was committed to a single pedagogical approach to Gregorian chant and believed that it alone was correct and the best. All this activity at the Sisters College and on the campus of the University during the summer, however, was contributing nothing toward the solution of the problem of a full-fledged department of music at the University itself.

The authorities of the University felt, chiefly for financial reasons, that they were not yet ready to set up a permanent department of music. It struck me that, if I could get a part-time teacher to give advanced courses in music on the campus during the regular year, this would open up the way to a fairly well-rounded department, and I succeeded in getting permission to engage such a person. I found two excellent musicologists in the music division of the Library of Congress. Musicology seemed the most appropriate phase of music to introduce under the circumstances, since it would fit in well with other fields of study in the Graduate School of Arts and Sciences as minor subjects for the Master's and Doctor's degrees. Accordingly, I first obtained the services of Dr. Oliver Strunk, and, when he felt obliged to give up the work, those of Dr. Edward N. Waters. No fault certainly could be found with the quality of their instruction, but for some unknown reason the seed would not sprout! Music as a graduate or undergraduate subject got nowhere. This little beginning was finally abandoned, and the University was back again doing business at the same old stand, the Sisters College and the Summer Session.

Then came World War II, and the idea of recruits being permitted to earn credits toward degrees or even to study for pleasure and self-improvement, while serving in one of the armed forces, was becoming very widespread. The authorities of the Navy School of Music sent representatives of the Navy Band to the University to see if some arrangement could not be made whereby members of this Band would be able to take general courses at the University which, combined with such courses in music as they might take at the base, would realize at least some progress toward a baccalaureate degree. It was through these negotiations that I met Dr. John Paul, who was usually the representative of the Navy in these discussions.

Thus when Dr. Paul separated himself from the Navy, we obtained his services for several Summer Sessions, but we were still unable to use him at the University proper during the regular year. The following memorandum illustrates the efforts made to solve the problem of procuring a well-developed University department of Music.

July 16, 1947

To THE
RIGHT REVEREND PATRICK JOSEPH McCORMICK:
    I have already spoken to you on several occasions about the great need of establishing a

Department of Music at the University. Hitherto, as you know, undergraduate work in music has been offered at the Sisters College during the regular year and both undergraduate and graduate work at the University during the Summer Session. In other words, there has been no work offered in music of any kind at the University proper during the regular year.

This is a source of great embarrassment always in that the outside world finds it most difficult to understand why a University of our professed quality does not include a regular Department of Music. Indeed, it is impossible for us at the University to give a satisfactory explanation for this situation.

I write now, first of all, to urge that arrangements be made in the budget of the University for the academic year 1948-1949 for the beginnings of a Department of Music at the University. I do not urge this for the coming academic year of 1947-1948 because I realize that the budget for this period has been definitely completed and no changes may ordinarily be made in it.

It would be highly desirable that the Department offer both undergraduate and graduate work and, as in the case of other departments, such work as may be necessary for the sisters at the Sisters College be duplicated there. This, of course, is the usual practice in the other departments of the University.

In any case, even if the University authorities decide on keeping all undergraduate work in music at the Sisters College and only graduate work at the University proper, the question of a good head of the department remains essentially the same. He should be a person of a broad academic training and not trained only in the usual narrow manner among musicians. He should be a person who knows American Universities and American academic practices so that he can deal with academic documents, such as transcripts of credits, which come in from other American institutions. He should also be acquainted with various academic agencies, especially those which examine schools and departments of music for approval. We have had many fine musicians at the University, but we have never had any good musician on a permanent appointment who was also a good American educator.

This brings me to my second point. I wish to suggest for appointment at the proper time, as head of the Department of Music, Mr. John Paul. Mr. Paul received his bachelor's degree from the University of Kansas in 1937 and his master's degree in 1942 from the University of Southern California. His teaching experience is as follows:

Supervisor of Music, Public Schools, Mulvane, Kansas, 1937-1940

Visiting Instructor, University of Kansas, Summer Session, 1937, 1938, 1939

Assistant to Dr. Krone, Music Department, University of Southern California, 1940-1941

Occidental College, Los Angeles and Hoover High School in Glendale, California, 1941-1942

Navy School of Music, Supervisor of Instruction, 1942-1945

Mount St. Joseph, Director of Music, Baltimore, Maryland, 1945-1946

Associate Professor of Music, William and Mary College (Norfolk Division), 1946-1947

Instructor of Piano at Bristow Hardin School of Music, Norfolk, Virginia, 1946-1947

Visiting Instructor at Catholic University, Summer Session, 1946-1947

He is, at present, Associate Professor of Music at the College of William and Mary at a salary which we, frankly, could not meet. However, both he and his wife like the University and Washington, especially since they are very much interested in the work of the Church in education and would like to have a part in it. I feel that he would come to the University as an Assistant Professor with a salary of $4,000 to start.

This summer he has been the head of the graduate section of our Department of Music and he has been working very hard indeed. We have had thirteen new candidates for the master's degree in music, all of whom come directly under the supervision of Mr. Paul. I can say that he has a very agreeable personality. The reports of all the students, religious and lay, with whom he comes in contact, speak very highly of him. The other members of his department, and especially the nuns, are also high in his praise.

I really do not know of anyone else who could fill the position of head of a new Department of Music at the University, bearing in mind the great task of its future development, as well as Mr. Paul.

ROY J. DEFERRARI
Secretary General

Finally, chiefly through the good offices of the Reverend James A. Magner, Mr. John Paul was asked to inaugurate a division, soon to become a department, of music during the regular academic year on the University campus. The old Cain residence, later used by the Phi Kappa fraternity, was given him as the headquarters of his division. In a very few years, however, these quarters had to be vacated because of the expansion of the National Shrine. But what at first appeared to be a disaster, as often happens in such circumstances, proved a blessing. Bishop McEntegart took a statesmanlike view of the problem and decided to build a wing on the Music building, which was then being used essentially entirely by the Department of Speech and Drama. The thought was that the Music group would use the new wing, and, as soon as the Department of Speech and Drama obtained quarters of its own and moved out to occupy them, it would take over the quarters so vacated. Thus the Music building would revert entirely to its original purpose.

The Department of Music has finally become full-fledged. It has become of age. It has grown steadily, and a great future lies ahead of it.

I have for several years been looking forward to the establishment of a School of Fine Arts. The basic elements for such a school are at hand: the Division of Art, the Department of Speech and Drama, and the Department of Music. All three started out as experiments in the Summer Session under my general supervision, and all three, although still very young as university departments and divisions go, are flourishing today. I feel sure that, if they were organized as a single school with a capable administrator as dean, not necessarily selected from the staff of one of the fields concerned, they would prosper even more.

SOME IMPORTANT
UNIVERSITY ACTIVITIES

The Library

When I first came to the University, the main library was on the first floor in the south corridor of McMahon Hall. There were, of course, many departmental libraries scattered all over the campus. Between the main library, the Semitics library, and the library of the Department of Greek and Latin, I personally was very well supplied with working tools for my courses and for my private studies. From the point of view of good university library facilities, giving appropriate service to faculty members and students, however, there was much to be desired. No one realized this more than Bishop Shahan himself, and in his mind he had evolved what he conceived as an outstanding modern university library building.

Moreover, the Bishop got Mr. John K. Mullen of Denver to donate enough money at least to start the building. Bishop Shahan's plans were, designedly on his part, far beyond the building potentiality of the funds donated by Mr. Mullen, but the Bishop was following his usual practice. He would start the kind of building that he wanted, and then count on Mr. Mullen to give more when he saw a beautiful building in his name unfinished.

Mr. Mullen did give an additional amount above his original donation, but still not enough to complete the structure as Bishop Shahan had planned it. The rear of the building, where the stacks were principally located, remained unfinished until 1958. Furthermore, when Mr. Mullen made his second donation to the cause of the library building, he did so for a "price." The library building was to be called not the John K. Mullen Library as was first planned, but the John K. Mullen *of Denver* Library. Also, the University was to offer annually ten scholarships (five for board, room, and tuition and five for tuition only) to prospective students from Denver or its environs. These students, after they had officially met all the requirements of the University's Committee on Admissions, were to be appointed by a special group consisting of members of Mr. Mullen's family. I have never gone into the details of this transaction, but the statement sometimes made that the University would have done better financially to have borrowed that money from a bank in the usual way, rather than to have been saddled in perpetuity with the obligation of granting these ten scholarships every year, seems to be very much to the point.

I cannot forbear mentioning another matter in connection with the library building. Bishop Shahan was a true lover of books. He once said to me: "If I hadn't become a bishop, I would have wanted to be a librarian." In this day and age, the fact that a person is a scholar or a lover of books does not qualify him to be a librarian in the modern professional sense of the word. No better proof of this can be found than the fact that Bishop Shahan, truly a scholar and a lover of books, planned and directed the construction of the present University library building. It is a beautiful building indeed, but far removed from what a modern university library building should be. As one person put it: "It seems to have been planned by someone who was in league with book-thieves. It offers so little protection and supervision over the withdrawal of books." But more important still, it is so constructed that no amount of remodeling would make it possible for a library staff, however well trained, to furnish the service expected in the way of professional assistance, especially for graduate students and university scholars, as is now provided by university libraries such as the Firestone Library of Princeton University and the Widener and Lamont Libraries of Harvard University. It would have been much wiser, in my opinion, to have diverted this building to another needed service, such as a union building or social center, and to have started all over again with a truly modern university library structure.

This seems to be the appropriate place to relate how the University obtained the services of the Reverend Francis A. Mullin as University Librarian. There is, of course, no connection between the names of the donor of the library building and the librarian. When the collection of books was on the first floor of McMahon Hall and during the early years after it was moved to the new building, Mr. Joseph Schneider was in charge. However, he never received the title of Director of the University Library, as described in the statutes of the University. Certainly no one could have found fault with Mr. Schneider's loyalty and disposition for hard work. He was always eager to help and to cooperate with members of the teaching staff in their library problems. Mr. Schneider, however, was not a professionally trained librarian in the modern sense of the phrase, so important in a university library today. His training was obtained in the apprentice manner in the Library of Congress. Bishop Ryan was determined to have a Director of the Library who was well trained in the profession itself and who had previously experienced advanced training to the Ph.D. degree in one of the major fields of learning. Moreover, he wanted the Director to be not a part-time person and more or less a figure-head, as he had been in the past, but someone who would give his whole time to the important work and would assume all of the responsibilities. In fact, Bishop Ryan had no other choice in the matter, if the University was to obtain and maintain the accreditation of the various educational groups which were just beginning in his time to become strong and to exert a powerful influence in the field of education. We scoured the field for just such a person but could find no one who was both acceptable and available.

We finally decided that we would have to train our own man, and I was given the task of finding the likely person. With the help of Dr. McGuire, we selected Father Francis Mullin, who had recently obtained his doctorate at the University in the field of medieval history and who, with his delightful personality, had the rare faculty of getting along with people. I reported our find to Bishop Ryan, and he immediately dispatched me to Dubuque, Iowa, in order to confer with Father Mullin regarding our plans, and, if agreeable to him, to lay the preliminary plans with Archbishop Beckmann for Father Mullin's transfer to the University. The entire matter was quickly settled, chiefly because Father Mullin was delighted with the proposal. Archbishop Beckmann, however, placed a condition on the transaction with Bishop Ryan, which was rather amusing. He insisted that the University pay him for the cost of his training Father Mullin for the Ph.D. degree in history at the University, since the University was going to receive the benefits of this training. This was reasonable enough, except for the fact that, as Father Mullin himself told me, the Archbishop of Dubuque had paid nothing for that training. Father Mullin had paid all his own expenses in this connection. His Excellency evidently had forgotten all about it. However, Bishop Ryan complied with the request, and the transaction was quickly completed.

The next question was where should Father Mullin be sent for his training in librarianship. The School of Library Science at the University of Michigan was selected for this purpose. There Father Mullin would be under the direct tutelage of Mr. William Bishop, one of the founders of the field of library science. Mr. Bishop had promised Bishop Ryan that he would take a personal interest in Father Mullin, in view of the very important post which he was being prepared to fill. Father Mullin spent two full years of very profitable study, as he often admitted, at this leading center of library studies at that time.

While Father Mullin was at the School of Library Science at the University of Michigan, Monsignor Corrigan came to the University as Rector. Under certain outside pressure he wavered seriously about going through with our plan to establish Dr. Mullin as University Librarian. The following letter is a good summary of my efforts to hold the new Rector to the plan worked out by Archbishop Ryan and myself for the University Library. Fortunately, our efforts were successful.

July 17, 1936

DEAR MONSIGNOR CORRIGAN

I am writing to give the substance of our conversation yesterday relative to Dr. Mullin and Library Science at the University.

The library of the University is a good working collection of books for the general purposes of a university. It also includes a good number of rare volumes. The organization and administration of this library is from the professional point of view about as bad as it can be. This situation is well known to both Catholic and non-Catholic educators and librarians throughout the country, and it is only because of confidence in the word of the authorities of this University that the situation would be remedied, that we have not encountered serious difficulties with those educational groups which have rated our institution so high as a university. The students and the religious superiors who send us students are aware of the condition, and complain bitterly about it. Were it not for the Congressional Library the Graduate School of Arts and Sciences could not proceed effectively, in spite of our good collection, because of the impossibility of finding so many books and the inadequate service in handling those that can be found. It is one of the duties of a graduate school to train its students to make their way through a large and well-organized library. This is impossible at the present time on the grounds of the Catholic University. Were the situation not so serious, it would be literally ludicrous.

The present condition of the library is due to the failure on the part of the authorities of this University throughout its history to realize that only a carefully and professionally trained person should be placed in charge of the University library. Neither a person without a truly scholarly background, regardless of his experience as a clerk in other libraries, nor a scholar without professional training in librarianship, will fill the need.

During the administration of Bishop Ryan, every effort was made to procure the services of a priest with the proper scholarly and professional training. Several were brought to the University during the summer mainly in order to get acquainted with them. In every case temperamental difficulties were discovered which disqualified them. Only slight consideration was given to the possibility of procuring the services of a layman, but here too no suitable person seemed to be available.

It was finally decided that the University would have to train its own man. Search was made for a priest with a Ph.D. degree in Church history and with a personality suited to the position, who would be willing at the University's expense and with the consent of his Ordinary, to receive professional training in library science. After much consideration Dr. Francis Mullin of the Archdiocese of Dubuque was selected. He holds a Ph.D. degree in Church history from the Catholic University of America, and has studied in some of the leading libraries of Europe. Up to the time of his acceptance of the proposition tendered him by Bishop Ryan, he was professor of history at Columbia [1] College, Dubuque, Iowa.

Since I had to go to Dubuque for the opening of the Mid-West Branch of our Sum-

[1] The name has since been changed to Loras College.

mer Session, Bishop Ryan asked me to arrange an interview with Archbishop Beckmann, and to present to him the great problem of the Library at the University and the great possibility for good to Catholic education throughout the country in our having a properly qualified person in charge of the Library. He authorized me to urge Archbishop Beckmann to release Dr. Mullin for the work in the Library at this University.

After much negotiation between the representatives of the University, Bishop Ryan and on several occasions myself at the Bishop's request, and representatives of the Archdiocese of Dubuque, it was agreed to release Dr. Mullin to the University provided the University would reimburse Columbia College of Dubuque to the amount of $2,000, the sum supposedly expended by that institution to train Dr. Mullin to serve as professor of history on its faculty. The University agreed to do this at the rate of $500 per annum, and this year's payment will be the third. In addition, Bishop Ryan proposed to send Dr. Mullin, at the University's expense, to the School of Library Science at the University of Michigan for professional training under the personal supervision of Dr. Bishop, Dean of that School. Incidentally, Dr. Bishop is president of the American Library Association and was advisor to the Holy See in its recent reorganization of the Vatican Library. Dr. Bishop reported that he would have to keep Dr. Mullin at Michigan for two years in order to fit him properly to reorganize the University Library and carry on its administration. Dr. Mullin has just returned to the University having fulfilled his apprenticeship. Dr. Bishop has reported very favorably of him on several occasions.

At this point it should be mentioned that in addition to reorganizing and administering the University Library, Bishop Ryan planned to have Dr. Mullin establish a department of library science on the graduate level within the Graduate School of Arts and Sciences. There is at present only one Catholic institution offering library science which has the approval of the American Library Association. This is the College of St. Catherine in St. Paul, Minnesota, but this is on the undergraduate level and does not train administrators and scholars in library science. The University has had an increasing demand from members of the hierarchy as well as from religious superiors to establish this work with the approval of the A.L.A. [2] We have been putting them off, telling them that the work would be established as soon as Dr. Mullin returned to the University. Moreover, Dr. Bishop who, as I have said above, is president of the American Library Association, has promised Dr. Mullin recognition for our work as soon as he, Dr. Mullin, has organized it as Dr. Bishop has every confidence that Dr. Mullin will organize it. Dr. Bishop furthermore, as he told me himself, is very anxious to have our library organized as it should be, and a department established, not only to meet the need of Catholic institutions, but also for the benefit of non-Catholic librarians engaged in problems involving Catholic books. It should be mentioned also that these plans have been announced to the Catholic Library Association on several occasions, and this organization, both collectively and individually, is looking forward to seeing the plans carried out. The members of this Association are giving serious

[2] The American Library Association.

consideration to having their permanent headquarters established at the University as soon as
the plans announced to them by University officials have been carried out.

Mention should also be made of the fact that
a continually growing group of courses in library
science have been offered during summer sessions
for the last seven years. The enrollment has held
up around 100 consistently in spite of many
obstacles, the chief one being lack of recognition
by the American Library Association. This recognition cannot be obtained, we have been definitely
told by representatives of the A.L.A., until our
library is properly reorganized. Furthermore,
many Sisters have written saying that they have
had to abandon their work in Library Science at
our summer session because of its lack of accredit-
ment.

Dr. Mullin was definitely promised that on
his return from the University of Michigan he
would be made Director of the Library, subject of
course to any necessary approval by higher authority. No definite salary was fixed. It was also distinctly understood that Mr. Schneider would
retain his present position but under the direction
of Dr. Mullin. Dr. Mullin was to get the reorganization of the Library underway as soon as possible. In about a year thereafter Dr. Mullin was
to start the Department of Library Science.

All the information which I have given here
can be found either in Bishop Ryan's correspondence on the matter or in my own. The latter I
gave over entirely some weeks ago to the Vice
Rector, Monsignor McCormick. I may say also
that a few days ago I had the opportunity of
speaking with Bishop Ryan, and, being greatly
concerned about this matter, I reviewed all the

details with him. He concurred in them absolutely, and he was himself disturbed that the matter was apparently not entirely clear to the present authorities of the University.

I can conceive of no step by the University which would do more for the University itself in all its branches, and which would benefit all Catholic education in the United States more, than the carrying out of the plans presented above. Regardless of the present financial condition of the University, I do not see how the present authorities can afford not to carry this project through. Failure to do so will be looked upon by both Catholic and non-Catholic educators as a step backward on the part of the Catholic University in as much as it will definitely indicate that the Catholic University has decided to endure the present deplorable conditions indefinitely. And personally I would be inclined to agree with them.

I feel very strongly on the matter, but please do not think that this is a temporary outburst of emotion. Your decision represents to me the success or failure of a project for which I have worked with Bishop Ryan during the entire period of his administration, and which, if carried out successfully, will establish any administration in the history of the University as prominent among all others.

I am ready to discuss this matter at any time and with anyone you may wish.

With best wishes, I am

Very sincerely yours,
(signed) ROY J. DEFERRARI
Dean

Father Mullin, after several years of very hard work in the University Library, died an untimely death. At first it seemed like a disaster for the University's plans to develop a modern university library. Father Mullin, however, perhaps because he knew very well that he was in very precarious health, had gathered capable people about him and had been training them to carry on the work both in the teaching of library science and in the service of the University Library itself. Thus the University was fortunate in having Mr. Eugene Willging on hand to succeed Father Mullin. Father Mullin and Mr. Willging had been very good friends. Mr. Willging has carried on Father Mullin's work with outstanding professional skill. The completion of the Library building and the improved library service which Mr. Willging plans to accompany the completed building will mark another milestone in the development of the University as an outstanding institution of higher education. [3] In planning service, however, it must always be kept in mind that a university library is not a general or municipal library. Its collections and books should be arranged in such a way as to serve best the needs of instruction and research in the respective departments and schools of the University.

[3] Since these words were written, the library building has been completed, and Mr. Willging has worked tirelessly to dispose the resources of the completed structure in a manner most beneficial to the University as a whole and at the same time pleasing to all the individuals concerned. It must be said, however, that the growing tendency to use the library building to house offices for activities far removed from the recognized purposes of a university library is greatly to be deplored. It is almost a public confession on the part of the University authorities of a failure to understand and appreciate fully the role of a library in an outstanding complex university.

Affiliation and Extension

(a) *Affiliation*

When Dr. Shields worked for the improvement of the Catholic elementary schools, he aimed especially for the better training of the teachers, which resulted, as we have seen, in the establishment of the Catholic Sisters College. [1] In the case of the Catholic secondary schools, he again worked through the Catholic Sisters College but supplemented this by a system of "Affiliation." [2] It is noteworthy that this plan was the first scheme of affiliation or accreditation ever established in the United States under Catholic auspices. At first it was concerned only with secondary schools, but very soon thereafter it included institutions of higher education. Affiliation expanded no further under Dr. Shields, but prospered greatly within these two areas.

On Dr. Shields' death the then Dr. P. J. Mc Cormick succeeded him as Chairman of the Committee on Affiliation, and when Dr. McCormick felt that the Deanship of the Catholic Sisters College and Headship of the Department of Education were sufficiently burdensome in themselves, Father Leo McVey relieved him of Affiliation.

[1] See The Catholic Sisters College
[2] The term "affiliation" is usually used in a loose and general sense, signifying any simple relationship of one group to another. Only at The Catholic University of America is it used to indicate a definite and systematic relationship of one academic institution to another.

As far as Affiliation was concerned, both Dr. McCormick and Father McVey did little more than hold the line as Dr. Shields had established it. In fact, a very unfortunate feature of Dr. Shields' career, as often happens in the case of great men, was that his colleagues and pupils loved and respected him so much that they would never change in the slightest the academic legacy which he had left them, regardless of new and unforeseen circumstances. With them loyalty demanded that all things, even ideas, remain just as he had conceived them. Knowing Dr. Shields as I did, I am sure that he would have desired that his basic philosophical ideas be ever kept in mind, but that they be modified to meet new conditions and thinking, always, however, in the light of the never changing ultimate goals. He himself, I am convinced, would have acted so.

The chief feature of Affiliation in those early days was an examination program for secondary schools, which for many years was very extensive and helpful and even financially prosperous to the University. Little, however, was done to assist affiliated institutions of higher education. When I urged systematic visitations of the colleges as well as of the secondary schools, the plan was promptly turned down by Father McVey, Monsignor Pace, and the other members of the Committee as impracticable. After a few years much complaint arose about the examinations on two scores: the high cost to the pupils and high schools concerned and the unreliability of the examinations them-

selves, which were, all in all, put together hurriedly
and carelessly and corrected in like manner. It
must be remembered also that this was the era of
the development of scientific test-making, and the
schools very properly looked for some results of
this latest thinking on the subject in the affiliated
school examinations. At any rate, for these two
good reasons, Affiliation gradually began to decline, and in 1939 was plunging downward. The
Rector, Bishop James Hugh Ryan, at that time
requested that I take over the work. Having served
for some years as a member of the Committee on
Affiliation of the University, as well as on the
Commission on Institutions of Higher Education of
the Middle States Association of Schools and Colleges, I was well acquainted with the ills involved
and the possible remedies to be applied.

On becoming Chairman of the Committee on
Affiliation in 1939, I made a detailed study of the
objectives, program, and organization of Affiliation.
The examination system for secondary schools was
made an optional service to the schools; the examinations furthermore were offered only for so-called
core-subjects, seven for the entire program, and the
cost to the students or to the schools was thus
greatly reduced. Every effort also was made to
improve the quality of the examinations. Moreover,
it was strongly felt that such service and assistance
should be given our affiliates as would attract
institutions to become affiliated with us. We hoped
to get rid of the question which was constantly

being raised: "What benefits are derived from being affiliated?" We wished to make these benefits clearly self-evident.

Most important of all was a restudy of the objectives of Affiliation and a clear statement of their significance. The Committee on Affiliation was established by the University to render to Catholic institutions of learning of all kinds such assistance as it could reasonably offer without prejudice to the autonomy of the affiliated institutions. In other words, the primary purpose of this Committee is to assist through Affiliation all Catholic institutions of learning which are willing and desirous of improving themselves. There should be, of course, numerous secondary objectives which accrue incidentally out of our periodic contacts with affiliated institutions, as we discover what their needs are. Frequently, for example, meeting the requirements for Affiliation prepares the way for accreditation with the voluntary associations of regional or national nature as well as for the approval by a state department of education. Accreditation as such, however, should be a secondary objective. Service should be the primary and all-important aim.

In the fifteen-year period following 1939, a gradual development took place as a result of changing attitudes throughout the country toward accreditation in general, and the enlargement of the purposes of accreditation to include the servicing and assisting of schools to raise educational standards. Thus, since the primary objective of Affiliation was one of service to Catholic educational institutions, its objective came to be very similar to that of the national and regional accrediting agencies. Perhaps the situation may well be stated as follows: Whereas the primary purpose of the recognized accrediting agencies is accrediting, and service is secondary, with Affiliation, service is the primary aim, accreditation is secondary. Along with this new concept of the nature of Affiliation, additional specific objectives were added from year to year, as the demands and needs of our affiliates became evident. The basic objectives, however, have always remained the same.

Whereas the program of Affiliation, as inherited by me in 1939, included the four-year general college and the secondary school, it now includes in addition the junior and community college, the teacher-training intitutions (the two-year institute and the four-year college), and the schools of nursing (the hospital school of nursing and the collegiate school of nursing). The minor seminary usually includes a four-year secondary school program and the first two years of a general college, while the major seminary includes two years of philosophy (the last two years of a general college) and the theology program. The secondary school division of a minor seminary may apply for affiliation as a secondary school; the two-year college program of the minor seminary may apply as a junior college or combine with the two years of philosophy of the major seminary and apply as a four-year general college. The affiliation of the theological division is conducted independently by the Director of Studies for Ecclesiastical Schools. With this last activity, the Chairman of the Committee on Affiliation has nothing to do.

We shall not go into details of the procedure through which any institution in these categories must pass before it is affiliated, although this is very important in our diagnosis of an institution and in our suggestions for its improvement. The procedure was worked out with great care and labor, and includes a visitation of a full day or more with a systematic evaluation, a process which was originally unanimously condemned by the Committee on Affiliation as impracticable and useless. It will, however, be of interest to list briefly the more important of the various special services that have been developed to supplement the usual individual services rendered to each affiliated institution.

(1) Publication of two Bulletins sent four times a year to affiliates: For Affiliated Institutions of Higher Education and for Affiliated Secondary Schools. These Bulletins contain original articles on current educational topics; results of special studies conducted at the University; current annotated bibliography, especially of periodical literature; and notices of various University activities of special interest to affiliates. Until recently, a third Bulletin for Affiliated Schools of Nursing was published; it is now combined with that for Affiliated Institutions of Higher Education.

(2) Production and dissemination of various mimeographed materials, giving standards, techniques, and general information relative to the organization of institutions, curriculum, grading, guidance, testing, library, and faculty. My chief aid in this work has been my assistant, Miss Rita Watrin, with occasional help from specialists.

(3) Stimulation and construction of new textbooks for Catholic schools and colleges. I have always encouraged qualified individuals to construct textbooks for both secondary schools and colleges to meet the special needs of Catholic educational institutions. This has been done by giving advice and editorial assistance to publishers as well as to authors. I have constructed such textbooks myself, as my bibliography will show.

(4) Three important services are in constant and frequent demand by affiliated secondary schools: an approved textbook list, curriculum studies, and a testing program. These three services have attained their present high standard chiefly through the efforts of my efficient assistant, Miss Rita Watrin. They were all in existence, but little more than that, when Affiliation was taken over in 1939. Indeed, the University authorities might well at that time have been ashamed of all three. The approved textbook list was far from complete, and was made up by a single individual passing judgment on textbooks without sufficient time to make a thorough study and evaluation of any one of them. This is in great contrast to the procedure now in force. The present list of approved textbooks covers

all textbooks published within approximately the last five years in the so-called "core subjects" of the curriculum or in closely related fields. Examination copies of new textbooks are furnished regularly by the publishers; these are distributed along with rating sheets to the members of the Textbook Committee. Each field is covered by two qualified secondary school teachers currently teaching in the field and the Catholic University consultant in the field. Ratings are made numerically and in detail with special emphasis given to criteria on Catholic educational philosophy. Rejected textbooks are omitted from the list; acceptable textbooks are placed thereon, without recommendations as to their specific use or their comparable standing with other similar textbooks. Affiliates are advised to obtain their own examination copies and to make their immediate choice based on their individual needs and preferences.

When we took over Affiliation there was a fixed curriculum mandatory for all affiliated secondary schools, regardless of where they were located or what their purposes were. The result was frequent clashes between the requirements of the Catholic University Affiliation program and those of diocesan authorities or those of state departments of education. At that time, 1939, a complete revision was made of the curriculum, and at the same time a strict policy was established by the Committee *not* to require affiliated high schools to follow any one curriculum. The course outlines were to serve merely as a guide, with complete freedom on the part of affiliates in the selection of textbooks, use of techniques, and detailed content. From 1939 on, minor changes have been made, but the basic principles as just described have remained the same.

A high school testing program had always been a feature of the University's secondary school affiliation plan, but up to 1939 it was compulsory, somewhat subjective, and anything but scientific and objective. In order to provide our Catholic high schools with a tool for testing the various results of their teaching program, giving due consideration to its Catholic features, a standardized testing program in the so-called "core" subjects, comprehensive in nature and optional to affiliates, was devised. Thirteen tests are published each year covering the following subject matter: (a) four years of English; (b) four years of religion; (c) two years of Latin, French, and Spanish; (d) one year each of algebra and geometry; (e) one year each of biology, chemistry, and physics; and (f) one year each of American history, world history, and Christian democracy.

The immediate purposes of the testing program are: (a) to determine a student's achievement over the four year secondary school period in what are considered the basic areas, (b) to make possible a comparison of the students' and the schools' achievements in relation to that of other students and other schools in the United States, (c) to check on teaching results by means of percentile rankings; on grading techniques; on general outcomes in relation to methods, remedial needs, intelligence quotients, etc., (d) to provide a Catholic University of America high school diploma granted on the fulfillment of all the requirements for graduation of the affiliated institution and the successful passing of the seven tests of The Catholic University of America, one in each field as stated above, with the exception of mathematics in which both algebra and geometry are required. The success of the revised testing program and its genuine value to our affiliated secondary schools are evident by the steady growth in the number of tests distributed each year. In 1950, when the scientific, standardized tests were introduced, a total of 16,239 tests were administered; in 1958, the total number of tests in the same thirteen subject fields reached 36,717. As of today (1961) the total has passed the 50,000 mark.

The following table, showing the number of affiliated institutions as of 1939 and using thereafter five-year intervals, gives some indication of the growth and development of the program as a whole.

GROWTH OF THE NUMBER OF AFFILIATES
FROM 1939 TO 1961 BY TYPES OF INSTITUTIONS

	1939-40	1945-46	1951-52	1956-57	1960-61
Senior Colleges	54	88	131	148	177
Junior Colleges	6	15	31	52	82
Teacher training	6	31	39	41	35
Nursing Schools	0	23	28	27	25
Misc. Higher Education	0	0	0	0	2
Secondary Schools	151	280	319	347	396
TOTAL	217	437	548	615	717

(b) *Extension*

Courses by extension were for many years considered to be those courses offered outside of the regular sessions of the institution, e.g., weekends, evenings, and summers. As the usual semesters gradually absorbed these programs, the term "extension" had no real significance as applied here, and the term became fixed in the sense of "off-campus" courses. It is so regularly used today.

The giving of courses by extension has thus far never been encouraged by the University authorities. This has probably been due to the lack of personnel for carrying on such instruction, and the almost inevitable flood of requests for extension centers which would follow if this kind of work were encouraged. Only when conditions have been quite urgent have extension centers been established. Thus in the early days of our School of Nursing, several leading nursing schools, e.g., that of Columbia University, began offering courses by extension in almost all subjects in many off-campus centers throughout the country. To give Catholic nurses in particular an opportunity to improve their professional development under Catholic auspices, the Catholic University established several centers for this purpose, chiefly in the vicinity of the University. This demand, however, has greatly decreased, until it has become quite negligible.

Two vigorous and very useful extension centers are those of the Xaverian Brothers in Silver Spring,

Maryland, and of the Christian Brothers in the District of Columbia. Recently (October, 1958), the Oblates of St. Francis de Sales established a similar center in Childs, Maryland. These three centers are peculiar in that they are under the direct control of the Dean of the College of Arts and Sciences, and only under the general supervision of the Chairman of the Committee on Affiliation and Extension. There is a good reason for this. These centers carry on the work of the lower division (the first two years) of the College curriculum, and send their students directly to the College for their upper division and concluding baccalaureate work.

Actually only one permanently established extension center has been conducted by the University through our committee. This was located at Xavier University in New Orleans, an institution for colored students under the direction of the Sisters of the Blessed Sacrament. The center was established in 1939 at the request of these Sisters. Mother Agatha, President of Xavier University, approached her Philadephia friend, Bishop Corrigan, with her problem. The State of Louisiana had a law which forbade white and colored students attending the same educational institution. Mother Agatha wished to conduct some in-service training for the Sisters of the Blessed Sacrament in that part of the country, if it possibly could be arranged. The Bishop sent Mother Agatha to me, and I suggested that The Catholic University of America set up an extension center at Xavier

University and employ such members of the Xavier faculty as were necessary on the extension staff. The Catholic University would itself grant credits by extension. Before embarking on this plan, I asked Mother Agatha to explain the arrangement to the State Department of Education of the State of Louisiana for its approval. This Mother Agatha did, and the necessary permission was readily granted. Extension work was carried on at Xavier until 1957, when the advent of antisegregation legislation did away with the need and the center was discontinued.

Work by extension is to be distinguished from the work of the so-called branches, which is discussed in its proper place, although the two kinds of instruction have much in common. There is no doubt but that the University could greatly expand its extension activity. It would be desirable to do so, if funds were available to set the work up properly to begin with and if the services of the necessary teaching personnel, well trained to carry on the work, could be procured. I am not at all sanguine about these resources being made available for the purpose in the near future. At any rate, it has been very satisfying to be able to help our Catholic co-workers in the field of education in a number of pressing situations such as I have described.

(c) *Novitiate Institutions*

Thanks to the increasing influence of the Sister-Formation Conference, a great interest has

arisen among religious communities in the establishment of academic institutions within the confines
of the motherhouse for the training of postulants
and novices. The general problem of where and
how to train subjects for the religious life is by no
means new. It is as old as the religious life itself. In
the United States the problem has simmered down
to two schools of thought, which I wish to discuss
here, pointing especially to the part which the University's Committee on Affiliation has played in this
movement.

One group of Catholic educators will argue
somewhat as follows: Many religious communities
are not large enough and do not have sufficient resources to conduct colleges of one type or another
of their own. They must, therefore, become connected somehow with a college or university already firmly established in their vicinity. This must
be done either by having the Sisters attend the institutions in question, or by having the institutions
send members of their faculties to teach by extension in the convents. By whatever way the contact
is maintained the religious communities usually pay
the colleges or universities involved the usual tuition fees for the instruction which their subjects
receive. There are several fundamental objections
to this plan. Many religious communities are not
located within such a distance from the institution
so as to make communication with ordinary facility
feasible. Another difficulty is the fact that the institutions of higher education do not have the faculty-

power to send teachers out to give courses in convents. What usually happens is that the institution will name Sisters within the community seeking instruction as members of its extension faculty, and gradually the religious community is planning and conducting its own program of studies with its own resources. The institution merely collects the fees and issues academic credit and degrees, all of which comes very close to being an academic racket. Again, this plan is extremely costly for the religious communities, although very profitable to the institutions concerned. Furthermore, it does not contribute what it should to the religious formation of Sisters.

The University's plan is based on this fundamental premise: If the young and prospective Sister is to be trained for teaching in the classroom simultaneously with her formation for the religious life, it is best for her to receive this training within her own convent and not outside in any teaching-training center, however excellent this center may be from the standpoint of professional education. Another principle of great importance in the execution of our plan is that the Sisters themselves in their own convents can do a far better educational job than an outside institution can by sending members of its own teaching staff to the convent. [3] Thus

[3] We have called attention above to the fact that the institution is unable to carry on this work by its own staff, but enlists the services of teachers within the convent, and eventually the religious community is carrying on its own work in the name of the outside institution, and is paying tuition and other fees to the outside institution for work which it is doing by itself.

the Sisters, by training a faculty of their own from their own personnel, will have a group of teachers who will be able to keep in close touch with their pupils for assistance and guidance and will have a strong personal interest in them. This is in sharp contrast to the other situation, where the instructor rushes in to give a lecture and rushes off again almost as soon as he has finished, or where the Sister herself rushes to an outside institution as a member of a large mixed class and can approach the teacher only with difficulty, and herself must hasten to return to her convent. Furthermore, the religious community under the University's plan will have an incentive to build up a good working library for teachers within the walls of its own convent, which will be not only a great convenience to the Sister students but will also be a great benefit to the community in general. The expense, especially when regarded in the light of value received, is fantastically less than the cost involved under the first plan.

The objections usually raised against the University's plan to meet the novitiate problem are two. First, since the Sisters will be within their own convents, because of this quasi-family relationship between the teacher and the students, educational standards will be low. The teacher will not grade the achievements of her students objectively, and will be reluctant to fail a Sister when she deserves to fail. All my experience in this work points to much greater objectivity and strictness within the reli-

gious community than on the part of the teachers of
an outside institution, who rush in and rush out of
a convent because they are very busy with other
duties and are anxious to get this extra chore completed with the slightest possible trouble and in-
convenience. Certainly the Sister of a religious community who has been named an extension instructor by a college or university to serve within her
own convent will not grade any differently if she
were assigned to teach in the community's educational program by her own Superior. A second
common criticism is that the teachers of religious
communities will not be as well trained as those
from outside. Certainly this need not be so. We
have found no difficulty in persuading Mothers
Superior that Sisters well-trained for this purpose
will yield fruit a hundredfold. As for experience
in teaching, the average Sister, all will agree, has
more of this asset in the best sense of the phrase
than the average teacher to be found on our college
faculties. Finally, permit me to recall again that
these very teachers within the convent, thus criti-
cized as instructors in novitiate institutions, are
themselves regularly named as teachers in extension
by the colleges and universities operating under the
first plan.

Some of the benefits to be derived from the
second plan, the program of Affiliation as set up by
The Catholic University of America, are as follows:

(1) The religious community is able to develop its own institution for the attaining of its various

objectives. This institution will belong to the community in the best sense of the word, without any entangling alliances of any kind.

(2) In keeping with the principles of non-interference with the institution's autonomy, the institution will issue its own transcripts of record. The University will accept the credits so issued at their face value. The institution, however, is in no way bound to send its students to the Catholic University. It may send them anywhere it chooses. In such cases, if necessary, the University will issue a statement that it itself will accept these credits in the usual way. All institutions of higher education and state departments of education, with very few exceptions, will accept these credits from an affiliate. The New Your State Board of Regents has cooperated splendidly with the University in this matter.

(3) The Catholic University, through its Committee on Affiliation, acts as a center of information for its affiliates on all educational matters, such as textbooks, administrative problems, and academic problems generally. The affiliate may use this service or not as it pleases.

(4) If the institution desires, the University jointly with the institution itself will issue a diploma of graduation at the minimum cost of fifty cents.

(5) If the institution wishes to grow from a two-year "normal" to one of three years, and eventually to a four-year college, the University through its Committee on Affiliation will go along with the institution, advising and supporting it at every step

of the way. Of course, at the college stage a charter or incorporation must be obtained from the state. Thereafter, the University will encourage and guide its affiliate to recognition by its own state department of education, its own state university, and finally its own regional association.

At present the Catholic University has over fifty affiliates of this kind—teacher training institutions and junior colleges within religious communities—and the number is increasing constantly. A few are recognized by their regional associations as four-year colleges; some are three-year and others are two-year institutions. All started from scratch, as it were, and all are progressing at various speeds, but essentially all are prospering. The Catholic University of America is proud of this achievement, and I am most grateful for having had a role in this accomplishment.

Approximately a hundred religious orders and congregations have established houses of study in the neighborhood of the University or in nearby Maryland for their own subjects. Some of these offer courses independently of the University, while others serve only as residences for their members who are pursuing studies at the University.

Some of those who conduct independent institutions of their own are affiliated with the University as described above, but others have no academic relationship with the University whatsoever. This causes some confusion in the outside academic world, although there is no good reason why this should be so. A long established axiom in the world of education is that the truly healthy and beneficial academic relationship is that based on voluntary action. These neighboring institutions, like all other Catholic academic groups throughout the country, are free to affiliate with the University or not, as they wish. This is as it should be.

The principle of a strictly voluntary relationship can well be carried still further with these neighboring institutions. Some administrators of the University have been somewhat critical of those religious groups which, while maintaining their houses within the immediate vicinity of the University, send few if any of their people to the University class-rooms. Some of the oldest established religious communities are among these. This is due to the fact that they feel that the University has little to contribute to their needs. They are more or less self-sufficient within their own houses.

This attitude on the part of the University authorities has always seemed to me to be most unreasonable. They should regard this situation as a challenge. It is reasonable to presume that, if they improved their academic offerings sufficiently and brought to the ranks of their faculty outstanding scholars and teachers, there would be no serious problem about attracting students to the University from the neighboring houses of study. In this way also the University would be living up more thoroughly to its name as The Catholic University of America.

The Catholic University of America Press, and the Catholic Education Press

The Catholic University of America Press was founded on November 14, 1939, and was incorporated on June 16, 1941. The period defined by these two dates includes a very interesting first chapter of the history of the press which has never been told.

Bishop Corrigan, Rector of the University, had just come into office and was soon very much preoccupied with arranging the various events which were to commemorate the fiftieth anniversary of the founding of the University. As one of the significant commemorations of this event, I suggested the establishment of a University Press. My presentation of the project was essentially as follows:

The need of such a Press is self evident, especially if one considers its particular objectives. It should be primarily interested in the publication of the following kinds of works:

(1) The result of original research of a scientific nature by members of the University faculty. Such publications ordinarily have to be subsidized, at least in part, from the general University Press or other funds. It cannot be expected that revenue from the sales of these works will contribute much to the cost of manufacture to the Press.

(2) Similar studies as indicated above under 1, conducted by persons outside the University, sometimes under the direction of members of the University faculty. It is understood that such work will not be published if by so doing funds will not be available for the publication of similar works by members of the University faculty.

(3) The Catholic University of America dissertations.

(4) Works of a semi-popular nature, the object of which is to acquaint the general reading public, especially within the Catholic Church, with new discoveries and advances in the sciences, the arts, and literature. These publications may be by members of the University faculty or others. Here it is expected that the revenue from sales will at least meet the cost of manufacture, and the customary arrangements for royalties should be made.

These aims as just described and as presented to Bishop Corrigan in 1939 were immediately approved; they were again examined and reaffirmed early in the academic year of 1955-56.

It was insisted also that the name of the Press be The Catholic University of America Press and not simply the Catholic University Press as many wished. One reason for this insistence was the fact that Bishop Shahan had actually permitted one member of the faculty to use "Catholic University Press" as the title of a private publishing venture of his own, and some of its books were still in circulation. Furthermore, there was at least one deliberate appropriation of the name without the formality even of asking permission to do so. In

any case the true name of the University is The
Catholic University of America and not the Catholic University. This fact in itself seemed to justify
the title as finally adopted.

The original plan as presented to Bishop Corrigan, moreover, contained what was thought to be
a solution of the problem of financing the Press. It
is common knowledge that university presses lose
money and need financial assistance from the university treasury or from other sources. At that time
Catholic schools were badly in need of textbooks
written by Catholics and skillfully integrated with
Catholic philosophy and theology. The most important of all textbooks, the religion and English
series for the four years of the Catholic secondary
school, were essentially *desiderata*. Then there
were the social sciences, the foreign languages and
literatures, and the natural sciences, all of which
were in need either of greatly improved textbooks
or of Catholic textbooks for the first time. My plan
was to develop such textbooks, which, if they were
to any degree satisfactory, would almost necessarily
have a large sale and bring in considerable revenue. This income could be used as a subsidy for
the publication of scholarly and technical works for
which there is little demand, and from which consequently little or no financial profit is derived.
The question naturally arose as to how an organization could be set up to handle these textbooks
in the process both of production and of sales. My
thought was that at least such textbooks as were

likely to have an extensive demand would be produced jointly with a publishing house of established reputation. In fact, an English series, a religion series, a biology textbook, a French series, and a Latin series for secondary schools were not only planned but eventually produced. The English series was actually published jointly and some royalty was received, but the Treasurer of the University had a strong aversion to the plan, the reasons for which I was never told. Consequently, I received word from the Procurator that I was to cease all publication of textbooks. I have always thought that this was an unfortunate step, especially in the light of subsequent developments.

Of course, I never for a moment entertained the idea of giving up my textbook projects and I so informed the Procurator. The very fact that I was asked to do so shows how little the authorities of the University realized the nature of my proposal. I was obliged simply to modify my plans with reference to them. The English series, previously a joint project, now became the sole concern of the Sadlier Corporation; the religion series is the property of Mentzer-Bush; the biology text of the American Book Company; the French series of the Loyola University Press; and the Latin series of the Bruce Publishing Company. I personally became the recipient of author's royalty, which I had been willing, according to our original plan, to assign to The Catholic University of America Press. All these textbooks, with the possible exception of the French series, have had an exceptional volume of sales. Had some way been found whereby these textbooks could have been published under the official patronage of the University, the problem of financing scholarly works of the highest order would unquestionably have been solved.

The Catholic Education Press was incorporated on a non-profit basis on June 30, 1947. The objectives of this corporation are, broadly speaking, the same as those of The Catholic University of America Press. The Catholic Education Press, however, is primarily concerned with the publication of textbooks and educational materials in general for elementary schools, secondary schools, and colleges. Had this Press been so constituted in 1939 or soon thereafter, it might have undertaken the publication of those series mentioned above. As matters stand now, the sales opportunity in this field has been greatly reduced not only by the publication of the series in question but also by the launching of several rival series in almost every field.

When The Catholic University of America Press was incorporated in 1941, it became firmly established for the first time. This was a genuine step forward. Before this it lacked direction and strictly defined powers.

As a result of incorporation, the officers of the University became the officers of the Press. The Committee of The Press exercised the editorial control and consisted [1] of:

[1] As of 1960-61.

> The Rector of the University, *ex officio*
> Professor Roy J. Deferrari, Director
> Professor Paul H. Furfey
> Monsignor Francis J. Houlahan
> Professor Martin R. P. McGuire
> Monsignor James A. Magner
> Professor Francis O. Rice
> Doctor Eugene P. Willging, Secretary

The same officers and committee of The Catholic University of America Press then served also for The Catholic Education Press.

The day-to-day business operations of the Presses are controlled by the Manager of the Press, Monsignor James A. Magner, and financial control rests with the Budget Committee of the University.

Workshops

While I was attending the meeting of the Association of Deans and Directors of Summer Sessions some fifteen years ago, I heard a great deal about the nature of academic workshops and the special techniques employed in them. The American Council of Education was at that time promoting this new approach to advanced study, and it had carefully described the nature of the work with recommended procedures. Unfortunately, the Council's definition and suggestions have not been followed by the numerous "workshops" which have since been undertaken throughout the country. At The Catholic University of America, however, we have endeavored from the beginning to maintain them. Bringing persons together who have completed their formal training and who in addition have had some experience in the field, in order to discuss problems which they have encountered and to get a fresh outlook on their work, summarizes very briefly the nature of a true workshop. This, to my mind, was a plan which could be of great benefit to Catholic educators. The absence of any thought of academic credit and the complete concentration on the solution of difficulties actually experienced should, I thought, have a special appeal to all serious minded teachers and administrators. Another attractive feature of the workshop plan is the opportunity which it offers the University to exercise the leadership in academic affairs which the Catholic educational world expects of it.

The financial problem involved was indeed great. State universities, which were the pioneers in this kind of education, were supported by substantial appropriations from the state treasury. The necessity of procuring outstanding specialists in all the ramifications of the subject under investigation and the importance of limited enrollments in order to make possible individual instruction and guidance make it impossible to conduct self-supporting workshops. This difficulty would have to be solved.

In 1945, the permission of the Rector was asked to discuss with possibly interested parties on the campus the feasibility of attempting at least one such workshop, and incidentally the first academic workshop in the true sense under Catholic auspices. This was granted. A group of about fifteen persons, including the Vice Rector, Monsignor Edward Jordan, and the Head of the Department of Education, Dr. George Foran, met in my office. The general outcomes of the deliberations were as follows: No one thought that any such program was practicable or useful. In fact, one person expressed a fear that the very title indicated a contact with and influence from communism, and this was long before the fairly recent period of witch-hunting! It was made clear that no special financial support was to be expected from the University and that any such activity as a workshop was to pay its own way. Furthermore, the facilities of the University were available for a workshop project only for a limited time during the entire year, namely, the period following the annual Commencement Day and preceeding the first registration day of the Summer Session.

With this assortment of chiefly negative and highly discouraging conclusions, a plan for the con ducting of academic workshops at The Catholic University of America was drawn up. Since, in spite of the many preliminary objections, several departments and individuals independently began to request permission to conduct workshops, without any very accurate knowledge of what they were undertaking, it became clear that all these and similar activities must be regulated by some one person directly responsible to the Rector of the University. In answer to my inquiry about this problem, Monsignor McCormick replied as follows:

August 1, 1947

In reply to your inquiry of July 8, I would advise that, for the present, you report on such activities as Workshops, Work Conferences, Forums, Institutes, etc., in your capacity as Secretary General. As I told you, the term Adult Education does not appeal to me as embracing these activities, and neither does the term Affiliation and Extension cover them adequately. Until some other individual is officially appointed for such activities, I believe it is better that they be under your direction as Secretary General.

(signed)   P. J. McCormick
Rector

No one was "officially appointed for such activities" until the time of my retirement in 1960, when the Reverend Robert P. Mohan S. S. was placed in charge of the Summer Session and Worshops.

The workshop period, then, has been set for ten days in the interim mentioned above, allowing sufficient time for the registration period of the Summer Session. Each workshop has its own officers, special lecturers, and consultants. Each also has its own budget. The officers usually include a director and assistant director of the workshop, a librarian, and a recorder. The workshop director is under the general supervision of the over-all Director of Workshops who is also the Director of the Summer Session and up to 1961 was also the Secretary General.

Workshop sessions are planned around the interests and problems identified by the participants under the general theme of the workshop. The problems selected by the group are delimited to such scope as will permit satisfactory progress during the time available.

In the morning, the sessions of the workshop consist of formal lectures followed by an opportunity for extended discussion. In the afternoon sessions, the group is divided into sections designed to give more detailed knowledge of particular phases of the subject. Each workshop participant is assigned to a section of his choice with which to work throughout his attendance at the workshop. By means of these small seminar groups opportunity is provided for working more intensively on chosen interests, while at the same time, through the morning sessions, each participant is enabled to keep in touch with the accomplishments of the workshop as a whole.

Because of the lack of any subsidy, compromise with the ideal has had to be made in two quarters. We have been obliged to accept more than the optimum number of participants, and we also have deemed it wise to grant academic credit under certain conditions to those who request it. The length of the period of the workshop has turned out to be very fortunate, although it was determined purely by unavoidable circumstances. Consultants are available for participation in group work and for individual conferences. Other resources such as secretarial services and work materials are available to facilitate progress in solving problems. The most significant resource is the membership of the workshop, i.e., the participants themselves, who live and work together and who contribute much from their vast and varied experiences.

As we have intimated above, the term workshop has been greatly abused ever since it was first employed and defined by the American Council on Education for a special technique. It probably is used more often now in the very loose sense of conference or round-table discussion. We, however, have tried to adhere to its original meaning as already described, although we too have been forced to make compromises. Since many members of religious communities cannot get permission to attend these workshops unless they can bring back academic credit, we have made it possible to gain such academic credit in any of our workshops, if a participant so desires. Again, according to the original definition and ideal, only persons with much practical experience in the field should be permitted to attend, and the deliberations accordingly should be on a very high academic level. But circumstances have made us consider it prudent on occasions to accept persons who have had no practical experience at all but who have been thrown into a job for which they have had no training whatsoever. For example, many deans and registrars, and even presidents in institutions of higher education today, owe whatever previous training they have had for their jobs to a single ten-day workshop at The Catholic University of America, and they are most grateful for it.

At any rate from 1946 through the present year there has been a rapid increase of from one to eight workshops per year. The total number of participants for these several workshops has grown from approximately one hundred to six hundred, which also represents the largest group that the present facilities can handle comfortably. [1]

As has been said, in the beginning the workshops were permitted or tolerated. Now they are considered a major operation of the University. Every workshop leaves a volume of proceedings behind it, most of which thus far have had a significant circulation. All this is good for the University, especially because the very nature of the activities of the workshops indicates educational leadership of a high order. It is our earnest hope that they will not be allowed to lapse.

Adult Education

Early in the period of World War II, I was invited by some of my friends in education within the city of Washington to attend a dinner meeting, at which certain representatives of labor from the British Isles were to be present to discuss adult edu-

[1] Cf. Appendix 3 for a list of the workshops which have been held at the Catholic University from 1946 through June of 1960.

cation as carried on in their own country. It was interesting to note that they were not to discuss labor schools but education for adults in general, who either did not have an opportunity to obtain the usual education in their early years or wished to improve their general academic training. This meeting was most interesting and profitable, for it gave us an introduction to facets of education to which many of us had given little thought and which were fast coming to the fore.

These Britishers seemed to encounter real difficulty in successfully describing the nature of adult education to us Americans, saturated, as we were, with the thought of obtaining credits for any studying that we might do and with the hope of attaining the magic number of such credits which would entitle us to a degree or a certificate. Also, and perhaps especially, the expectancy of some material gain accruing to us from these extra studies is often found in the mind of the American adult student. Learning for the sake of learning is a principle which could well be increasingly promulgated in our American educational system. These gentlemen, however, were very patient with us, as one after another of our group spoke in the educational jargon of American professional educators. Speaking for myself, I can say that they gave me, in spite of the handicaps under which they labored, an understanding of adult education which has stood me in good stead ever since. The following points with regard to adult education were made very clear and have been used to form the basis on which adult education has been carried on at The Catholic University of America.

(1) Adult education aims to train a person to be a better citizen: to have a better understanding of world problems, to be able to exercise the privilege of the vote more intelligently and wisely, and to avoid the pitfalls of erroneous political philosophies such as communism. How well this purpose can be applied to Catholic adult education, with particular reference to training the layman to serve his Church better!

(2) Academic credits are in no way involved, only the needs of the individuals who present themselves for instruction.

(3) The organization of the courses must break away entirely from the traditional plan of formal instruction leading to certificates and degrees. It must be very flexible so as to meet the needs of any given group. All programs of study should be brief, consisting of comparatively few lectures or classes, and not be long drawn out. The adult who is giving of his leisure time to attend these classes cannot count on being able to attend regularly an extensive series of meetings.

(4) The instruction must be arranged wherever it is most convenient for the participants, e.g., in parish halls, even in priests' homes, as well as in college classrooms.

(5) Teachers must be selected with great care, keeping in mind their ability to lecture well,

because here instruction is carried on best through lectures as the participants can do no serious extra-curriculum study beyond a little outside reading on a very uncertain schedule. The teacher, however, must never talk down to the members of his class but must treat them as the adults that they are. It is also desirable that some discussion follow the lectures or even interrupt them, if properly controlled.

Of course, much other information was also received, but these principles represent the basic thinking in this vast and important field of educational activity.

The importance of adult education in the scheme of Catholic education struck me very forcefully, especially when thought was given to the extensive operations of the National Educational Association and the various state universities in this field, and when we realized that the most popular subjects today for adults are theology, psychology and psychiatry, and history and politics. Surely, in the light of all this, Catholic education cannot consider adult education as outside its province. Yet today very little adult education, far less than conditions require, is being carried on under Catholic auspices. It seems evident that adult education is just as important in the sphere of Catholic education as any of the well-established and traditional fields. Just as much harm can come to Catholics from attending adult education classes given by the National Educational Association and those offered by a state university, as by enrolling as a candidate for a degree in a state or any other non-sectarian institution of higher education.

At the University, however, several hindrances were encountered in the way of starting even a small program of adult education. Adult education, it was said, had been tried several times in the past but had not attracted enough people to make it worthwhile. Of course, what these objectors had in mind were night courses with or without credit; they were not adult education in the true sense and, therefore, were not germaine to our consideration. The Rector himself, Bishop McCormick, who understood the nature of adult education better than most of the others, thought that it was beneath the dignity of the University to undertake such instruction. We explained that in England the Universities of Oxford and Cambridge with all their traditional learning of the highest order did not consider it beneath their dignity to cooperate with the labor unions of Great Britain in carrying on genuine adult education.

In any case, regardless of these objections, permission was granted to plan a program of adult education under the auspices of the University according as we thought best. The following letter led to the final favorable decision.

May 8, 1945

To the Rt. Rev. Msgr. P. J. McCormick:

I meant to speak to you long ago regarding the possibility of the University offering, in a serious way, some courses for adults. A regular program of adult education seems to be of genuine importance to every wide-awake university at this time. In fact, many educators, especially in the state institutions, are regarding this phase of their work as one of the most important forward steps for the university after the war.

If our own University here should take the matter seriously, someone should be appointed to the task who will have at least the major portion of his time available to planning the work and administering it, possibly with a small advisory committee to assist him. The work in its entire conception should be divorced from any connection with the regular courses offered by the University. The courses in adult education should be organized from an entirely different point of view and should not be influenced by the units of work in planning for our regular curricula. The person put in charge also should be given an opportunty to visit some of the institutions of the country where this work has been proceeding on an elaborate scale for the last year or two. I have in mind especially the University of Michigan.

I really believe that this program of adult education is extremely important as I have said above and if it is going to be considered at all for next year, plans should be made in connection with it as soon as possible. I have talked this matter over with several of the deans and with Monsignor Jordan. I shall, of course, be glad to talk to you about it in more detail if you so desire.

Roy J. Deferrari
Secretary General

The chief difficulty was the lack of any person at the time with enough leisure to be able to direct a serious program in the field. I myself did not have the leisure. Then Dr. John W. Stafford, C.S.V., Head of the Department of Psychology, and Psychiatry, reminded me that the Reverend Sebastian Miklas, O.F.M. Cap. was conducting a very successful Adult Education Institute within the Archdiocese of Washington, with the approbation and great interest of the Archbishop, and that he probably would be willing to transfer it to the University and carry on the work under the auspices of our institution. A conference with both the Rector and Father Miklas was soon arranged, and plans were made for the beginning of the present Catholic University of America Adult Education Institute. Father Miklas has been very successful in carrying on a general type of adult education. In this connection he gave me an opportunity to give a series of lectures in the Institute on the Fathers of the Church. This was a delightful, if strenuous, experience; it is recommended to anyone who wishes to sharpen up his teaching methods.

However, complete satisfaction with our present scheme of adult education has not yet been attained. We have not gone far enough. The adult education project is not yet an official part of the University family. Furthermore, it does not, as of this date, appear on the organization chart of the University. Father Miklas does not yet have a regular faculty rank. Moreover, all these matters were brought out by the Middle States Association of Colleges and Secondary Schools in its recent evaluation of the University. Besides all this, there are a number of other kinds of adult education which the University should introduce, for example, special sessions of several days duration for groups of our alumni, especially our graduates in the professions. All this, we strongly believe is a definite responsibility of the University. Incidentally, it gives another opportunity for some profitable public relations. The present condition of adult education in The Catholic University of America might be summed up as follows: the University authorities have not yet taken adult education seriously enough, but have left it on the fringe of things, as something which is good but by no means indispensable.

SPECIAL UNIVERSITY PROBLEMS

The Admission of Women

A very interesting fact about the several sets of constitutions or statutes of the University is that women or men as such are nowhere mentioned. While serving on the committee appointed by Bishop Ryan to compose a recommended revision of the statutes, I mentioned this, and had the effrontery to insert "women" in one of the proposed new statements. Monsignor Pace declared sharply that neither men nor women as such should be mentioned in our planned new set of constitutions. All this raised the suspicion in my mind that the various authorities of the University always had an unexpressed feeling that some day women would have a place in The Catholic University of America. Of course, like all institutions for men only and those which evolved from such into a coeducational status, our University always had its small group

of "women-haters," both clerical and lay. Even up
to my most recent days on the campus I have been
reminded that woman's place in the University is
a very precarious one. As a priest put it not long
ago: "Don't think for a minute, Deferrari, that
women are definitely here in the University to
stay." Then he related a nebulous conversation
which he had overheard between important persons that would indicate an uncertain status for
women at the University even now! These rather
persistent and vigorous protests always remind me
of the young boy whistling as he walked in the
dark through a cemetery. As far as I know, they
were never taken very seriously by anyone.

At any rate, Dr. Thomas Edward Shields deserves credit for bringing women at least to the
fringes of the University, when he established the
Sisters College in 1912. To be sure, they were on
the outside looking in! They were not permitted
to appear on the campus proper, to say nothing
of using the library and attending classes on the
campus. For many years the only woman on the
University campus in any official capacity was Miss
Frances Brawner, Secretary to the Vice Rector,
Monsignor Pace.

The first women to appear on the campus to
use the educational facilities of the University were
the Sisters whom I brought to the University in
1920 from the Sisters College to use the Greek and
Latin libraries on the second floor of McMahon

Hall. [1] The first woman to be admitted officially as a student to one of the regular classes at the University proper was Sister M. Inez Hilger, O.S.B., then of St. Benedict's Convent, St. Joseph, Minnesota, who enrolled in September, 1924. She had sought the permission of her Ordinary, Bishop Joseph F. Busch, to attend the University of Minnesota to study economics and social studies generally, because she could not get such graduate instruction, by reason of being a woman, in The Catholic University of America! Bishop Busch made a great issue of this case before the Board of Trustees of the University and obtained permission for this special student only, which decision was not to be taken as a precedent! How this decision was to take care of hundreds of similar cases of Catholic women, both religious and lay, was never made known. The following excerpts from Sister M. Inez' letter to Dr. Kerby gives a vivid description of the problems involved:

June 10, 1929

Rev. Dr. William J. Kerby
1828 Lamont Street
Washington, D.C.

Dear Dr. Kerby,

At your request, I am sending you this account of my efforts of August 1924, to attend the Graduate School of the Catholic University.

Early in June 1924, Mother Louise Walz, Superior of our Community, told me she wished

---

[1] Cf. The Catholic Sisters College.

me to be transferred from St. Mary's Academy, Altoona, Wisconsin, to the College of St. Benedict. I was to establish a Department of Sociology at the College, and in order to prepare myself, I was to spend the school year 1924-25 at the University of Minnesota. I registered as a student in the Sociology Department of the University of Minnesota in the Summer Session which opened at the end of that June.

Upon my return to the Motherhouse, I conferred with Mother Louise, telling her of probable difficulties in my work. I gave her instances of differences and of arguments that had arisen between the Catholic and the non-Catholic members of the classes. I told her that I could hardly keep out of the arguments since I knew that the Catholic boys and girls in the classes expected me as a Sister to defend the Catholic position and teachings. I recall one argument quite distinctly even now. Christ was spoken of by one of the students as a splendid social worker but His divinity was questioned,—I think even denied. The controversy was carried on entirely by the students; the professor did not take part in the discussions. In the other course, a student asked one day, whether she were correct in stating that old-maids, bachelors, and people leading voluntary celibate lives were not completely developed normal human beings, for if they were they would all be married; to which the instructor answered, "Yes, to a very large extent."

While doing my work at the University of Minnesota for a B.A. degree, priests had on various occasions remarked to me that they thought it quite out of place to have Sisters attend State Universities; that Sisters become lax in doing so;

that their attendance gave approval to parents in sending their own sons and daughters to State universities.

I had now made an honest but unsuccessful attempt to enter a graduate school in the most outstanding of our Catholic institutions of higher learning. Since I feared criticism from the Clergy and from Catholic institutions of higher learning who would not know of my unsuccessful efforts, I thought it well to submit the entire matter to the Right Reverend Joseph F. Busch, Bishop of St. Cloud Diocese. So with Mother Louise's permission I submitted the answers which I had received from the various schools to him, and communicated to him the obvious fact that there was nothing else for me to do but to attend the University of Minnesota during the school year. He read the letters and commented upon the lack of opportunities for Sisters wishing to do graduate work in Catholic institutions, and noted the fact that two highly notable Catholic schools did not admit women as students. He said that he was going to Washington, for the Bishops' Annual Meeting in a few days, and that he would take the opportunity of bringing these facts to the attention of the Bishops. However, he too realized that all I could do was to register at the University of Minnesota, which I did the following week. Dr. Chapin as well as all the faculty members of the Sociology department extended every courtesy and help to me.

Upon his arrival in Washington, Bishop Busch was able to arrange for my attendance at the Catholic University, and wired immediately to that effect to the Motherhouse at St. Joseph, Minnesota. The telegrapher, however, made an error in the

spelling of the Bishop's signature, so that the
signature was unidentified. Mother Louise was in
the State of Washington when the wire arrived,
and the acting superior did not interpret the message as of any importance. Therefore, no action
was taken until the Bishop arrived from Washington. At this time I was registered at the University
of Minnesota and ready for work. Two Sisters
from St. Benedict's, Sister Rita Marshall and my
sister, Sister Marie Hilger, immediately brought
word to me at Minneapolis that Bishop Busch had
laid the matter of my attendance at the Catholic
University before the Bishops at their Annual
Meeting, and that because of Bishop Busch's
efforts and the Bishops' kind response, I was to
be admitted to the Graduate School at the Catholic University.

I left Minneapolis the following day, September 29, and registered at the Catholic University
on October 1, 1924. Courtesy was extended to me
by all members of the faculty of the Catholic
University whom I met or with whom I had any
dealings, and that courtesy and good will was
manifested by them throughout the entire year.
The student body, too, consisting of priests, semi-
narians, and laymen, at all times were most courteous and respectful. At no time was I embarrassed
in any way.

My courses consisted of five hours a week in
Principles of Sociology and three hours a week in
Poverty and Relief with Reverend Doctor William
J. Kerby; three hours a week in Industrial Ethics
with Reverend Doctor John A. Ryan; three hours
a week in Social Case Work and two days a week
in Field Work under Reverend Doctor John
O'Grady; one hour a week in Outlines of Psychiatry with Reverend Doctor Verner Moore O.S.B.;

one hour a week in Mental Measurements with Mr. John W. Rauth; and two hours of Seminar a week.

Before the first week of school had ended, I felt convinced that I had gained everything by the transfer. Catholic thought, of which there was so little before, pervaded everything at the Catholic University. Even the atmosphere one breathed seemed charged with Catholic principles. Since there was no need of being on the defensive, I settled down to a life of mental and spiritual growth. My appreciation of the contacts with the superb minds of my instructors, I cannot express in words. The knowledge I gained was saturated with Catholic principles and interpretations. The response of the student body during class hours was at all times an inspiration to me. My field work was intensely interesting. I gained a keen appreciation of the struggling though beautiful lives of the poor and needy. My visits with these in poverty and distress made deep and lasting impressions. My contact with the Social Workers in the various agencies in the District of Columbia and with their work, were and still are most valuable and helpful.

(signed)   SISTER M. INEZ HILGER, O.S.B.

All Sisters were admitted to the University for graduate study in the first year of Bishop Ryan's rectorship (1928), and he was directly responsible for it. Very soon thereafter laywomen were admitted for graduate study only in all departments of arts and sciences and in the non-ecclesiastical professional schools. Bishop William Turner of Buffalo, formerly Professor of Philosophy at the University, was very much interested in promoting the cause of the laywomen on this occasion. Indeed, a relative of his, Mrs. Mary Mahoney, then Miss Mary Hannon, was the first laywoman to register as a candidate for the Ph.D. degree and to receive that degree. She enrolled in September 1929, and received the degree in 1933. Mrs. Florence McGuire, the former Florence Mattimore and wife of Dr. Martin R. P. McGuire, Head of the Department of Greek and Latin, was the first woman to register at the University for the Master's degree. She enrolled in September 1927 and obtained that degree in 1928. They were both students of mine in the Department of Greek and Latin at about the same time.

There was always a good argument to support the admission of women to graduate instruction. They could not get their instruction anywhere else under Catholic auspices. This essentially was a true statement of the situation at that time. There was then, however, a strict ban against women, lay or religious, entering any of the undergraduate courses of instruction at the University. I am afraid that I myself unconsciously caused some confusion in this connection and a good deal of annoyance to Bishop Ryan. With the Rector's permission, I had introduced a program of studies leading to the A.B. degree in education, principally for the lay-teachers of the public schools of the District of Columbia. In fact, whenever Sisters of the District Catholic schools, not registered at the Sisters College, came to me and begged me to admit them for undergraduate credit to courses in the Graduate School of Arts and Sciences, labeled as for either graduate or undergraduate credit, I was inclined to give in to them. This was direct interference with the Sisters College as the sacrosanct center for the registration of undergraduate Sisters. Naturally, this caused great resentment on the part of the authorities of the Sisters College and some one of them presented the matter to the Board of Trustees. Shortly thereafter I received a curt note from the Rector to the effect that the Board of Trustees had ruled that women were *not* to be admitted to the undergraduate courses of the University proper and that he wished this rule to be "rigorously" enforced. But the undergraduate program for the teachers of the District had been accepted by the University authorities, and a good many women teachers had enrolled. I could not very well kick them out now! The Sisters College, however, was in an impossible position, and as an academic institution it was doomed. Whatever it attempted to do academically was being done on the University campus with far better resources and thus much more efficiently. It became essentially a matter of competition, with the advantage distinctly on the side of the University proper.

When the nursing program was introduced on the University campus, the University authorities found themselves with a rather large group of women who had to receive instruction in practically all the basic courses of general education over and above the strictly professional courses in nursing. Certainly the University authorities could not be expected to duplicate courses already being given in English, philosophy, science, religion, and other fields for the nursing students alone. This would have been financially impossible. Thus the women broke the barrier on the undergraduate level at last.

Women, however, were not yet admitted to the College of Arts and Sciences as candidates for undergraduate degrees. The great argument against so admitting them was that the University would be treading upon the territory of Trinity College and Dunbarton College of Holy Cross, which were devoted solely to the Catholic higher education of women. When the question of admitting undergraduate women to the Department of Speech and Drama was presented to the Academic Senate under Bishop Corrigan, I was delegated by that body to interview the Sister presidents of those institutions to see how they would feel about any such action on our part. Sister Catherine Dorothea of Trinity expressed herself as opposed in principle to coeducation on the higher level under Catholic auspices, but had no objection to the University entering upon it, if it so saw fit. Sister Mary Frederick of Dunbarton College said that her institution was not offering any courses in speech and drama, and thus the opening of our program in this field to women would not affect her college. She did, however, express misgivings as to the reaction on Dunbarton College of a general University policy of admitting women to the College of Arts and Sciences as candidates for degrees. Shortly before this, pressure had been successfully brought to bear on admitting women to our pre-medical programs. This meant accepting under-graduate women as concentrators in the Depart-ments of Biology, Chemistry, and Physics. More-over, this was easily brought about because the university authorities of the time were convinced that our Catholic colleges for women were not emi-nently successful in training students to enter medical schools. I was and am still inclined to doubt this opinion, but it did have the desired effect.

This is as far as the movement to admit women to the College has gone up until now. The oppo-nents of this educational development hold fast, not so much because they seek to maintain the integrity of Trinity College and Dunbarton Col-lege, [2] but because they labor under the delusion that they are keeping at least some portions of the University free from women. There may not be concentrators in English, Greek and Latin, history, and other subjects, but it can be safely said that essentially all the courses of these departments have many women students in them, that is, those women students from the School of Nursing, the departments of the sciences and speech and drama, who in fulfilling the requirements of their own particular programs must take courses in English,

[2] After all, both these institutions can and are getting along very successfully without any special help from anyone else.

Greek and Latin, history, and the rest. Thus there seems to be no valid reason for barring women from any of the departments of the College at all.

One may ask: "Why be concerned about this? We now have many excellent Catholic colleges for women which are doing outstanding work in these departments." My reply to this is very simple. "The Catholic University of America is the one Catholic university in the United States devoted primarily to training for research. As such, its aims are peculiar to itself. It is especially devoted to scholarship in the highest sense of the term. Even in the College, it trains for scholarship and thus for thinking and leadership, not in the sense commonly bandied about, but in a very definite and demonstrable way. If young Catholic women wish to enter upon such an exacting regime under Catholic auspices, available to them only at The Catholic University of America, why should they not be permitted to do so?" As a matter of fact, students in the College are taught by some of the most distinguished scholars of the University.

Appointments and Promotions
of Members of the Faculty

A great problem indeed to university administrators is the appointment and promotion of members of the faculty. Of course, this involves salaries, but I do not intend to touch upon this phase of the subject. Suffice it to say that in the case of salaries, as with appointments and promotions, unless a university president has a scale or a plan within which he can operate, he faces a great deal of trouble. It may be necessary at times in order to obtain the services of a very desirable person or to retain an essentially indispensable man to break the scale or general plan of operation, but if this policy becomes anything more than a genuine rarity, there is chaos. The morale of the faculty becomes very low, which is close to disaster for any educational institution of high repute.

I came to the University in the late years of Bishop Shahan's rectorship. The general morale of the faculty was extremely low at that time for this very reason. Essentially all of the lay faculty and some of the clergy openly expressed a wish to move elsewhere, if other positions were available to them. Some of the clergy advised the laymen to move out as soon as possible, on the ground that conditions would not improve within the foreseeable future. Actually Bishop Shahan had no plan with which to cope with this problem. He bargained with each individual to give him as low a faculty grade as possible and the lowest possible salary as well. The principles for appointments and promotions were laid down in a very general way in the statutes of the University, but even these were followed only vaguely. They were used chiefly as a reason for not hiring or promoting an undesirable person but never in a positive way. There was a feeling among the faculty, largely true, that unless you did something drastic about it yourself, you would always remain in the same grade and at the same salary. Regular unsollicited promotions were essentially non-existent.

Bishop Ryan was obliged to deal with this condition at once. He appointed me chairman of a committee to make recommendations on promotions to the Rector. At first appointments were not within its province. All that our committee had to go on were the statutes of the University, which obviously needed interpretation and amplification. The Rector, however, had told me very definitely that from now on the members of the faculty who did research were the ones who would receive promotions. While the quality of teaching was important, by itself alone it would not warrant promotion beyond the assistant-professorship. Hitherto, promotions had been made entirely by the Rector as he saw fit, and high quality of teaching, in addition to the time requirement, was the only criterion used. In many instances the quality of teaching was not exactly high.

The Committee soon felt it necessary to define the various kinds of acceptable research, and on March 1, 1932, it succeeded in getting the Academic Senate to accept the following definitions

(a) That the following should not be regarded as scientific contributions: essays; compilations;

articles of a popular character in newspapers or non-scientific magazines; textbooks without new features or original treatment; translations of works in foreign languages; book reviews and encyclopedia articles, involving no critical study or historical research; assistance to students preparing dissertations.

(b) That published articles, monographs or larger works be regarded as contributions to science which embody results of scientific and original investigation. Such results may be: the discovery of new facts; the solution of a problem hitherto unsolved; the establishment of new relations among facts already known; the construction of a theory involving new principles; critical study correcting errors; editing of manuscripts hitherto unpublished; improved editions of important scientific or literary works; translation, with critical apparatus, of works in foreign languages—especially classical and oriental; formulation of an improved method or creation of a better technique.

This was a tremendous step forward and has proven to be a very stabilizing force for the Committee in its work ever since. I can think of only one occasion when these definitions were violated, and this was done by the Committee itself on a very close vote, when I was in the hospital suffering from the results of an automobile accident. The person appointed to take my place as Chairman of the Committee suffered a very curious case of qualms of conscience!

It was my rather idealistic belief that one could be quite objective as an administrator without regard for personal friendships. In other words, I felt that one could make a just decision which was unfavorable to a friend and still in private life continue that friendship without any noticeable change. This, of course, is unfortunately not true. Nearly everyone, as Archbishop Ryan once put it, thinks of the University as a big cheese. He passes by it and takes as large a hunk out of it as he can manage without regard to anything or anybody else. In general, rarely does one consider the rights of the University or justice toward it. The student or the faculty member, as the case may be, is always to receive preeminent consideration. The University is to receive no or little thought in the settlement of a problem of conflicting interests. Anyone who attempts to see that justice is done the University is a terrible ogre. This may seem like extreme cynicism, but my experience leads me into it.

In these early days when all were still more or less beset with the belief that promotions depended essentially on one's bargaining powers and not on a set of objective principles, it was not uncommon for the chairman of this committee to be attacked verbally by a disappointed candidate, and occasionally by the candidate's wife as well. But fortunately I was relieved of the duties of this committee by Bishop Corrigan, when he became Rector, and Dr. Landry was appointed chairman of a new committee on appointments as well as promotions. Moreover, all cases of appointments or promotions to instructor and assistant professor were still to be made directly by the Rector with such consultation as he might wish to make, but appointments and promotions to the ranks of associate professor and professor were to be made by the Rector after consulting the Academic Senate which was to act through the Committee. All cases involving the professorship had to obtain in addition the approval of the Board of Trustees.

Bishop McCormick continued the same committee, but in 1946 this committee demanded further clarification of the criteria to be used in making their recommendations. I was then appointed chairman of a "Committee on Regulations and Procedures Regarding Promotions and Appointments of Members of the Faculties," which made its report to the Academic Senate on February 27, 1947, when it was approved. This document attempted to define very specifically such matters as quality of work, amount of new knowledge required, and the value of applied knowledge. The Committee, after using the new interpretations for about three years, was still dissatisfied with a number of features, and again appealed to the Academic Senate for further clarification. The same committee was then revived and produced a report which was accepted by the Senate and essentially replaced the previous report. There were still two important omissions in these two reports, namely, the proper interpretation of the phrase "opera aequalia", commonly translated "equally important services" and used in connection with appointments and promotions to the rank of Associate Professor, and a definition of the value of creative work in relation to research for purposes of promotion and appointment. The Committee requested information on these two points. A new committee of the Academic Senate was appointed to go into these matters, and I was again appointed the chairman. A report, which was approved, was made to the Academic Senate on January 26, 1956.

When Dr. Landry was about to retire in 1951, the Rector asked me to rejoin the Committee on Appointments and Promotions, and to take Dr. Landry's place as chairman. Frankly, from a purely personal point of view there was little disposition on my part to return to that job. My recollections of it in the past were far from pleasant. But Bishop McCormick was most anxious that I do so, and I have never refused to do anything that anyone of the six Rectors under whom I have served wished me to do. He said that he knew that I already had more than enough to do, but that he wished that I would try it; if I found it overburdensome, he would relieve me of it. And so I was back again in a work that had no pleasant memories for me. However, all went well.

When the last clarification of those sections of the statutes on appointments and promotions had been made by the Senate Committee, Bishop McEntegart felt that the work of this committee should be digested and put into easily usable form. On thinking the matter over, it seemed that a manual for members of the faculty and administration containing a digest of all legislation, including the statutes of the University, on appointments and promotions was very much needed. Moreover, this should contain the documentary evidence for every statement. When this plan was presented to the Rector, he readily agreed, and so, with the not insignificant help of Miss Watrin, in 1956 the present "A Manual for Faculty Promotions and Appointments at The Catholic University of America" was produced.

Candidly, the Manual is worthy of pride. There is no institution of higher education that has worked out so systematically its set of principles for appointments and promotions and has published them for all to see. Nearly all colleges and universities within the United States have no systematic plan of any kind. Usually one person, the President, with such consultation as he sees fit to carry on, makes all appointments and promotions. The Catholic University plan is a striking bit of evidence of the integrity of the institution. It is very much to be hoped that the principles therein enunciated will be strictly followed in the future as they have in the recent past. We can think of no more powerful instrument for maintaining the morale of the faculty than this. If changes become necessary in the future, as will probably be true, it should then be revised accordingly but always maintained.

Scholarships, Fellowships,
and Student Aid

Shortly after having been made Dean of the Graduate School of Arts and Sciences and while attending a meeting of the Association of American Universities, I was struck by the fact that all the other member institutions of the Association enjoyed a large number of scholarships and fellowships and that The Catholic University of America had only the Knights of Columbus Scholarships (then so-called and then fifty in number). My astonishment was even greater when it was learned that the founding Fathers of the University had proclaimed the basic elements of their institution to be faculty, students, and buildings, in that order of importance, and had been very emphatic in presenting the high importance of a faculty of high quality and of students of great promise. The buildings were relegated to a very poor third place. The acquisition of funds for scholarships and fellowships in order to attract students of the highest quality was put on the same level of importance as the establishment of a scale of salaries that would draw and retain a strong faculty. Further investigation revealed that we did at one time have endowment for a moderate number of scholarships and fellowships but that the capital funds had been used to meet current expenses.

When this condition of things was called to the attention of the Rector, Bishop Ryan, he was indeed troubled. He asked me with the help of the Procurator, Mr. Harvey Cain, to discover just what scholarship and fellowship funds were supposed, according to the record, to be available and to restore and offer them to worthy students. They would be continued out of current funds until such time as the original funds could be replaced. These funds, incidentally, were replaced within a comparatively short time. Thus within that year it was possible to announce for the first time a fairly respectable number of scholarships and fellowships for graduate study at the University. On this occasion also the term Knights of Columbus Scholarships was changed to Knights of Columbus Fellowships, since the value of these benefits amount to far more than the maximum of $500 usually attributed to scholarships. I also took it upon myself to study the number and the nature of scholarships and fellowships being offered in representative universities of the country and to compare them with our own meager offerings. The results of this study were organized into an article which was published in *Columbia*, the official organ of the Knights of Columbus. The leading educational institutions of the land have from 300 to 600 endowed scholarships and fellowships of substantial value (from $500.00 to $3,500.00), with which to attract truly promising graduate students annually, as compared with our own merely 50 to 75, depending on the amount of income from the various endowments. Of course, the University does much charity in connection with the religious students, all of whom regularly receive half tuition rates as undergraduate students, the Sisters also as graduate students, but this represents something of a special nature in the way of student aid. All these benefits are not granted from an established endowment. They represent a substantial curtailment of the income from current fees. I had hoped that when these facts were forcefully presented, persons of means, either within the Knights of Columbus or without the support of that organization, would contribute such funds as would enable the authorities of the University to develop their scholarship and fellowship program to the extent envisioned by the founding Fathers. In this, however, I was doomed to disappointment.

The group of scholarships and fellowships accumulated for this first formal announcement makes up the nucleus of such forms of grants as have been announced ever since. The total value of the first collection of stipends is probably fully as great as that of today, since at that time we had the original number of fifty Knights of Columbus Scholarships, which today, owing to a great decline of income from the initial investments, has been reduced to from eight to ten, varying according to circumstances from year to year. The scholarship and fellowship aid added to our holdings has not to any great extent made up for this great loss.

It is, of course, still highly desirable, as in the days of our founding Fathers, for the good of the University, that a strong scholarship and fellowship program be developed. The very arguments then used in support of it still hold today. If one looks at the practice of the University of offering half rate of tuition to Sisters and Brothers, the program is indeed large and extensive, but a quick glance at our offerings will show that we are doing little to attract promising research minds from among the laity. It is an easily demonstrable fact that entirely too many of our able undergraduate Catholic students are being taken into the leading non-setarian universities by the lure of the large stipends of scholarships and fellowships which are offered by these institutions. Certainly there is enough Catholic wealth in the land to solve this problem. The chief stumbling block in accomplishing this is the difficulty of convincing our wealthy Catholic brethren of the fundamental importance of establishing strong scholarship and fellowship programs in our Catholic institutions of higher education, at least in some degree comparable to those of non-Catholic Institutions. Any such comparison made today would be simply too ridiculous for words. Only by this means can we bring to our classrooms in creditable numbers the potentially strong Catholic thinkers and leaders. After all, genuine leadership must depend on well-trained minds and not on over-developed muscles and limitless "brass"!

The practice of negotiating loans for needy students, even without interest, has never been a great success in any institution in which it has been tried. Young people do not wish to face the prospect of going out into the world after graduation with a formidable debt on their hands. The present practice of the Treasurer's Office of the University of assisting a student in a real emergency to negotiate a loan from a bank is about as much as can be done in this way to help a student.

The University and Accreditation

To understand the University in its relation to the accrediting process in the United States, it is necessary to understand accrediting. First of all it must be understood that "accrediting" is a procedure worked out by the institutions themselves, not only to screen out the colleges and universities which have reached a certain minimum of excellence but also to stimulate these same colleges and universities to continue to improve themselves. It came into being because of a purely political reason. Our founding fathers, when making the Constitution of our country, had taken many powers away from the individual states and placed them in the hands of the Federal Government. In seeking to build up the authority of the states, accordingly, among other things they left the supervision of education in the hands of the individual states. Since most of the states were slow to use this power and for practical reasons could not do so on a very high educational level, the institutions themselves took the matter in hand and developed the process of accreditation or, as it is preferably called today, evaluation.

Because the process is rather complex and is still being refined, it is very much misunderstood generally, even by responsible educators themselves. The following is a brief and more or less graphic description of the supervision of education in the United States.

I. Main Line of Accreditation

1. National Commission on Accrediting.
2. National Committee of Regional Accrediting Associations.
3. Regional Accrediting Associations.
   a. New England Association of Colleges and Secondary Schools.
   b. Middle States Association of Colleges and Secondary Schools.
   c. Southern Association of Colleges and Secondary Schools.
   d. North Central Association of Colleges and Secondary Schools.
   e. Western College Association.
   f. Northwest Association of Secondary and Higher Schools.
4. Associations of Colleges and Secondary Schools, in a few states only.
   N.B. Religious communities may be incorporated in a general way including colleges, but this is a bad policy, e.g., foundations are in general reluctant, if not opposed, to giving

college funds to a corporation which includes more than the college.

II. Departmental Accreditation.

1. American Chemical Society.
2. American Association of Departments and Schools of Music.
3. Association of Teachers of Business Subjects and others.

III.   Professional Groups.

1. Engineering Council for Professional Development.
2. American Medical Association.
3. The National League for Nursing.
4. The Council on Social Work Education.
5. The American Library Association.
6. The National Council for Accrediting Teacher Education, and a few others.

IV. Groups having accreditation value, but which are not really accrediting agencies.

1. The Association of American Colleges.
2. American Council on Education.
3. Phi Beta Kappa.
4. Sigma Xi.
5. Sigma Delta Epsilon and others.

V. The Association of American Universities

The Association of American Universities was established in 1899, and its constitution was adopted on February 28, 1900. It was "founded for the purpose of considering matters of common interest relating to graduate study and research." It was "composed of institutions of the North American continent engaged in giving advanced or graduate instruction. Its initial membership consisted of the following institutions:

> University of California, The Catholic University of America, University of Chicago, Clark University, Columbia University, Cornell University, Harvard University, Johns Hopkins University, Leland Stanford Junior University, University of Michigan, University of Pennsylvania, Princeton University, University of Wisconsin, Yale University. Other institutions may be admitted, at the annual conference, on the invitation of the Executive Committee, indorsed by a three-fourths vote of the members of the Association."

In 1914, the United States Office of Education, by a decision of the United States Attorney General, was forced to give up its list of approved colleges, and it passed this list, with the responsibility of carrying it on, over to this Association. The wisdom of the Association's accepting this responsibility was long a hotly debated point. It appeared in the publication of the Association as "List of Approved Institutions Whose Qualified Graduates Are Admitted to the Graduate Schools of the Association of American Universities." This activity was terminated in October of 1948, and the list was published for the last time in the "Journal of Proceedings" of that year.

In 1948 likewise, the Association of American Universities was reorganized with the following changes among others in its constitution. "Its purpose is to consider and express opinions on matters of common interest relating to university policy." "It is composed of institutions of the North American continent, the quality of whose graduate work in certain fields is high and, in addition, whose claims for inclusion are strong either because of the general high standing of their programs or because of the high standing of one or more of their professional schools. New members may be admitted by a three-fourths vote of the membership."

The list of members is published annually in the "Journal of Proceedings of the Association."

Comments

The actual process of accreditation in I (Main Line of Accreditation) begins with 5 (Charter or Incorporation by State) and proceeds upward.

The National Commission on Accrediting (I,1) is not itself an accrediting association. Its chief work is to effect smooth procedures and cooperation between existing accrediting groups and to prevent the needless duplication of accrediting agencies.

The National Committee of Regional Accrediting Associations (I,2) is made up of representatives of the six regional accrediting associations, and its purpose is to procure cooperation and, insofar as practicable, uniformity of principles and procedures.

These regional associations (I,3) represent the heart of the accrediting process. While they do not operate in exactly the same manner, there is a great deal of uniformity among them. It is here that the problems of accrediting are studied systematically and eventually solved. The entire accrediting process as it exists and operates today and as it continues to evolve is the chief concern and the product of the regional associations.

The various associations of colleges and secondary schools (I,4) within certain states have in general the same criteria as those of the regional associations, but their procedures are usually simpler and their standards may be said to be at least slightly lower and properly so.

The charter or incorporation of the state concerned (I,5) establishes the legal status of the college or university, and the institution cannot possibly exist without it. In the case of an old charter or incorporation, it is important that it be reviewed by a competent person in order to reestablish its validity.

Departmental accreditation (II) is not to be encouraged. It is the spread of this kind of accreditation that has brought the patience of college and university administrators to the breaking point. Those groups cause much duplication of work and a great increase in operating costs. A few have become well-established and may be said to have justified their existence to some extent, but in general they are not to be desired.

The accrediting professional groups (III) have very definite and proper fields of operation. For the most part, however, they must do much in the way of refining their procedures so as to eliminate unnecessary duplication of the work of the regional associations. This, it would seem, can best be achieved by closer and more efficient cooperation with the regional associations.

The groups having accreditation value, but which are not accrediting associations (IV) in the strict sense of the word, may be of great value to institutions of higher education. This certainly is true of the Association of American Colleges and the American Council on Education. The value to be gained by any institution from any of the others depends on the nature and character of individual institutions.

Much space has been given to an explanation of the Association of American Universities (V) because this group has been and is greatly misunderstood especially in Catholic educational circles. Some of this misunderstanding may be deliberate and purposeful and not entirely through lack of information. In spite of statements to the contrary, this association is definitely of an accrediting nature, as can be seen from the quotations above taken from its constitution. It is, however, somewhat off the "Main Stem" because it is concerned especially with institutions the quality of whose graduate work is high, or one or more of whose professional schools are of high standing. In Catholic educational circles, there seems to be a reluctance to admit that there is any significance in the fact that The Catholic University of America is still the only Catholic institution in the present annually published list of members of this Association. The total number of members is now thirty-four. This Association incidentally is often, wilfully or otherwise, confused with the Association of American Colleges.

When Monsignor Ryan became Rector, he found that the University Rectors before him had been comparatively unconcerned about accreditation. Monsignor Pace told me about how Professor Hall of Clark University, a friend of his from old University of Leipsic days, became interested, along with President Charles Eliot of Harvard, in founding the Association of American Universities, in order that the American people through this instrument might be able to distinguish those institutions truly worthy of the name "university." They were very anxious to have a Catholic representative in the group and had selected The Catholic University of America for this purpose. Professor Hall got in touch with Monsignor Pace and asked if the University authorities would be interested in including the University's name in the membership of their organization. Monsignor Pace took the matter at once to the Rector, the Most Reverend Thomas Joseph Conaty, who replied: "Do you think that it would be worthwhile?" It is difficult to conceive of anything more worthwhile for the University than this outstanding recognition of graduate studies and research, both at that time and through the years until the present. Yet it cannot be said that the University authorities before Bishop Ryan ever fully appreciated or were very enthusiastic about the membership.

Bishop Ryan insisted that I, as Dean of the Graduate School of Arts and Sciences, attend every annual meeting of the Association of American Universities, and it was of incomparable benefit to me, a young and inexperienced dean. I found my colleagues in the graduate deanship most kind and generous in their willingness to answer my many questions on administrative problems. This has been a notable characteristic of this group throughout the years. Even while serving in the post of Secretary General, it was very helpful to consult them on one question or another, for they always responded with the same wholehearted cooperation and helpfulness. It might be added that for many years I was the only Catholic member of the group, and on a number of occasions was invited to present papers to my colleagues, as the back-numbers of the Proceedings of the Association will show. I was very active also in connection with the work of special committees, chiefly that charged with the passing on prospective new members of the Association; that which maintained the list of approved institutions whose graduates were admitted to the graduate schools of the Association without examination; and that concerned with the developing, in cooperation with the Education Testing Service, new and needed tests for the administration of graduate studies. Furthermore, requests were frequently made to join in passing final judgment on the worthiness of Catholic and non-Catholic institutions alike.

Bishop Ryan was very anxious also to mend our relations with other accrediting agencies, especially the Middle States Association of Colleges and Secondary Schools, which had been sadly neglected. The annual meetings of this Association then became a regular contact for me to cultivate. The chairman of the Commission on Institutions of Higher Education of this Association at this time was Adam Leroy Jones, Director of Admissions at Columbia University. He was also in charge of maintaining for the A.A.U. the list of institutions approved for college work which has been mentioned above. There had never been a Catholic representative on this Commission, and he was being pressed hard by Father Aloysius Hogan, President of Fordham University, to name a Catholic to the group. Mr. Jones promised to do so and then caused a little consternation in some Catholic circles by not naming a Jesuit Father to the post but rather myself. I have already served on this commission longer than anyone else and hold an emeritus but active status. It would be difficult indeed to gauge the value to the University and to me personally of the experiences which have come from serving with this group. Among other things, I have been able to follow and to contribute directly to the evolution of the process of accreditation or, more specifically, of evaluation from a more or less haphazard one man inspection to the present scheme based on scientific criteria conducted by a team of evaluators, each an expert in his field, varying in number from five to fifty according to the size and nature of the institution concerned. I have also been able, as a representative of The Catholic University of America, to take part in and contribute to the development of the so-called "unit evaluations," whereby all the professional accrediting agencies evaluate through their representatives simultaneously with the evaluators of the Middle States Association. Moreover, all the benefits gained by these contacts have been applied to the work of the University's Committee on Affiliation, although, I am happy to state, the University's Committee on Affiliation anticipated the Commission on Higher Education of the Middle States Association in some of its principles and policies.

The experience gained from this work with the Commission on Higher Education of the Middle States Association proved to be very useful in preparing the University for its first evaluation by the Middle States Association, which took place from March 17th through the 20th, 1957. It was extremely difficult to convince the Rector and many others at the University that it was important and even necessary to begin this preparation two and a half years in advance. The obvious purpose for beginning so early was not only to record the *status quo* as fully and accurately as possible, but also to remedy the obvious weaknesses that would come to light. Even when the start was made nearly two years and a half early, in spite of careful planning it lagged at times, largely because the higher powers did not push the work vigorously enough, and thus permitted much valuable time to be lost. In fact the last three months of the period of preparation, devoted chiefly to sifting and organizing the findings into convenient book form, were hectic indeed. The rush to meet the date line unavoidably resulted in apparent editorial carelessness here and there, and thus a less impressive showing resulted than would otherwise have been made.

Another episode of 1950 (November) in connection with the Middle States Association, in which I personally rather than the University was involved, should be related. The so-called evaluative criteria, used in the evaluation of secondary schools and developed in large measure by one or two members of the Commission on Secondary Schools of the M.S.A. came in for a vigorous attack by a group of Catholic educators who were intent on making a holy crusade out of the affair. The evaluative criteria, published in book form for Catholic and non-Catholic schools alike, contained a place in the beginning for the presentation of the school's educational philosophy. Admittedly, the space supplied was not large, but, little as it was, non-Catholic and especially public schools were greatly embarrassed to make any use of this place at all. These institutions were unconscious of any positive educational philosophy. Theirs was rather a negative one. For example, they had to beware lest the religious feelings of any one, even those of atheists, be offended. Also, there could not be the faintest semblance of cooperation of any sort between church and state. In any case, nothing prevented any school official from expanding on his philosophy of education to his heart's content by the simple expediency of adding more pages to the space supplied, and this was so indicated on the form. This Catholic group, however, insisted that the full expression of the philosophy of the Catholic secondary school was deliberately and maliciously curtailed to the detriment of those schools. They could not, however, point to a single instance where a Catholic school had been prevented from presenting as extensive a picture of its educational philosophy as it wished, and where this had worked to the damage of the institution.

It has always been my experience in dealing with accrediting agencies that harm, to be sure, may come to a Catholic institution through the ignorance of an evaluator, but I cannot recall an instance where it happened from wilful malice. By getting together with the parties concerned and discussing the problem frankly a solution can always be reached. I will give only one out of many possible illustrations of this in my own experience.

There is a requirement of at least fifty students in some states, and of a hundred in others, before any college can receive permission to grant degrees. This requirement is made obviously to guarantee a certain financial income from tuition fees to help stabilize an institution. Equally as obvious is the fact that any religious community wishing to operate a college for its own subjects will have to get the necessary funds for the purpose from other sources than tuition fees which do not exist for religious. Thus the purpose of the requirements of a certain number of students for a college conducted by a religious community for its own members has no validity. Whenever, in behalf of a religious group, this has been called to the attention of the state authorities, a concession has been readily granted.

In the case under discussion here, it was my contention that the matter could and should have been amicably settled without compromise of any sort through a meeting of the parties concerned. The insistence of some on bringing the matter to the floor, at the meeting of the Secondary School Department of the M.S.A., with a threat to withdraw all Catholic secondary schools from the Association certainly was not wise at least at this point. It seemed very doubtful to me at the time that any Catholic educator present at that meeting had the authority to make such a threat. But the threat was made and some of those present definitely wanted all Catholic secondary schools to withdraw from the Middle States Association.

When the various meetings of the M.S.A. were taking place at Atlantic City, I had a choice of attending either one of two important gatherings being held simultaneously: one, the meeting of those interested in the evaluation of secondary schools; the other, that of the Commission on Institutions of Higher Education. The latter was the one for which I was primarily sent to the convention by the University, and so I decided to attend it. This meeting lasted a normal length of time, and I went to the dining room for lunch. In the middle of my meal, I was startled by constant and vigorous paging of me by various forms of my difficult family name. I rushed out, leaving my unfinished meal, and found myself in the midst of a group of my secondary school friends, who excitedly urged me to rush to the Catholic secondary school meeting, which was in the midst of a prolonged and very agitated session. The advisability of all Catholic secondary schools withdrawing from the M.S.A. was being seriously discussed, and it looked as if a motion would be made to that effect and that there might well be enough strength to carry it. I went into the meeting, but when there I did not see how I could say anything, as my friends wished me to do, because this was the end of a long meeting and I really did not know what had gone on before. The resolution was finally made and put to a vote but it failed by a substantial majority. Later the matter was settled quickly and amicably to the entire satisfaction of all, even the most violent.

But this was not the end for me. The evening before I was discussing the matter with an old friend of mine from Erie, Pa. She said: "The whole thing started in *upstate Pennsylvania,* when Father——gave a talk to the secondary school teachers there." Later that evening I was talking with someone else about this same burning question of the convention. I remarked that I had heard that the whole affair had started in *upstate Pennsylvania,* and I gave other particulars that I had gathered regarding it. Shortly after I had returned to Washington from the convention, I received one of the most shocking letters that it has ever been my misfortune to receive. It came from the Superintendent of one of the largest Catholic secondary school systems in the United States. I bring it up chiefly because of its humorous aspects, and I will quote both the letter itself and my answer to it. Please note the reference not to *upstate Pennsylvanians* but to *upstart Pennsylvanians,* a curious lapse indeed! Also consider that while I was a member of the Commission on Higher Education, I never had anything to do with the Commission on Secondary Schools. Catholic representation here was the duty of Father Edward B. Rooney, S.J., although the spleen of the crusaders was vented not on him but on me!

November 27, 1950

Dear Dr. Deferrari:

During the recent meeting of the Middle States Association I believe that you were rather

outspoken in your criticism of the protest made by
Catholic secondary school representatives concerning the new evaluative criteria. I would charitably
interpret your attitude as the result of a lack of
knowledge concerning the nature and content of
the criteria. It has been admitted by responsible
people in the Association that the new criteria
are based largely upon and slanted toward the
philosophy of John Dewey. Certainly even you
will admit that the Catholic philosophy of education and that of Mr. Dewey are highly incompatible. A survey of the criteria by Catholic educators
in Pennsylvania prompted grave concern and a
sincere effort to meet what seemed a danger and a
challenge to the Catholic schools. Several people
to whom you talked later asked my reaction to
your alleged statements that this was a "tempest
in a teapot" started by "upstarts from Pennsylvania." I find it difficult to believe that you would
thus publicly question the integrity and intelligence of those responsible for the protest. If my
information is true, then you have done a disser-
vice to the cause of Catholic education.

You attended the regional unit meeting on
Saturday and prompted someone else to ask why
something had not been done before this. I think
that to be the responsibility of our supposed
leaders in Catholic education such as yourself
who are officially connected with the Middle
States Association. Perhaps if our schools had
been given the type of leadership they had a right
to expect, and the Catholic viewpoint had been
considered and not utterly ignored, the present
situation would never have eventuated. I would
regret to think that you are more Middle States
minded than Catholic minded. Certainly there
must be some limit beyond which Catholic princi-

ples cannot compromise with secular agencies. It is our honest and sincere opinion that this limit has been reached in the 1950 Criteria.

With best wishes, I remain

Sincerely yours,

In reply I wrote very briefly as follows:

November 29, 1950

DEAR FATHER:

In spite of the intemperance of your letter of November 27, I wish to make the following statements for the record:

1. I did say that I believed the whole matter to be a "tempest in a teapot."

2. I did *not* call any people "upstarts from Pennsylvania."

3. I am not a member of the Commission on Secondary Schools and I have taken no part in their work.

Your letter contains a number of innuendos and general criticisms of me which are untrue. I shall be glad to discuss with you in person any of the above or any other matters connected with the problem, if you are so inclined.

Very sincerely yours,

ROY J. DEFERRARI

Another incident involving the University and an accrediting agency was of extreme importance. The School of Social Work, now absorbed into the National Catholic School of Social Service, was established with Monsignor John O'Grady as Dean during the rectorship of Bishop Ryan. When Bishop Corrigan became Rector, he was beset by the then Monsignor Francis J. Haas and Monsignor John J. Burke, C.S.P., to change the nature of the School of Social Work from an institution of a strictly professional kind to one centering around philosophical social studies, on the ground that only in this way (not in the training of students in the mechanics of case work) could the Catholic leaders needed so badly in this field be obtained. [1] This, of course, meant the elimination of Monsignor O'Grady as Dean of the School, which was actually brought about. The American Association of Schools of Social Work, however, threatened to withdraw its approval of the School, if such action were taken, because obviously the School would no longer be a professional school and thus not within the purview of the Association. Accordingly, the School of Social Work was left as it was, and the new School of Social Science midst all the resulting chaos was established. [2]

Another serious conflict between the University and an accrediting agency arose in the regime of Bishop McCormick, when the School of Engineering and Architecture lost its accreditations by the Engineering Council for Professional Development. The obvious chief cause of this unfortunate occurrence was the failure on the part of many of the faculty to give primary consideration to their duties

[1] Cf. Organization.
[2] Cf. Organization for further details.

at the University, but rather to give first thought to private engineering projects of their own. To be sure, it is expected that a good teacher of engineering will do a certain amount of outside work, but it should be work that will enhance his value as a teacher and will not take up more than the equivalent of one day a week. Furthermore, it should have the approval of the authorities of the University. These considerations were entirely out of mind on the part of most of the faculty of Engineering and Architecture, and the final disastrous result was inevitable. Bishop Ryan saw the problem, and made good progress in solving it. When he was succeeded by Bishop Corrigan, however, the old policies prevailed again, and the School of Engineering and Architecture fell back into its old ways.

The next Rector, Bishop McCormick, although told of the danger and even warned by the Engineering Council for Professional Development, did not see fit to do anything about it. He accepted the assurance of those then in control of the School that all was well, until finally the School lost the accreditations of its various divisions completely. This was not only damaging to the School of Engineering and Architecture but very harmful to the University as a whole. Rumors of little or no veracity spread rapidly over the country. For example, one persistent rumor was to the effect that all the University's work in science had lost academic approval! Furthermore, there was chaos in the thinking of the University authorities as to how to meet the problem. The old guard in the School of Engineering and

Architecture who were responsible for the disaster insisted that it was all due to the lack of a new engineering building and this they did in the face of written and verbal reports to the contrary. Hasty plans for a new building had been drawn up which on more careful consideration exhibited absurd shortcomings and were later completely abandoned. This was in the closing months of the academic year 1952-1953. It was evident that something needed to be done quickly to clear the atmosphere and to discover what positive steps needed to be taken to regain the accreditation of the E.C.P.D. I took the liberty of approaching Bishop McCormick, offering a positive plan. He was delighted with it, and said that it was the first ray of light that he had seen since the distaster struck. He appointed a Committee on the School of Engineering and Architecture, whose duties were to discover in detail the causes of the debacle and to offer suggestions as to the proper steps to be taken for the regaining of the lost accreditation.

Leading engineering educators were invited to the University for consultation with the Committee. I myself visited several, including President Whittaker of Lehigh University and Dean Thorndike Saville of the School of Engineering of New York University and then chairman of the Evaluating Committee of the E.C.P.D. On one point all agreed: The real cause of the debacle was a deficient faculty and not inadequate housing. As Thorndike Saville put it: "If you have the proper faculty, you can have a good engineering school in a shack!" Everywhere we received the same advice: "You need men!" To rehabilitate the faculty was a very difficult task, but it had to be faced. Furthermore, it was something which could not be done in a year or in all likelihood two years. In the meantime, it was felt that we might introduce a program of studies in engineering which for the first two years would be within the jurisdiction of the College. The thought was that by the time the two years had passed, the accreditation of the E.C.P.D. would have been regained, and all could then be restored to the School of Engineering and Architecture again. This was actually carried out, chiefly through the work of the Dean of the College, the Very Reverend James M. Campbell. While it did much good by keeping things going, at least in a partially approved status, through this hazardous period, it was thought best after two years to revert to a complete engineering program, even though the accreditation had not been regained.

One very important step which was taken at this time was the appointment of the Reverend Francis E. Fox, O.S.F.S., as Acting Dean. He was an outstanding scholar in the field of physics and very much aware of the needs of the School of Engineering and Architecture. Unfortunately he died suddenly early in the academic year of 1953-1954, shortly after his appointment. I firmly believe that if Dr. Fox had lived all would have gone well from this point on.

Bishop McCormick had passed away even before Dr. Fox, and Bishop McEntegart had suc-

ceeded him as Rector. The following is a report sent
by me to the Rector on January 25, 1954, summariz-
ing all the events leading to the status of the School
of Engineering and Architecture as of that date:

Summary of Events Leading to the Present
Status of the School of Engineering and
Architecture

I. Loss of Accreditation by E.C.P.D.
   Early in September, 1952, the Rector of the
Catholic University of America received a communication dated September 5th from the Engineers' Council for Professional Development, of
which the following paragraph is the salient part:
   At the annual meeting of the Engineers'
   Council for Professional Development held
   on this date, the following action was
   taken with regard to the curricula submitted by the Catholic University of
   America for consideration by the ECPD
   Education Committee.

Aeronautical	Not to accredit
Architectural	To accredit for two years
Civil	Not to accredit
Electrical	Not to accredit
Mechanical	Not to accredit

   This action should not have been unexpected.
The curricula in Aeronautical, Architectural, Civil,
Electrical and Mechanical Engineering were inspected in 1948 and granted provisional accreditation for two years. On October 13, 1949, the
Dean of the School of Engineering and Architecture received a statement from the E.C.P.D.

listing thirteen points of major weaknesses accounting for the provisional accreditation. This was accompanied by the following comment: 'Some of these deficiencies are deepseated and will require considerable time to correct. At the time of its next re-inspection, the Committee would expect to find at least a reasonable degree of progress toward removing some of the more serious of the deficiencies noted.'

On March 28, 1950, the Dean of the School requested of the E.C.P.D. an extension of one year of the provisional accreditation on the ground that more time was required to prepare for the inspection. He reported progress in eliminating some of the weaknesses, and indicated more progress as probable before 1951. Provisional accreditation was accordingly extended until 1952.

However, in 1952, when the blow fell, the E.C.P.D. in summary, expressed itself thus: 'Apparently there has been little or no change for the better since the last inspection except that there are fewer students enrolled and therefore classes are less crowded and the teaching load is generally lighter. In general, the housing has not been improved; the laboratories are generally still obsolete; there is a continued high degree of inbreeding, little or no research or creative work, general routine instruction of a descriptive character lacking in fundamental and quantitative phase, inadequate libraries and a general lackadaisical attitude on the part of the staff. The departmental libraries are highly unsatisfactory and wholly inadequate.'

A considerable correspondence followed between the Rector and the officials of the E.C.P.D., which served chiefly to bring out the weaknesses of the School in greater detail. One step forward, perhaps, did result. The University authorities decided to bring in engineering educators, as suggested by the E.C.P.D., for consultation.

The University authorities also proceeded to establish a series of committees to work out plans for the eventual reaccreditation of the School.
II. The Committees.

        A. The Engineering School Visitation Committee

This committee consisted of Frank A. Biberstein, Harry P. Gallogly, Joseph C. Michalowicz, and Maurice E. Weschler, and, according to the Chairman's final report, dated February 14, 1953, was appointed by the Reverend James A. Magner. The work of this committee is characterized by its stress on the erection of a new engineering building just as soon as possible.

        B. Committee on the School of Engineering and Architecture

This committee consisted of Roy J .Deferrari, Karl Herzfeld, Frank O. Rice, Anthony Scullen, and Frank A. Biberstein, and was appointed by the Rector early in February, 1953. It at once superseded 'The Engineering School Visitation Committee.' This Committee made a report in late February, 1953, another including budgets for 1953-54 and for 1954-55, and a final report on May 6, 1953.

The work of this committee consisted of a restudy of the aims of the School of Engineering and Architecture, the reorganization of the various programs of study, including graduate work, preliminary consideration of the problems of the faculty, and of housing and equipment. It is to be noted that this committee shifted the emphasis to the more fundamental matters of curriculum and faculty, and while aware of the importance of equipment, including a new building, regarded the latter as coming after the first, chronologically at least. This decision was reached after consulting a number of the leading engineering educators of the country, including Thorndike Saville, Chairman of the Education Committee of the E.C.P.D.

The present committee concluded its report of May 6, 1953, with these words:

'Since the next step in solving the problems of the School of Engineering and Architecture is the reorganization and development of the faculty, and since this step should be taken immediately with vigor, the present committee feels that it should be discharged as having essentially completed the work of establishing a plan of procedure. The next and subsequent steps can best be taken by a new committee properly selected.'

The committee was accordingly discharged; and the Very Reverend Francis E. Fox was appointed Acting Dean of the School of Engineering and Architecture, Professor Scullen meanwhile having resigned as Dean.

C. The Advisory Committee on the School of Engineering and Architecture.

When Father Fox was appointed Acting Dean of the School of Engineering and Architecture, to assume his duties officially with the conclusion of the academic year 1952-53, an Advisory Committee was appointed to work with him. This committee consisted of Doctors Herzfeld, Rice, Deferrari, and the Very Reverend James M. Campbell, with Father Fox, Acting Dean, as Chairman.

The chief accomplishments of this committee, before the opening of the academic year 1953-54, are well summarized in the words of the late Father Fox himself:

'(a) The appointment of two men to the faculty, Dr. Max Munk, and Mr. Glenn Larson.

(b) The decision to recommend the inclusion of the Department of Architecture in the Pre-Engineering curriculum.

(c) The decision to recommend that Architectural Engineering be absorbed into Architecture.'

With the opening of the academic year 1953-54, the Acting Dean was occupied largely with the care and direction of students. However, together with his Advisory Committee, he devoted himself also to furnishing the Rector with budgetary information and information on long-range planning for the future of the School.

III. Planning for the Future.

With the progress of the first semester of the present academic year, the Rector of the University became more and more concerned with bringing in engineering educators from the outside, especially from Catholic engineering schools, to help solve the great fundamental problems: an economical reorganization of the School of Engineering and Architecture and the selection of the permanent Dean and a few key members of the faculty. In November, the Rector called a meeting of the Advisory Committee to confer with representatives from the Schools of Engineering of Manhattan College and the Univeristy of Notre Dame. In December, a similar meeting was called by the Rector with the Deans of three Catholic Schools of Engineering: those of the University of Detroit, Manhattan College, and the University of Notre Dame. It was on the very day of this meeting, just before it was called to order, that Dr. Fox met his untimely end.

The chief results of this last meeting were:

1) A decision to refer the task of making a more economical budget to the Advisory Committee.

2) A decision to form an advisory committee chiefly of engineering educators of other institutions, including, if possible, persons close to the E.C.P.D., to select the new and permanent Dean and to assist him in his problems, especially that of reorganizing the faculty.

In the meantime, the Rector appointed Mr. Valade, Acting Dean, to replace the late Dr. Fox principally to carry on the daily matters concerned with the School, such as the care of students, and to give such assistance as he can to those directly responsible for settling the over-all problem of restoring the School of Engineering and Architecture to the approved list of the E.C.P.D.

(signed)   ROY J. DEFERRARI
Secretary General

Bishop McEntegart soon became convinced that what was needed was a committee made up of engineers from industry as well as of engineering educators to replace the old committee of which I had been chairman. This was a very wise decision. I was asked to serve on this second committee, of which Brother Amandus Leo, Dean of the School of Engineering of Manhattan College, was chairman. I have also had the satisfaction of seeing the School of Engineering and Architecture, first under Thomas Killian and then under Donald Marlowe, in 1957 regain the full accreditation of the Engineering Council on Professional Development. [3]

Several Rectors of the University have questioned the value of accrediting agencies in general. I believe that this is due to a failure to understand the nature of modern accrediting procedures. The whole manner of accrediting has changed greatly within the last ten years, and the process is still evolving. It is nothing less than shocking to hear college and university presidents assail accrediting agencies, as they sometimes do, and to listen to tirades against the accrediting process of thirty-five or fifty years ago. It is not overly surprising to hear a college or university graduate talk confidently but erroneously about these groups, as if the fact that he holds a college or university degree gave him complete knowledge of this subject. But college and university presidents should know their accrediting agencies thoroughly and accurately, and should keep in close touch with them always. The college and university president should attend at least some of the meetings of the groups in the main stem described above. In addition some one of his close advisors should have the responsibility of keeping him informed of all developments in the field, and the significance of these developments for the appropriate activities within his institution. Unless the Federal Government, through the Department of Health, Education, and Wel-

[3] For another crisis in the field of accreditation, this on a national scale, see The Beginning of Instruction in Nursing at The Catholic University of America.

fare, actually takes over the supervision of all education in the United States, which God forbid, the
accrediting agencies will become more and more
powerful and important. Thus any institution laying claim to even the slightest amount of educational leadership should through its representative
or representatives take an active part in their work.
On my own initiative, always with the full consent
of the various Rectors, but rarely with any understanding on their part of the importance of the
work, I have endeavored for the last generation or
more to perform this service for The Catholic University of America, and I believe that it has been
very beneficial to the University and most rewarding to myself.

The Integration of the Races

Shortly after I had arrived at the University,
early in the academic year of 1919-20, the Director
of Studies and Vice Rector took me aside to tell me
about the local race problem. During the previous
summer session there had been race disturbances
just outside Gibbons Hall, and the feeling between
the races was still rather sensitive and bitter. He
told me how from the foundation of the University
there had been no bars of any kind against the Negro race, but that the enrollment of Negroes in the
University had grown steadily and appeared likely

to dominate the institution completely. Accordingly, The Catholic University of America was going
to bar Negroes entirely from registering as students
and to take its stand with all the other so-called
white institutions of the area. However, there was
one colored student left who had finished all his
work for the Master's degree in Latin except for
the writing of an acceptable dissertation. Would I
please direct this work, and, when finished, see
that his diploma was mailed to him. By no means
was I to permit him to appear at the regular commencement exercises. To say that this was a shock
and even a scandal to me would be putting it
mildly.

The Vice Rector at that time, as great a man
as he was in many respects, could not rise above his
Florida origin in the matter of the treatment of Negroes. The Negro student in question was Professor
George Morton Lightfoot [1] of Howard University,
Head of the Department of Latin and Director of
the Summer Session at Howard University. His
undergraduate work had been done at Williams
College in Williamstown, Massachusetts, and he
was very well trained. Indeed, he was a splendid
gentleman, and I never enjoyed the directing of a
dissertation more than I did supervising his. Although he wished to go on for the doctorate and
would certainly have done a very creditable piece

---

[1] Dr. Lennox, Dean of the School of Letters, as Dr. Butin used
to say, got both the noun and the adjective confused, and regularly
called him "Armstrong"! Professor Lightfoot had first registered at the
University on October 15, 1898.

of work, he was not permitted to do so. He was the last of the Negro students for many years at the University.

Just as it was my lot to see the end of an era in the education of Negroes at the University, so did it fall upon me to see the beginning and the *floruit* of the present period of enlightenment in this phase of our history. When I became Dean of the Graduate School of Arts and Sciences, one of my first problems was that of the admission of Negroes. Applications for admission came in regularly, and, what was still more embarrassing, letters from responsible champions of the Negro cause protesting our policy. The Reverend Mother Agatha, then President of Xavier University in New Orleans, occasionally placed her difficulties before me. After nurturing the young Negro student through his undergraduate studies and endeavoring to make the faith strong within him, where could she send him for his graduate work? Surely, The Catholic University of America, the papal university of the country for which an annual collection was taken up in *all* the Catholic churches of the land, should take him in. Mr. David Goldstein, as he went all over the country preaching and as he made clear in several letters addressed to me, found it most difficult to answer similar questions as they cropped up in his question-box. Thus the protests, nearly always polite and only mildly complaining, came steadily into my office. For a time I brought all the credentials of Negro students to the Rector, feeling that he himself should share some of the mortification of turning them down. But he soon grew weary of this and requested that I bring no more to him. Nothing was then left to be done but to live as quietly as possible with the problem.

Shortly after Bishop Corrigan assumed his duties at the University, I received several more applications for the admission of Negroes, and it struck me that it would be well to try out this new man from Philadelphia. So, following my usual practice when bringing matters before the Rector, I made a list of agenda for our meeting, including "the admission of Negroes" as one item. I waited with some anxiety for his reaction when he would come to this topic, but it was nothing alarming; he reacted simply by saying: "Why not?" As I returned to my office after the conference, I met Dean Campbell, who was also anxiously waiting the result of my meeting with the Rector. To his question: "How did you come out?", I replied: "He said: 'Why not?' which I suppose means: 'Yes. Admit them.' " "Does this mean graduate as well as undergraduate students?", he asked further. "He did not say, but I think it reasonable to assume that he meant both," I replied. Of course, I realized that the Rector should have brought the matter before the Board of Trustees, because it was clearly within their province to decide, but very frankly I was quite ready in this matter to take advantage of Bishop Corrigan's tendency to overlook regular procedures. I knew that Bishop Ryan only a few years earlier had placed the question before them for a decision, and had received a negative answer.

Thus Father Campbell and I opened the doors of the College and the Graduate School of Arts and Sciences respectively to Negro students, making The Catholic University of America the first so-called white school in many years to do so in the District of Columbia. The word spread rapidly, and within a week nearly a hundred Negro students had registered in the Graduate School of Arts and Sciences alone. But our troubles were only beginning. One morning, soon after the lowering of the bars, I received a stern call by telephone from the Rector telling me to come to his office immediately. I complied with his request, realizing full well what it was all about. I had no sooner put my head within the door of his office than he shouted: "I never gave you permission to admit Negro students." I asked that he have his secretary bring him the copy of the agenda of our last conference, and there neatly initialed after the item "Admission of Negroes" was "O.K., J.M.C." A great commotion had been stirred up almost entirely by the members of the faculty and, not least of all, by their wives, but there was very little complaint from the white students. A few parents called by telephone to ask by what right we had admitted Negroes without first announcing our change in policy to them! The Board of Trustees later approved the new practice in a piece of post-factum legislation, and the entire problem was quickly resolved as far as the University administration was concerned. There were, of course, for the first few years several minor difficulties to settle in connection with the implementation of the new legislation, but these were caused by outside interference such as we experienced from sensation-minded newspaper reporters, prejudiced clerks and employees of the University, and managers of hotels where the students wished to carry on some of their social affairs. All in all, however, everything went very smoothly, thanks principally to the good sense and feeling for fair play on the part of the students themselves.

The matter of the common use of the dormitories was not settled at this time. There seemed to be no difficulty involved here, as far as the School of Nursing was concerned. Both students and members of this faculty were always very sound in their thinking during this entire controversy, but there was some timidity on the part of the administration in openly declaring a status of complete equality between Negro and white students in every phase of their university life: social, religious, and academic. Bishop McCormick deserves the credit for making this principle clear beyond any doubt.

The entire process of achieving the complete integration of the races at The Catholic University of America had serious repercussions at the American University, a neighboring institution conducted by the Methodist Church. After all, a very large percentage of the Negroes in Washington were Methodists, and only a comparatively small number were Catholics, although this number has been growing very rapidly in recent years. Naturally many of them went to their white co-religionists and complained about their reluctance and unwillingness to accept them on equal terms, while the Catholics were proceeding so rapidly toward full integration. At this time I received a telephone call from Dr. Paul Douglas, then President of American University, with whom I was rather well acquainted. He had difficulty in believing that we had gone all the way in solving the problem. He had admitted Negroes to the down-town graduate and undergraduate classes, where there was no question of sharing residence halls and dining facilities, but uptown where the problems of the common use of sleeping quarters and accommodations for meals were inevitable, the situation was quite different.

From the beginning I insisted again and again that it was the responsibility of the University, as The Catholic University of America, both for Church and country, to take the leadership in ending a gross injustice and a damaging disgrace to our democracy. I insisted also that the Lord would bless the University for playing a leading role in this difficult struggle, and I believe that this has come to pass. The students, both white and colored, developed a maturity and an outlook on life which could never have been achieved without this experience.

The following is a letter which I addressed to to the Rector, Monsignor McCormick, which gives evidence to the smoothness with which the integration of the races proceeded at the University.

July 5, 1949

DEAR MONSIGNOR McCORMICK:

I am replying to your note of July 1 with the enclosed letter from the Baltimore Urban League which, incidentally, I am returning herewith.

I would say that our experience with the admission of Negroes has been pretty much as follows. From the beginning we have had no on-campus difficulties. As far as our student body is concerned the admission of Negroes from the beginning has caused no difficulty whatsoever. Furthermore, it is true that the numbers of Negroes who have sought admission here has always been a very small minority of the total student body. We have never had any mass applications from Negro students.

In the very earliest days, as you recall, when Negro students were first admitted, whatever difficulties we had, and these were very slight, were caused by persons outside the University who were taking an interest in this particular affair of the University with which they had absolutely nothing to do.

I do not know whether this is the sort of thing that you want but I hope that it will enable you to give some sort of an answer to the letter from the Baltimore Urban League.

Sincerely yours,
ROY J. DEFERRARI
Secretary General

Certainly the University, as a result of its change of policy toward the integration of the races, has avoided much embarrassment as the struggle has gone on during recent years. What could have been more difficult for the University authorities to explain than a policy of segregation of the races in the face of the pronouncements on racism by the Holy See!

While integration of the races was taking place at the University, a movement working toward the same end nationally had started in Massachusetts and was developing fast under the patronage of His Excellency, Archbishop Cushing. Mrs. Roger Putnam conceived the idea of helping the Negro to help himself, and organized the group known as "Catholic Scholarships for Negroes, Inc." The thought was that promising Negro girls and boys should be encouraged, principally by financial support, to go on for higher education, and that some or most of them would return to work among their own people. Archbishop Cushing asked me to serve on the Board of Directors and to help especially with the selection of those to receive the scholarships. This I have been glad to do. It has been a genuine pleasure to work with Mrs. Putnam all these years, i.e., since 1950. Thanks to Mrs. Putnam's own energetic devotion to the work, the support of His Excellency, Archbishop Cushing, and the splendid cooperation of the Catholic colleges and universities, the organization has been able to send approximately 125 Negro girls and boys into higher education annually in recent years. The Catholic University of America has received from seven to ten of these students every year. Mrs. Putnam almost singlehandedly has contributed a tremendous force for the advancement of integration among the races on a national scale.

Research [1]

During the period of my graduate studies at Princeton University I was given both the training and the zeal for research. Starting off with a great eagerness for taking courses, I gradually reached the stage where I became impatient with the limitations of the classroom and wished to work independently, consulting only with others who were undergoing similar experiences. This was as it should have been in the normal evolution of one being well trained for a life of scholarship. It was always a great pleasure for me to note my own students as they reached this stage of their intellectual growth.

As I look back upon this period, I feel that there were two teachers who did most to prepare me for such scholarship as I have attempted. One was Edward Capps, Professor of Greek, who transmitted much of his natural love for Greek civilization to me; and the other was Paul van den Ven,

[1] Cf. also the Graduate School of Arts and Sciences.

Professor of Byzantine Civilization at the University of Louvain, who came to Princeton University after the burning of Louvain library in World War I and who taught me especially the practical procedures of scholarship. I have heard it said at times that a certain person on a teaching staff violated all the recognized principles for good teaching and yet was probably the best teacher in the institution. That description would fit Professor Capps perfectly. He was a warm personality, easily approachable, always interested in another's research, and ever ready with worthwhile suggestions and advice. Professor van den Ven did me the invaluable service of unwittingly convincing me that research was a very practical thing: something which could be carried on with appreciable results and not something about which one talked but did little or nothing, or, as a well-known priest put it: a state of mind! He worked with me in the spirit of partnership, an equal with an equal. I have long since learned that in every University there are some members of the faculty who, either through inability or laziness or a little of both, accomplish little or nothing in the way of original investigation. They try to make up for their deficiency by talking a lot about scientific research and by adopting the role of "the watch-dog of research." Either through book-reviews or in daily conversations they become very critical of everything that another does, but yet never themselves give a practical demonstration of how something should be done. I was reaching a state of cynicism in scholarship when I met Pro-

fessor van den Ven. He opened up all the vast store
of research possibilities in both the Greek and Latin
Fathers, in which I together with my students have
labored these forty odd years. On reaching the University I found kindred spirits of Professor van den
Ven in Monsignor Henri Hyvernat and Dr. Romanus Butin. I shall never forget their sympathetic
understanding of my weaknesses as well as appreciation for my strengths in scholarship. I was in my
middle twenties when I was obliged to direct the
doctoral dissertations of students easily old enough
to be my parents. Naturally I sometimes needed
support of both a moral and scholarly nature as
problems of personality and scholarship necessarily
arose between us. Father Butin especially, as time
went on, was my great support and last court of
appeal.

Although, when I first arrived at the University, as I have indicated elsewhere, I was teaching
an absurdly heavy schedule of an average of
twenty-five hours per week and was directing an
equally absurdly large number of masters and
doctors dissertations, I was determined not to give
up or neglect my own investigations. When I left
Princeton University, I had already published, be-
side my dissertation, a college textbook and several
articles. Also I had started a long article (published later in two installments in the *American
Journal of Philology*) on St. Augustine's manner
of delivering sermons and a translation of St. Basil's
letters in four volumes for the *Loeb Classical*

Library. These last two projects I completed comparatively soon after I took up my work at the Catholic University.

When in 1928 I was asked by the Rector, Bishop Ryan, to enter administrative work, one member of the faculty actually had the effrontery to accuse me of taking an administrative office so as to have a good excuse for not doing another bit of research for the rest of my life, in other words, of being intellectually lazy and the type that does research solely for the purpose of obtaining a promotion in faculty rank and not through any real love of it! Actually, when I became Dean of the Graduate School of Arts and Sciences, I considered one of my immediate problems the stimulating of research within my school; certainly I could not succeed in this by doing no research myself. [2] Furthermore, I found myself much more refreshed for my personal studies at home after a day's activity in an administrative office than I did after a day of teaching and directing dissertations of graduate students. I never did give up all my teaching or all directing of students in research until 1956-1957, when all my time was needed for the work of the University's self-evaluation in preparation for the evaluation of the committee of the Middle States Association of Schools and Colleges, but I was obliged to curtail this work greatly.

Because of my being obliged to remain in my office almost constantly during the day with little

[2] Cf. Graduate School of Arts and Sciences.

time for library work so necessary to most kinds of research, I did turn more and more to the work of making concordances and translations for which a minimum of activity in a library is necessary. However, the *Latin-English Lexicon of St. Thomas Aquinas* is an exception to this generalization.

In this connection, I must mention Sister M. Inviolata Barry of the Congregation of Divine Providence. Her Superior permitted me to have her as a colleague in research while she served as the Superior of the community's house of studies at the Sisters College. Sister Inviolata was one of my very first graduate students in the days when we all worked as *pares inter pares* in McMahon Hall on Sundays. [3] A glance at the appended bibliography will show both how long we worked together on research projects and how much we accomplished. Sister's industry and ingenuity in solving research problems, especially those of procedures, were of indispensable value to me. She was also amiable and ready to run down library problems which required such time as I was unable to give. Without her, I would, of course, have accomplished much less.

That I should publish herewith [4] a list of my publications minus some journal articles, which frankly I have lost track of, may be regarded by some as a colossal act of egotism. It seems to me,

[3] Cf. Catholic Sisters College.
[4] Cf. Appendix 4.

however, that it must go into my recollections of the University, since during all my years at the University scarcely a moment was spent, whether as teacher or administrator, without thought of my students' or my own research projects, both naturally being closely interwoven.

SPECIAL CAMPUS MATTERS

The National Shrine of
the Immaculate Conception

Already, as early as 1918, when I first came to the University, Bishop Shahan was thinking of the Shrine of the Immaculate Conception as the University church and meeting place of the hierarchy of the United States. It is impossible to say how long before that he had had this on his mind. The laying of the cornerstone took place on September 23, 1920. The following entry in the diary of Sister Lucida Savage, C.S.J., of St. Louis, Missouri, is of interest:

> Sept. 23, 1920. Grand ceremony of laying cornerstone of National Shrine. Cardinals Gibbons and O'Connell, Apostolic Delegate, many prelates, and estimated 10,000 visitors. Scene very beautiful. Sermon by Bishop McNicholls, O.P. of Dubuque.

As he began promulgating the idea, hoping to get supporters with substantial funds, he had to suffer the inevitable gibes of severe critics.

First there were those who felt that it would be ruinous financially and otherwise to the University. It would completely dominate the University and divert to itself funds, which the University sorely needed. People would become more interested in the Shrine than in the University; those who would come to the campus to admire the University would become completely engrossed in the Shrine. The immense structure of the Shrine would completely dwarf the other buildings of the campus and make the campus scene an architectural monstrosity.

"If we must have the Shrine, let us place it at some distance away from the University" was the plea of a kind of middle group of critics. Several different locations were suggested, among them the site of old Fort Totten in back of the University near the Marist House of Studies. Monsignor Edward A. Pace at that time owned this land, and he offered to donate the property as a site for the Shrine.

Bitter opponents of the Shrine said many unkind and unpleasant things about the whole idea. To mention only two and these of the milder sort, the Shrine was referred to as "Shahan's folly"; others remarked that all that Bishop Shahan had in mind was to build himself a tomb. He is, of course, the only person buried in it today.

The Bishop, however, who had held his ground before in bitter controversy, maintained his position firmly. The Shrine, as he conceived it, would interest people otherwise unconcerned about the University. They would come to admire the Shrine and would go away with a knowledge of the University. The money received from the Shrine would not be diverted from the University. It would come from an entirely different source, i.e., another stratum of society other than that which contributed to the University. Architecturally, it would dominate the campus, to be sure, but in an harmonious and inspiring manner. More important than all, Our Blessed Mother, the patron of the United States of America, would be honored in a special manner on the campus of The Catholic University of America. There was something very fitting about this. Our Blessed Mother, furthermore, would entirely dominate her University in spirit. Her presence would be felt by all who in anyway shared in the activities of the University—members of the teaching staff, the administration, the student body, the clerical staff, and the other workers.

The words of Bishop Shahan have often come to mind in recent years as the Shrine, beginning with the year of 1956, has pushed forward rapidly and taken definite shape. How true they have proven to be! When Bishop McEntegart, as Rector in 1956, was about to address the student body of the Summer Session and was searching for an appropriate subject to discuss, I suggested this very thing, the influence which the Shrine was exerting on all phases of the University and would increasingly exert as time goes on. He grasped the idea immediately and gave a most impressive discourse.

The financing of this project in the early days gave much concern. The following quotation from Monsignor Ryan's "Aide Memoir"[1] illustrates this.

The Shrine of the Immaculate Conception, situated on the University campus, presents a real problem to the University. In the future it may become a much more grave one and the Sacred Congregation should be put au courant of some of the facts in the case.

The Shrine was started about twelve years ago as a University Church and $2,000,000 were to be expended in its construction. Since that time the ultimate cost has been revised repeatedly until this summer Monsignor McKenna stated it would cost $40,000,000 when completed. If this estimate is true, it will cost five per cent, or $2,000,000 annually simply to maintain the Shrine.

Begun as a University Church, the founder, Bishop Shahan, now contends that it is a *national* Shrine, not a University Church at all, and that it is *independent* of the University in every way. He acts even in detail on this assumption. Since my advent as Rector, I have had no voice in the construction or management of the Shrine. Its only relationship to the University is that a Committee of the Board of Trustees is supposed to have supervision of the work of Bishop Shahan and Monsignor McKenna. As a matter of fact, the Committee knows little or nothing about this

[1] Cf. The School of Sacred Theology.

work, which is in essence the personal task of two men. Bishop Shahan and Monsignor McKenna claim *absolute* freedom from University control. The sum of $2,738,970.63 has been collected up to June 30, 1931 and it is costing 55¢ to 60¢ to collect every dollar, a significant and ominous fact.

There is not one member of the Board of Trustees, with the exception of Cardinal Dougherty, who does not look upon the completing of this immense church as an over-ambitious project, to put it mildly, and who does not predict that on the death of Bishop Shahan it will be thrown back on the University. The Hierarchy in general accepts this viewpoint of the Board of Trustees.

That the Board of Trustees should take some action in the premises is conceded by all, but a personal equation enters the problem which makes action next to impossible. As far as I can see, all we can do is to wait and to pray that when the burden is transferred to the shoulders of the University, it will not be too heavy to carry. The Sacred Congregation may look forward to the day when this problem will cause us serious trouble.

Fortunately, all has turned out well. The National Shrine is serving its twofold function of national shrine and university church. The financial problem has been solved without any damage to the University, and the National Shrine, moreover, is regarded as part of the University family.

There is much criticism today as to the propriety of the particular kind of architecture which the National Shrine represents. Many believe that a modern style designed for practicality would have been more appropriate. To me, as to many others, the National Shrine is a work of great beauty and edification.

Athletics and Physical Education

Athletics and physical education in the past, at least in many institutions of higher education, have been inseparably linked together. This has always been the policy of The Catholic University of America. The wisdom of this practice, however, is highly doubtful. It must be remembered that today physical education is no longer regarded merely as a matter of building up one's physique or taking regular exercise. It involves taking instruction and study in a field of solid content, that the student may learn about the nature of his body and all of his being that is affected by it, and how to take care of it, and also, if he so desires, how to teach others these same things. If no academic credit is given for courses taken in physical education, it may reasonably be assumed that it is a program of the traditional kind, involving the usual setting-up exercises, little more than spending time in the gymnasium. Certainly such studies should not carry university credit. A well-organized Department of Physical Education, disassociated from athletics at least in concept, is badly needed at the Catholic Univeristy of America.

While athletics at the University have always been more or less tied up with physical education, athletics have by no means always dominated the department. Moreover, so-called "big-time" football has hit the University only twice thus far in its history, the first time in an incipient form under Bishop Shahan and the second time in full bloom in the early days of Bishop Ryan's rectorship. Both were indications that the real nature or purpose of our college was not well understood by important members of the administration. In fact the numerous and persistent controversies over whether or not the University family should include the College depends on one's understanding of the nature and purpose of the College. Since we have discussed this elsewhere, [1] suffice it to say here that our College should, in harmony with the general purpose of the University itself, give a good general education and at the same time train for advanced or university work beyond the baccalaureate degree, whether the undergraduate actually proceeds further in his studies or not. Certainly such a kind of college should have no place for "big-time" athletics, especially football. Acting as a training place or minor league team for the professional football leagues is hardly an activity for the College of The Catholic University of America. Furthermore, as long as so many institutions of higher education, in spite of all efforts to prevent them, have indulged in a horrible abuse of football, it is much better to

[1] Cf. Reorganization.

abandon the sport on an intercollegiate basis, as the authorities of the University have done in recent years, until such time as a general reform takes place. It should be said also that it is very unwise, because of obvious reasons, for an institution which avoids the abuses of football to send its teams against those of colleges and universities which make no effort to do so, and thus to expose its *bona fide* student athletes to humiliating defeat and even physical injury. The abuses and the ill-effects of "big-time" athletics are becoming more and more flagrant, and a reaction is bound to take place. Football by its very nature is the worst offender. Once this has been cleaned up, the other sports will follow.

The arguments always put forth to justify this great emphasis on football are: that the contests bring the alumni together as a unit and promote alumni giving; that they stimulate interest in the institution on the part of the alumni; that they weld the students themselves into a closely knit group filled with pride for their institution; and finally that they make the college or university well known throughout the land and attract students to attend the institution and others to contribute to its support. It is futile to attempt to refute these arguments. Suffice it to say that the last, the possibility of building up the undergraduate student body in particular, appealed to both Bishop Shahan and Bishop Ryan.

I recall Bishop Shahan declaiming vehemently against the administrators of the leading universities of the country for introducing the blight of athletic professionalism into their institutions and setting a horrible example for all others to follow, even those with barely sufficient funds to carry on their usual academic activities. He was especially incensed at Harvard University for building the first mammoth stadium. When I ventured to say that these large private institutions did insist on their athletes maintaining the same academic standards as other students, his Excellency promptly put me in my place in no uncertain terms. But the Bishop did yield in this regard to the persuasive arguments of Professors Thomas J. MacKavanagh and Louis Henry Crook, and permitted them, since they represented the faculty control of athletics, to offer valuable scholarships to attract outstanding athletes and, in particular, football players. This effort, however, did not achieve any great success. Only a very few truly excellent athletes were persuaded to attend the University, and it cannot be said that these brought any real or creditable attention to our institution. This movement did, to be sure, result in the erection of the stadium with University funds distracted from other badly needed purposes. It did bring in representatives of the tramp professional athlete; it clearly lowered academic standards; it spread discontent among the undergraduates; and it did *not* increase the student body.

Subsidization of athletes was one of only a few University policies on which Bishop Ryan and I disagreed. It is worthy of note that we could disagree strongly on various questions without any deleterious effect on our mutual friendship. He would argue that the undergraduate body of the University needed to be built up, which indeed was very true; that the University of Notre Dame did it through football, and what "Notre Dame" did, we could do. Obviously, this was not a very well thought-out argument, as Bishop Ryan himself showed later when he planned the reform of the College. [2] Perhaps he was led off the track of his usual good sense in settling academic problems by his great love of collegiate sports. A later Rector very timidly went astray in this respect, on a much smaller scale, for the same reason. At any rate, Bishop Ryan deliberately entered the entangling mesh of difficulties created by "big-time" athletics, particularly football, on a large scale. First of all he engaged the services of a nationally-known football coach from the University of Minnesota, to serve also as athletic director, at a salary far in excess of that of any member of the teaching staff. He was Mr. Arthur J. "Dutch" Bergman. There was nothing new in the excessive salary, because it had long since become rather common for institutions of higher education to pay successful football coaches more than they did the presidents themselves. This policy, however, did cause much bitter criticism and discontent on the campus of The Catholic University of America, where such a practice was hitherto quite unknown. It did not help matters

[2] Cf. The College of Arts and Sciences.

any when Mr. Bergman let the deans know that if any one of them permitted the academic failure of any of his star performers, especially during the football season, he would go directly to the Rector, who had promised to support him in every way. His Excellency's reply to those who had the courage to face him with their criticisms was: "Just wait five years until you see the great growth of the College and the great glory which our athletes will bring the University!" But five years passed, and the results promised Bishop Ryan by Mr. Bergman never materialized. There was no perceptible increase in the student enrollment of the College, and there was no great stir in the world of intercollegiate athletics caused by the achievements of our star performers, unless one was impressed by the football victory of The Catholic University of America over the University of Mississippi in the Orange Bowl!

In the meantime the tremendous cost of maintaining the football program did not diminish. The chief item of expense was the sums of money which had to be guaranteed to such teams as the University of Detroit and the University of South Carolina. These contests supposedly would bring paying spectators to the University stadium in sufficient numbers not only to meet the guarantees but to accumulate a considerable surplus. But comparatively few of these spectators ever came out to Brookland to watch our star athletes, and the guarantees and salaries had to be paid. Word got out among the faculty that the football deficit was approximately $100,000.00 and speculation was rife as to the sorely needed increase in faculty salaries which this amount would make possible if thus applied. The Procurator himself told me one year that it was slightly over $60,000.00. This should not surprise anyone, especially since just recently the president of a neighboring university told me that he would be very happy indeed, if his deficit for big-time football could be kept to $100,000.00.

Nothing was done, however, to remedy conditions until after Bishop Ryan went to Omaha. Then Bishop Corrigan's Committee on Administration and the Budget took the matter in hand by abolishing all subsidizing of athletes. This meant abandoning intercollegiate football as a University sport. Mr. Bergman was offered the opportunity of continuing at the University as Director of Athletics in charge of physical education, but he refused. His capable assistant of long standing, Mr. Edmund La Fond, was then tendered the post, and he accepted.

From this time on emphasis has been on intramural sports, and very successfully so. Mr. La Fond has gathered about him a group of coaches and assistants who receive moderate salaries and who are doing their work to a great extent out of a genuine love of sports and the University. The attitude of the students on the campus in relation to sports is essentially good. The vast majority prefer the present condition of things, where no one is being paid to represent the University in the field of athletics. At least the deplorable state of students with athletic ability refusing to compete in a given sport unless they are given some financial compensation, even though they do not need the money, no longer exists. Not all problems have been solved by any means, but we no longer have any major difficulties as in the past.

Intercollegiate football was brought back for a few years at the insistent demand of the students, and it was played with teams supposedly of our own stature. However, a number of considerations, chiefly a decline in interest on the part of the students, caused it to be abandoned again. All other so-called major and some minor sports are being conducted both on an intramural basis and with our peers, chiefly in the Mason-Dixon League. It is to be noted that during the period of big-time football, only four varsity sports were conducted. Today, with a smaller budget and no deficit, nine varsity sports within the Mason-Dixon Conference are being carried on. The University authorities, I believe, are well satisfied with the present state of athletic affairs. The one serious criticism that might be raised against it is the failure thus far to take proper care of the strictly physical education of all students and the athletic interests of women students. Provision has been made recently (1958) to care for women in this field.

Before closing this chapter I must add that I shudder at the repeated efforts of well-meaning alumni and some newly appointed administrative officers to abandon our present plan, which has been reached at such a costly price, and to restore the "big-time" policy again. I beg these persons for the good of the University to examine the record, to see what the cost was both in dollars and cents and in the lowering of the student intellectual outlook, and to note that few, if any, worthwhile students came to the University because of athletics. Study after study has been made of this subject with the same findings. It is still to be shown that a single good student ever came to The Catholic University of America because of athletics even in the palmiest days. But more important than all these considerations, undue stress on athletics is diametrically opposed to the spirit and the specific instructions of the University's statutes.

The American Association
of University Professors:
The Catholic University of America Chapter

The American Association of University Professors was established in 1915, when I was an instructor in the Classics at Princeton University. One of my greatest teachers and a close personal friend, Professor Edward Capps, was among its founders, and he often spoke to me about it. In fact, at his urging I joined the Association in its earliest years, 1920.

Whether the conception which I have of it meets with the approval of the present day authorities of the Association, I do not know, but it is what I assimilated from my conversations with Professor Capps. He used to say: "It is not a labor union, but rather an organization of teachers who seek to cooperate with the authorities of educational institutions. The teachers can see certain phases of college and university life better than administrators can, because they themselves make up the faculty and are much closer to the student body. They know best what the students wish to know by way of information in general and on current questions in particular, and so can arrange public lectures most effectively. They can reach the students much more quickly and thoroughly on matters pertaining to University policies and problems, and can be very useful instruments in the implementation of administrative decisions. The teachers on their part will be more loyal and more enthusiastic about the institution if they feel that the institution's authorities trust them and realize that they can contribute something to the development and improvement of the institution over and above the routine work of the classroom. The A.A.U.P. should also be able to perform valuable services by acting as arbiter between university authorities and faculty members in amicably settling disputes and misunderstandings. In short, it is an attempt to bring the faculty and administration closer together, without in any way condoning any infringement on the rights and du-

ties of either." This is what I learned from Professor
Capps, and it was with this concept of the A.A.U.P.
that I came to The Catholic University of America.

When I arrived on the campus, I found that
I was the only member of the A.A.U.P. in the
institution. I remained such for several years, when
Dr. J. De Sigeira Coutinho, Associate Professor of
Economics, shared that honor with me. At the suggestion of the national office of the organization, I
approached the Rector, Bishop Shahan, about the
possibility of establishing a chapter of the A.A.U.P.
on the University campus. This was not well received. The answer was a vigorous "No!" Later,
after Bishop Ryan had succeeded Bishop Shahan as
Rector, I received another letter from the A.A.U.P.
headquarters urging me again to attempt the establishment of a C.U.A. chapter. Bishop Ryan had
a much different feeling toward the proposal.
When we first discussed the subject he was by no
means enthusiastic about it, but he finally adopted
the attitude that the University had nothing to con-
ceal or to fear in the matter, and that it might prove
very valuable as a means of letting off steam and of
maintaining pleasant relations between the administration and members of the faculty.

Thus I wrote to Joseph Mayer of the A.A.U.P.
on April 30th, 1934 as follows:

> I would be glad to start the ball rolling again.
> Accordingly, if you will tell me what is necessary
> to do, I shall call the group together and we will

> organize at once. I might add that the University authorities would be very pleased to have us organize.

Accordingly, I communicated with the members of the faculty and invited them to join the A.A.U.P. and to attend the organization meeting of the local chapter. I myself refused to accept any office in the chapter because I was literally overwhelmed by my regular duties and many small additional responsibilities such as this. There were only about ten persons present in this first meeting, but the chapter grew steadily thereafter.

The first officers elected were Arthur R. Barwick of Geology, President; Francis L. Talbott of Physics, Secretary; and Father Charles A. Hart of Philosophy, Treasurer.

The early years of the University's A.A.U.P. chapter were quiet enough. They might easily be considered fruitless or "do nothing" years. A sudden change took place at the beginning of Bishop McCormick's rectorship and continued into the brief period of Bishop McEntegart's regime. While the Chapter did present a number of very outstanding lecturers during the years, its chief activity was complaining about faculty salaries, which indeed were very low. The manner, however, in which they approached the problem could hardly be called a move of cooperation with the administrators. It was rather one of frontal attack, not so much on the administrators as a group but on one or two individuals seemingly responsible and selected as scape goats. Monsignor Magner, Procurator of the University, bore the brunt of the attack for the regular year, and I was subjected to it for the Summer Session. The pitiful part of this unpleasantness was the fact that, led by a few inexperienced and notoriety-seeking individuals, the chapter made charges in private for the most part, but in a few instances in writing to the Rector. It assumed that it knew all the facts involved; actually it was woefully ignorant of them. Without going into the harrowing details, I wish to state simply that the Director of the Summer Session is given a budget by the administration, within which he must work; furthermore, it is a contingent budget. If the enrollment does not bring in the funds necessary to meet the requirements of the budget, the available funds are curtailed; on the other hand, the funds are not increased if an unexpectedly large number of students brings extra funds into the treasury. Within this framework the Director of the Summer Session labors as well as he can. Although suggestions have been requested again and again for improving the Summer Session and for meeting its problems, none have ever been received which could be put into practice. As a matter of fact, the salary scale of the University's Summer Session has always been higher than that of any other institution of higher education in this area. This was verified year after year. Speaking for the University as a whole, its financial woes have always been the same as those that have plagued all similar institutions in the land, and its faculty salaries, according to the results of special studies of the problem, have always been above the national median.

When Bishop McEntegart became Rector of the University, one of the first University problems to which he put his mind, being sensitive as a trained social worker to the social and economic ills of the country, was faculty salaries. He asked me to get him some representative literature on the subject, which I gladly did. Included therein was material which had appeared recently in the Bulletin of the A.A.U.P. At the first meeting of the faculty of the College of Arts and Sciences which I was able to attend after a serious automobile accident, representatives of the A.A.U.P. presented a communication on the salary difficulty which they proposed to have the Dean take to the Rector in the name of the Faculty. I objected strenuously, pleading that the Rector was giving the matter serious consideration and begging that he be given a chance to do something about it on his own (which he seemed on the point of doing) before the A.A.U.P. chapter or the faculty approached him about it. My efforts were of no avail. The motion was passed, but I honestly believe that most of the members of the faculty refrained from voting. Furthermore, the petition might well have been called impertinent in its phraseology. The result of this unfortunate affair was that the Rector was inclined to have little confidence in the local chapter of the A.A.U.P. with respect to receiving helpful advice in meeting his difficulties. It should be said also that subsequent experience served to confirm him in this feeling.

The leaders of the local chapter at this time were very anxious to take credit for preserving the integrity of faculty tenure, and at a celebration of the twentieth anniversary of the founding of the chapter, they went to great length to demonstrate this. [1] As a matter of fact, faculty tenure has been rigidly maintained by the statutes of the University and by the ecclesiastical court that backs up these statutes. No institution of higher education in the world has a better record than The Catholic University of America in this respect. Every instance cited on this occasion was inaccurately presented.

However, as in other institutions of the land, thanks greatly to the contributions of the Ford Foundation, faculty salaries have greatly improved, and the local chapter of the A.A.U.P. has apparently become somewhat appeased. Certainly it can be said that in the last two rectorships, the administration has been deeply conscious of the problem of faculty salaries, and has done all in its power to solve it. I would say that at the present moment (1958), the problem has been well solved.

Student Societies: Social and Honorary

When Bishop Ryan became Rector of the University, our campus was entirely free of societies of any kind, except for the purely academic kind

[1] See an unpublished essay by Father Henry J. Browne in the University Archives entitled: "The A.A.U.P. on Campus: A Score of Years."

such as the debating society and the French club. The administration had from the beginning taken a firm stand against the social Greek letter fraternity. The new Rector, however, listened with favor to the several petitions that immediately came to him for the establishment of this kind of campus activity, and soon several of these organizations were operating. When more tried to move in, however, it was thought wise to place a ban on any increase in their number. The usual arguments against fraternities had no affect on Bishop Ryan, but all their short-comings as presented to him have been amply demonstrated by experience. In an institution like the Catholic University of America, where the chief aim is to work the student within reason up to his highest capacity, fraternities and social clubs are a distraction. The American college as a whole is a much more serious institution today than it was when these social organizations first began to flourish. There is now much less time for these diversions. Naturally, we all need some social relaxation, but this can readily and amply be obtained through functions planned on an institutional basis. Moreover, fraternities and social clubs damage institutional solidarity and spirit. These statements are almost bromidic, yet they are so true and apparently are so much overlooked that they can stand repetition. It appears clear that the University would be much better off without these organizations. Such good as may be derived from them certainly does not compensate for the harm which they do.

Honorary academic societies, however, are quite a different thing. Bishop Ryan almost at the beginning of his rectorship charged me specifically with the task of obtaining chapters of Phi Beta Kappa and Sigma Xi for our campus. Phi Beta Kappa, of course, is the honorary fraternity which recognizes high scholastic achievement in a program of studies which emphasizes the liberal arts, and Sigma Xi stresses rather high attainment in the natural sciences. There is also another important difference which should be brought out. Sigma Xi insists upon serious accomplishment in research within the fields of the natural sciences on the part of the appropriate members of the faculty of the institution which is seeking a chapter. Phi Beta Kappa does not directly mention research but does refer to qualities of leadership on the part of those who are selected for membership in any chapter. But since good leadership depends so much on a well trained mind, it may be said that membership in Phi Beta Kappa depends essentially on high academic accomplishment.

Communication was immediately established with the executive secretaries of both groups, and prompt replies were received from each. It was clear, however, that at that moment we could not meet the research requirements of Sigma Xi. Accordingly, we devoted our entire attention to obtaining a chapter of Phi Beta Kappa. Dr. Wm. A. Shimer, the executive secretary of this society, was very helpful, as well as sympathetic, toward us as we faced our first obstacle. No Catholic institution of higher education up to that time had received a chapter, and there was a very definite hostility within the organization against Catholic institutions. Several of us on the University campus were determined to have a show-down on the matter. A chapter of Phi Beta Kappa in any college meant definitely that that institution was a liberal arts college of the highest quality. Furthermore, the possessor of a Phi Beta Kappa key, the symbol of membership in the group, was recognized, whether rightly or wrongly, wherever he appeared in the land as a superior person intellectually. Woodrow Wilson was keenly aware of the supposed intellectual superiority of the Phi Beta Kappa man, and displayed this attitude on many occasions, especially in his newspaper conferences. Surely some Catholic institutions of higher education and some of their students deserved such recognition. Hence our persistent quest for a chapter.

The procedure at that time for obtaining a chapter of Phi Beta Kappa was as follows. First of all, the members of Phi Beta Kappa on the University faculty had to organize themselves into a group, which would be responsible for making the petition for a chapter to the United Chapters of Phi Beta Kappa. The authorities of the institution may not make such a petition. The country, furthermore, was divided into regions, and the central office of Phi Beta Kappa sent the petitions to the headquarters of the appropriate regions for consideration by ballot. At this time there was no investigation of any kind of the petitioning institution.

The Catholic University of America was on the northern fringe of the Southern Region, and when the balloting, which was carried on by the traditional black and white balls, took place, the University got only three white balls! It was obvious, that, located as we were, we could never get a chapter of Phi Beta Kappa under this system. If we had succeeded in procuring the approval of our region, we would have been presented to the next triennial national meeting of all the chapters. Here the ballotting as in the regions would be repeated, but an exception was allowed in that an individual might take it upon himself to present an institution for a chapter directly to the triennial meeting without having it go to the regional group. This procedure was rarely followed, but it is known to have been successful.

Dr. Shimer recognized the weakness of this system and the potential danger which it had for the good name of Phi Beta Kappa. He accordingly determined to reform the scheme. Instead of the preliminary voting on an institution by the members in its region, he established an evaluating committee whose task it was to examine the institution up for consideration very much as the regional accrediting associations have been doing. The applying institutions first fill out detailed questionnaires, on the basis of which some are eliminated at once. A visitor or inspector or, to use the most recent term, evaluator is then sent to each of the others. After a study of the reports of the evaluators and the questionnaires as well, still more are eliminated; the remainder, usually about fifteen, are sent to the national triennial meeting for final action. When this was tried for the first time, the College of St. Catherine of St. Paul, Minnesota, was the first Catholic college which had reached this final point in the procedure. This triennial meeting took place in Cincinnati, and it was marked by a terrific debate on the floor as to whether the selections of the evaluating committee were to be regarded as final and the triennial conclave was to be a rubber stamp! Some members, whose names are better left unmentioned, indulged in such remarks as: "No Catholic institution should have a chapter of Phi Beta Kappa, since the Catholic Church does not permit freedom of thinking!" and "No Catholic institution can merit a chapter of Phi Beta Kappa, since there are facts in the history of the Catholic Church which no Catholic educational institution can afford to let its students know." Each institution up for consideration may have a representative, a member of Phi Beta Kappa, present at the deliberations of the triennial meeting to defend it and to correct erroneous statements made about it, if necessary. Unfortunately, the College of St. Catherine had as its representative a prominent member of the administration of the University of Minnesota who was not a Catholic and had absolutely nothing to say in the face of these ignorant and perhaps vicious remarks. At any rate, St. Catherine's did not at that time receive the required number of affirmative votes. The triennial meeting, however, did go on record as believing that the recommendations of the evaluating committee should ordinarily be accepted unless some very compelling reasons dictated otherwise.

Dr. Shimer urged the authorities of the College of St. Catherine to apply again and to ask to be considered at the next triennial meeting which would take place in 1937 at Atlanta, Georgia. He later came to me in alarm to say that St. Catherine's had decided to send the same person from the University of Minnesota, who had represented or rather had failed to represent it in Cincinnati, to lead its defense in Atlanta. He did not want the same disaster to strike again. To prevent this he had a very unique suggestion. I, as a member of Phi Beta Kappa, was to write to various chapters to see if any of them would accept me as one of their two regularly allotted representatives. Only in this capacity could I speak from the floor if there should be need, it being understood that I would at least attempt to stop any more of the canards such as were brought up at the Cincinnati meeting. I wrote to institution after institution, even my own alma mater. Although I volunteered in every instance to pay my own expenses, I was regularly turned down when my purpose in asking for the privilege became known. As I was beginning to lose hope, one of my Phi Beta Kappa friends at Hobart College, to whom I had written last, replied that his chapter would be glad to have me go to the Atlanta meeting as one of its representatives.

At Atlanta I had a most interesting experience. It had been the custom, wisely abandoned after this meeting, for the representatives to electioneer the day and night before and to carry on a kind of campaign in behalf of their respective institutions, if, of course, they were to be voted on. Since Hobart College already had a chapter and needed no publicity, I worked hard for St. Catherine's. I might add that I appeared to be alone in this particular work. When the time came for the final voting the next morning, I met the other representative of the Hobart College Chapter for the first time, and he was not at all inclined to vote in favor of St. Catherine's. We argued the matter right up to the urn into which we were to drop our vote (one vote for the two of us), and we even held up the proceedings as we debated. At the last second he agreed to casting our vote in the affirmative. At the counting of the ballots, the College of St. Catherine had the bare number necessary for approval. Without the Hobart vote, it would have failed again.

The ban against Catholic colleges seemed now to have been broken, but there is a little postlude which I am tempted to present. On my return to Washington, I found a telegram on my desk from the President of the College of St. Catherine to this effect: "You will be glad to learn that St. Catherine's has been awarded a chapter of Phi Beta Kappa." I was very happy to reply, with my congratulations, simply that I had been present at the meeting and was quite aware of it.

In the meantime, The Catholic University of America had decided to delay its second application until the next triennium, which was to take place in San Francisco. We had to put our own house in order. Father James M. Campbell, as Dean of the College of Arts and Sciences, had just been appointed and had inherited a rather dismal state of affairs. There was much work to be done, but we felt that we would be ready by that time. President David A. Robertson, of Goucher College, was the evaluator sent to us by the evaluating committee. Several untoward incidents happened during his visit, not the least of which took place in the Registrar's office. Mr. Charles Fox Borden was Registrar of the University at the time. When we took President Robertson into the Registrar's office to examine the students' records, one of the regular procedures even today for any evaluation, Mr. Borden rudely turned his back on the Phi Beta Kappa evaluator and vowed that no one was going to examine his records! After a little discussion, this difficulty was patched up. Then, when President Robertson was examining the grades given students by our teaching staff, he was amazed at the consistently high grades given by the teachers of the Department of Religious Education. In those days numbers rather than letters were used in grading students. One well known teacher in his two classes of over fifty students each gave 100% for the most part, with only an occasional change to 99%! At this point Dr. Robertson asked two very cogent questions: "Are these all football players?", to which the answer, of course, was "No." Then he said: "Are these grades based on the success with which students practice their religion or on their knowledge of content?" When we told him the latter, he replied: "I would be ashamed to admit that everyone could get either 99% or 100% in any course on the content of my religion." Mr. Robertson asked further what we did with regard to the teaching of religion to non-Catholics, and we answered very smugly: "Nothing. We do not compel them to take courses in religion. They are free to go where they please with regard to their religious instruction and worship." To this he replied: "Non-Catholic students need religious instruction more than Catholic students do. You should do something for them!" From this time on, non-Catholic students at The Catholic University of America have been obliged to take courses in religion specially designed for them. They are, of course, permitted to take additional courses in the subject, if they so desire, and many of them do. All in all, however, the evaluation went well, and the evaluating committee recommended the University for a chapter at the San Francisco triennial meeting.

The following announcement appeared in the edition of the Tower [1] that came from press after the Christmas and New Year holiday of 1939 and 1940.

---

[1] The undergraduate student newspaper of the campus.

IMPORTANT ANNOUNCEMENT

In view of radio announcements and press releases of December 14, the *Tower* prints the following statement of facts relative to the status of a hoped for chapter of Phi Beta Kappa at the University.

(1) On December 6 President Robertson of Goucher College inspected the College of Arts and Sciences here in behalf of the United Chapters of Phi Beta Kappa. The College was reported favorably by the inspector.

(2) On Monday, December 11, the Executive Committee of the United Chapters began to study reports on between thirty-five and forty other colleges which had likewise been approved by inspectors.

(3) On Wednesday, December 13, the Secretary of the United Chapters released to the press a statement which listed the Catholic University as one of nine institutions which were to be recommended to the triennial convention of Phi Beta Kappa as deserving a chapter.

(4) The University will be nominated for a chapter of Phi Beta Kappa at the triennial convention in San Francisco in September, 1940. If it receives a majority of the ballots cast on its nomination, it will be granted a chapter. If it does not receive a majority, it will not again be eligible for a chapter earlier than 1943.

I attended this gathering and experienced great pleasure in seeing this chapter voted through with very few dissenting votes, which gave me the impression that Phi Beta Kappa on a national scale did not have as much anti-Catholic prejudice as was at first suspected.

Those of us who had labored for this cause were overjoyed; and my telegram to Bishop Ryan was happily received. But all the difficulties were not over yet. In the meantime, Bishop Ryan had been succeeded by Bishop Corrigan as Rector, and letters began coming to him condemning our acceptance of a chapter of Phi Beta Kappa. It was a Masonic secret society, they said, pointing to a Catholic pamphlet on forbidden secret societies, on the middle of whose cover was a picture of the symbol of Phi Beta Kappa, the key! Incidentally, I wrote to the author of this pamphlet and pointed out to him the slanderous nature of the cover of the publication, but I never received the courtesy of a reply. Some also referred the Rector to a rare volume in the Library of Congress which exposed all secret groups including Phi Beta Kappa. The Rector called me to his office and demanded that I refute each and every one of the charges. I did the best I could, but he apparently was not satisfied with my explanations. He then sent the Librarian, Father Francis Mullin, to the Library of Congress to examine the whole question, making use of the references supplied in the various communications on the subject. Father Mullin's report, however, did satisfy Bishop Corrigan, and plans were made for the installation of the Beta Chapter of Phi Beta Kappa in the District of Columbia at The Catholic University of America.

The installation ceremonies were executed without a flaw, and the Rector spared nothing in order to make them a success. I had asked Bishop Corrigan if we might give Archbishop Ryan an honorary membership and a key symbolizing that membership. I did not think, in the light of the last minute difficulties which I had experienced with Bishop Corrigan, that he himself would be interested in receiving one. To my amazement, in answer to my question with regard to Archbishop Ryan, he replied: "Of course, give one to Archbishop Ryan, but I think that you ought also to give one to me!" To this I readily agreed. Thus, at the installation of our chapter, we increased the membership of the Catholic hierarchy in Phi Beta Kappa from two to four, Bishop Duane G. Hunt of Salt Lake City and Bishop Robert Joyce of Burlington, Vermont, having already merited earned memberships.

The chapters of Phi Beta Kappa at the College of St. Catherine and at The Catholic University of America are still the only chapters possessed by Catholic institutions of higher education. The reasons for this need to be explored by a non-partisan investigation, and I do not hesitate to say that the fault does not lie entirely with the society of Phi Beta Kappa itself.

Now that we had a chapter of Phi Beta Kappa, I turned my attention again to gaining the recognition of Sigma Xi. The University had recently procured the services of several scientists of national reputations on our teaching staff. In view of Sigma Xi's emphasis on research, I thought it appropriate that the responsibility of procuring the desired chapter should be turned over to one of these. Dr. Karl Herzfeld agreed to take charge of the petition. In a few years the University had the honor of being the second Catholic institution to receive a chapter of Sigma Xi. The first Catholic institution to be so honored is St. Louis University. At this point also I asked what is to some extent a rhetorical question: "Why do not more Catholic institutions of higher education have a chapter of Sigma Xi?"

A freshman honorary society, Phi Eta Sigma, is represented by a chapter on our campus. Monsignor Charles A. Hart was responsible for starting and promoting it. It may be said that its purpose is to prepare freshmen for membership in Phi Beta Kappa. I am proud to possess honorary membership in it.

When Father Edward A. Fitzgerald was Registrar of Loras College, he took it upon himself to launch a Catholic honorary society, which he hoped would rival Phi Beta Kappa. He argued that it was apparently impossible for any appreciable number of Catholic colleges to receive chapters of Phi Beta Kappa, although they deserved them, and so why should they not start their own organization! As a matter of fact, the authorities of Phi Beta Kappa openly admit that they cannot possibly process all the applications that come in, and so necessarily many worthy institutions will not receive chapters. This is a definite weakness in the organization. Father Fitzgerald visited me at the University just before he presented his project to the College and University Department of the National Catholic Educational Association, and asked my feeling in the matter. He inquired, moreover, whether we at the University would be interested in having a chapter of his organization, even though we already had a chapter of Phi Beta Kappa. I replied that I personally would be very much interested in it and that I saw nothing incompatible in our having a chapter of both honorary societies. I felt that the requirements for membership in our chapter of Delta Epsilon Sigma, the name of his society, could be distinguished from those of Phi Beta Kappa by including special emphasis on excellence in philosophy and theology (religion). This seemed to please Father Fitzgerald, but nothing was done about our procuring the chapter until very recently (1955), when the newly elected President of Delta Epsilon Sigma, Mr. Thomas Garrett, Registrar of St. Michael's College, Winooski, Vermont, pressed the matter. A chapter of Delta Epsilon Sigma was at last installed in our College and has been going along very successfully. It has its special place, by reason of its requirements of excellence in philosophy and theology, and while its roster of members overlaps a little with that of Phi Beta Kappa, it is different enough to make it distinctive. The students of The Catholic University of America are very much interested in Delta Epsilon Sigma and cherish membership in that organization.

The Teaching of Religion
and Theology

When I came to the University in 1918, I looked forward to the opportunity of learning my own religion more thoroughly and more scientifically. It had been my lot to go to public schools and secular institutions of higher education, not by deliberate choice but by force of circumstances which we need not discuss here. The point which I wish to bring out is that I was conscious of this gap in my training, even though I had made every reasonable effort to make up for it by private reading and study. Furthermore, I was resolved not to let my children go through their academic life without a good training in the subject, and I expected to find the ideal program in my own institution, The Catholic University of America.

What I am about to say is not intended to cast any reflection on any individual or on the Religion program at the University when I arrived there or thereafter. I am depicting a more or less general condition and a Catholic educational problem which has plagued Catholic educators in the United States from the beginning. Thank the Lord, they have gone far in recent years toward the solution of the difficulty.

The trouble has stemmed, I think, from two chief causes: a superficial delineation of the aims of the teaching of religion in college and the crusading (I am tempted to say "fanatical") nature of so many of those who are primarily engaged in it. As for the former, we will all agree that unless the student, as he studies religion, improves his living of it, the whole process is a rather empty thing. But how is a teacher to get the student to live his religion? Upon what does learning to live one's religion depend? A more thorough understanding of one's religion? Association with those who are truly living their religion and witnessing their example? Exhortation of the pastoral kind? Probably upon all three but with distinct emphasis on the first: a more thorough understanding of one's religion. At least as far as the college and university are concerned, a well planned intellectual approach accompanied by very well directed serious study is a *sine qua non*, the very basis for teaching the subject. This is the classroom activity so important to all successful teaching. The other two are by no means to be discounted but are to be brought in for the most part by a carefully organized program of religious activities and social life on the campus. An appropriate combination of the three is the desideratum of the college.

A serious block to the development of good college departments of theology (religion) is the crusading teacher! He regards himself almost as if specially chosen by God for the work. There is only one correct method for teaching religion (with him it is always religion, not theology), and that is *his* method. Furthermore, woe betide anyone who would even dare to discuss the matter with him (especially if he be a layman). I have suffered much from religion instructors of this kind.

Before proceeding further, be it understood that I have had no sympathy with the long debates and meticulous arguments over whether we should use the term "religion" or "theology" for the program of studies followed in the college curriculum. Let each one use the term which he prefers. It makes little difference as long as the job is done. To me, this is simply a matter of semantics. The body of knowledge which we study is rather theology, whether on the college or major seminary level. The actual living of the teachings of theology is religion, in whatever stratum of society we may be. These are the usual dictionary definitions of the two terms. Religion certainly seems to refer primarily to the moral virtue by which we give homage to God.

The Department of Religious Education, when I arrived at the University, was devoted chiefly to the last two of the basic principles which I have mentioned, namely, association with those who are truly living their religion and witnessing their example, and exhortation of the pastoral type. It must be said that Monsignor John Cooper, himself, did an outsanding job in this manner. But very little was done by way of an intellectual approach to the learning of Catholic theology, such as we would expect the graduate of a Catholic college to know. While occasionally an instructor or two would depart from the adopted texts and attempt to do some serious systematic work of this kind, such instruction was decidedly the exception. The several persons who have served as head of the department refused to hire full-time teachers as a general policy, and insisted on having classes so large that they had to be placed in the auditorium of McMahon Hall. Obviously there could be no serious teaching under these conditions. We were merely lending support to the common saying, which I have heard so often among my non-Catholic colleagues in the Commission on Higher Education of the Middle States Association of Colleges and Secondary Schools: "You say that Catholic Education centers around philosophy and theology, yet these sections of the library are the weakest of all, and the courses in these fields are the poorest taught." It must be remembered that this state of affairs was not peculiar to The Catholic University of America, but until recently a rather general condition in Catholic higher education.

For about five years just before World War II, I was rather close to the work of this department by reason of the fact that my son and three companions, graduates of St. Anthony's High School in Brookland, D.C., were taking these courses and by their comments were unwittingly reporting to me. While at St. Anthony's, one of the curates, Father Sweeney, was very much interested in teaching theology and asked permission to carry on this task in the school. He took his notes, made while he was in the Seminary, and out of them constructed a strong high school program in the subject. He certainly was most successful in developing a genuine and solid interest in theology on the part of these four boys. They all looked forward to the continuance of their study of theology in college and to continued advancement in the subject. Again, with the exception of the classes of one teacher, the instruction was a decided anticlimax. The effect on the boys was at times pathetic.

When Bishop Ryan planned the reorganization of the University, he appointed a committee to study and reform the undergraduate curriculum. I was happy to be a member of this Committee, because I felt that here was my chance to do something about religious instruction in the College. I soon learned that no one should criticize religion as it was being taught, least of all a layman. The Department was in the hands of a group of three who passed the headship back and forth among them. The founder and first head of the Department was Dr. John Cooper, and, if anyone could make a success of the teaching of religion according to the principles enunciated, it was he. The other two, however, whose names are best left unmentioned, were in my opinion unsuccessful teachers and did little to advance religious instruction at the University for over a generation.

My own interest in the teaching of theology did not falter in spite of its set-backs. I succeeded in promoting the publication of the high school series of texts entitled, "Our Quest for Happiness", published by the Mentzer-Bush Company of Chicago.

It is important to keep the record clear here. Monsignor Elwell of Cleveland was the chief author, owner, and director of this series. I aided only in its publication. Actually, I tried to have it published by The Catholic University of America Press, but the Department of Religious Education would have none of it. This, however, did not mar the tremendous success of the series. At the time of its first appearance, it probably was the best series of its kind. The series by Sister Jane Marie, O.P., seems to be a genuine step forward. What we want, of course, is a series that will stimulate a theological thinking of the faith in addition to presenting facts, even for students on the secondary school level.

It was because of my interest in the teaching of college theology that I published a *Latin-English Lexicon of St. Thomas Aquinas* (The Catholic University of America Press). While attending a secular college, I was very conscious of the need of a knowledge of Catholic philosophy, and attempted to read the *Summa Theologica* of St. Thomas by myself. This, of course, proved to be an impossible task, but I felt that I might have made some headway with it, if I had had an appropriate lexicon. This I was determined to make, if it possibly could be done sometime in my life.

While gathering the material for the lexicon, I also obtained the material for a complete *Index of the Summa Theologica of St. Thomas,* and from this same material to construct a handy one volume *Latin-English Dictionary of St. Thomas* (St. Paul

Editions, Daughters of St. Paul, 50 St. Paul's Ave., Jam. Pl., Boston 30, Mass.). All together these works on St. Thomas Aquinas involved one and a half million 3x5 cards, and a period of sixteen years. They could not have been accomplished without the assistance of Sister M. Inviolata Barry of the Sisters of Divine Providence, Our Lady of the Lake College, San Antonio, Texas.

This same interest in Theology (Religion) as a secondary school and college subject prompted me to introduce courses strictly on the content of theology into the Summer Session. When I first attempted this, the opposition on the part of the Department of Religious Education, that is, of its head at the time, was almost fanatical. But when Bishop McCormick approved, we went ahead with great success. The present Archbishop Francesco Lardone organized the program. After a few years I became uneasy over the fact that the Department of Religious Education and the School of Theology were so publicly separated. The sharp disagreement between certain persons in each group was being paraded before the general public. After some maneuvering the two were brought together in the Summer Session under the Head of the Department of Religious Education. This proved to be a great mistake as far as the enrollment in the theology courses was concerned. The Head of the Department showed little interest in the theology program and some students felt that he was openly hostile to it. The theologian in direct charge of these studies was very busy at other things and had very little time to devote to this important work. As a result the enrollment in theology almost disappeared. In the Summer Session of 1957, I attempted to separate the two fields again and to set up the work in theology independently as it had been originally. I thought that all concerned were in full agreement with the change, but unfortunately we did not have all the necessary agreements *in writing*. Suffice it to say that we were not successful in our attempt to effect this separation.

All, however, seems to be well established now. With the appointment of the Reverend Gerard Sloyan in 1957 as Head of the Department of Religious Education, all the reforms that could be desired have been or are being brought about. To mention but a few: full-time teachers are being appointed to the teaching staff as a general policy; small classes are being organized as in other subjects; due consideration is being given both to theological content and methods of teaching; from the point of view of an intellectual challenge the content of all the courses is comparable with the content of courses in other departments. We all feel very confident that at last the Department of Religious Education is being made truly worthy of the College of which it is a part.

Something should be said about the graduate work in the Department of Religious Education. Most of the graduate studies thus far have been directed toward the Master's degree, and very few students have been candidates for the doctorate. When I was Dean of the Graduate School of Arts and Sciences, my experiences in line of duty did not permit me to hold a very high regard for the academic excellence of this department. In a certain sense it was a *refugium peccatorum*. Students who had difficulty fulfilling requirements for graduate degrees in other departments frequently requested transfer here, where they regularly had little difficulty. But all this, we believe, has passed, and none too soon. Thanks to the impetus of the recent Sister-Formation Conference, religious superiors everywhere are seeking solid programs in theology leading to the Master's and Doctor's degrees. The generally weak courses of study in this field will no longer satisfy. Superiors, if need be, will send their subjects to the countries of Europe for the best possible training in the most fundamental of all subjects. The Catholic University of America should lead the way in the development of such programs. It has already done so for the Master's degree, and is already well on its way to establishing strong programs for the doctorate. Moreover, the quality of these studies is fast being recognized especially by the Superiors of religious communities of women.

In conclusion, a few words should be said about the Society for Catholic College Teachers of Sacred Doctrine. The idea of this Association came out of the Seminar on Theology and the Social Sciences given in the college workshop held at the

University in June of 1953. Specifically, it came from the person of Sister M. Rose Eileen of the Sisters of the Holy Cross, a member of this seminar. She and I had discussed the matter on several occasions before. She now presented her plan to Father Cyril Vollert, S. J., and Father Gerald Van Acheren, S. J., whom I had been fortunate enough to induce to conduct this particular seminar. They too became very enthusiastic about establishing the Society for Catholic College Teachers of Sacred Doctrine. Incidentally, the name was arrived at only after much debate and serious thought. The founders were most anxious to include in their organization *all* teachers of religion, theology, and what have you, and so to avoid the old battle of semantics. The results have proven the wisdom of this decision. The founders, moreover, very thoughtfully invited me to take part in the planning of their organization, but unfortunately this took place when circumstances made it impossible for me to attend. However, they kept me informed of all progress. Again the Head of the Department of Religious Education at The Catholic University of America opposed any person representing the University having anything to do with the organization. He later relented to the extent that he approved Father Sloyan's attendance at the first regular meeting of the Association. He especially objected to my having anything officially to do with the group, among other reasons, because this might indicate that the University approved the Association, which he said was being set up at my instigation to promote the study of theology as opposed to religious education. But again, enough of these ridiculous details.

In any case, the Association has been established, and it has been enthusiastically received all over the country as something urgently needed. I have not taken an active part in its work for obvious reasons, but I am proud to be one of its deeply interested members.

Members of the Clergy and the Laity

In an institution of higher education such as The Catholic University of America one may expect to hear much about the advisibility or even propriety of the clergy or laity holding this or that office. I heard much along this line even before I came to the University as well as after my arrival here. In fact, soon after I appeared on the campus I was advised by members of both estates to move elsewhere while the moving was easy, being still unmarried and having no strong ties to hold me here. My own impression is that this favorite topic of discussion, especially when the conversation is lagging, is fast losing its popularity. It has not, however, completely died out.

The Statutes of the University specifically indicate that the Rector and Vice Rector must be priests, and I have heard much complaint about this mandate on the part of both laymen and occasionally even by priests. These protests, however, are unreasonable. The Catholic University of America, as a papal institution, with the Sacred Sciences forming the backbone of its academic organization, is in a special sense a custodian of the dogmas and the teachings of the Church. Only the properly trained priest can appropriately take over the responsibilities of directing and guarding the teaching function of the Church in all its ramifications as carried on in the University.

For the same reason we should expect to find a vast majority of priests as members of the faculties of the Schools of the Sacred Sciences (theology, canon law, and philosophy). However, in the field of philosophy the activity of members of the laity has been noteworthy, and laymen successfully pursuing their scientific investigation in theology and canon law are by no means unknown.

As regards other positions of importance in the University's organization, many might be called indifferent. They should be assigned to the persons best fitted for them, whether members of the clergy or laity. Still others could better be filled by priests or lay persons, according to their nature and the good judgment of the University authorities.

Because of the great concern of a few persons on the University campus, chiefly those who have joined us recently, and especially because of the curiosity of so many persons, Catholics and others, outside the University, I have thought it wise to make these statements. The discussion by Dr. Perlmutter of Xavier College for Women in Chicago on the place of the laity on Catholic college faculties, which appeared in a recent issue of the Commonweal, [1] contains little that is applicable to The Catholic University of America. Indeed, for many years now, there have been no feelings of discontent or rivalry within the University family on this or any similar score. This is a very pleasing recollection to record. [2]

---

[1] The Lay Professor, by Oscar W. Perlmutter, in the *Commonweal*, Vol. LXVIII, No. 2, pp. 31-34. The key statement of the author as he summarizes this article, "If a college is in one sense a community of scholars, then a Catholic college is two communities, one lay, the other religious, which are separate but not equal," is quite out of place with reference to The Catholic University of America. At our University the two groups are definitely integrated into one genuine community of scholars.

[2] As I go to press with these Memoirs, I feel obliged to chronicle what seems to me to be a growing tendency on the part of the last two administrations, at least in administrative matters, to push the laity aside in favor of members of the clergy. This involves the matter of easy and full communication between all parties concerned, religious and lay, on both academic and administrative matters, in addition to actual appointments to responsible positions.

OUTSIDE THE UNIVERSITY

Trinity College

Early in my career at The Catholic University of America, I was invited to join the faculty of Trinity College as a lecturer to teach a course in methods of teaching Latin and one other in some phase of Latin literature, usually Roman comedy. It was a distinct pleasure to cooperate with this institution, which was the first Catholic college for women to be established on an independent basis, apart from an academy or any other kind of academic foundation. It was also a real honor to join with such distinguished University professors as Monsignor Edward A. Pace, Doctors William Kerby, John A. Ryan, Thomas V. Moore, Nicholas Weber, and others who were at that time members of the Trinity College teaching staff.

The students in my classes proved to be well-trained, and were very much interested in their work, all of which was a source of great satisfaction to me. A good number of these students have made their mark in public life as well as in the home. Several went on into the religious life of the Sisters of Notre Dame of Namur, today holding positions of importance in the religious community itself and in the administration of Trinity College.

In addition to this undergraduate work, I was invited to train and direct members of the community toward the Ph.D. degree. My first class of this kind consisted of Sisters Wilfrid Parsons, Julia Stokes, and Albania Burns. The last two have long since passed to their eternal reward. Sister Wilfrid is still active as Professor of Latin at Emmanuel College in Boston, and very recently completed an outstanding translation of St. Augustine's letters in five volumes for our series, The Fathers of the Church. In later classes there were, among others, Sister Angela Elizabeth Keenan and Sister Thérèse of the Blessed Sacrament Sullivan. The former translated, as well as furnished a commentary for the famous treatise of St. Cyprian, *De Habitu Virginum*, which has also appeared in a volume of "The Fathers of the Church." Sister Angela Elizabeth is now Dean of Emmanuel College. Sister Thérèse established, as her dissertation for the doctorate, a new Latin text, also an excellent English translation with a commentary, of the third book of the *De Doctrina Christiana* of St. Augustine.

I continued this work until I became Dean of the Graduate School of Arts and Sciences, when I was obliged to resign from this delightful occupation because of the pressure of my new duties. As Dean of the Graduate School of Arts and Sciences, and with the support of the Graduate Council, I was able to persuade the authorities of the Sisters of Notre Dame of Namur to permit their nuns stationed at Trinity College to go to the University campus for graduate courses and guidance in the fulfilling of the requirements for graduate degrees. This was distinctly a step forward for Trinity College.

Since that time the Sisters have been attending courses at the University in ever-increasing numbers. During the current school year over seventy Sisters of Notre Dame of Namur have been in attendance during the fall and spring semesters, the workshops, and the summer session.

The Sisters of the Holy Cross and Dunbarton College of the Holy Cross

The Sisters of the Holy Cross with their historic Academy were closely allied with the University from the beginning, even though they were located at a considerable distance from the University on Upton Street near Connecticut Avenue in the Northwest section of Washington. The previous and first location of the Academy of the Holy Cross had been at 1312 Massachusetts Avenue, but, on the advice of Bishop Shahan, the Sisters sold this property to the National Catholic Welfare Conference. It was Bishop Shahan also, who, together with Dr. Shields and Dr. Kerby, found the Dunbarton estate on Upton Street as the new location of the Academy.

Bishop Shahan and Monsignor Pace were welcome friends at the Academy at all times. In fact, Bishop Shahan retired from the Rectorship of the University to live the remaining years of his life and to die at Holy Cross Academy in March, 1932. I recall also that, when I made the trip to Cleveland with Bishop Shahan at the invitation of Father John Burns, C.S.C., later the Provincial of the Congregation of the Holy Cross, ostensibly to establish a Catholic Classical League, [1] Father Burns urged Bishop Shahan after the meetings were over to stop off at the University of Notre Dame on his way back to Washington. His arguments among others were that Bishop Shahan needed a rest and that I had never seen the University of Notre Dame. The clinching consideration, however, was that the Bishop could visit his old friends at St. Mary's, among them Sister M. Angelice and Sister M. Scholastica. I recall also our having dinner at that time as guests of the Sisters alfresco behind the building where the postulants were housed and trained.

When the University authorities began thinking of the establishment of a Catholic college for women in the immediate vicinity of the University, their first thought was of the Sisters of the Holy

[1] Cf. Rectors under Whom I Have Served, Bishop Shahan.

Cross. These Sisters, however, because they were considering the launching of a collegiate program at St. Mary's, Notre Dame, Indiana, were not prepared to enter upon what appeared at the time as a tremendous venture.

In 1929, when Monsignor Ryan made the Summer Session an integral part of the University and appointed me its Director, the superiors of several large religious communities, contrary to the expectation of some critics, visited me with a view to making arrangements for sending rather large groups of their nuns to the Summer Session. Among these were Mother Marie de Lourdes, provincial superior of the Sisters of the Holy Names in the East; Mother Blanche and Mother Rose of Lima of the Sisters of St. Joseph in Albany, New York; and Mother M. Bettina, Provincial Superior in the East of the Sisters of the Holy Cross. I was, of course, delighted to see them all, especially under the circumstances of my taking charge of the Summer Session,[2] but I was pleased to see Mother M. Bettina for a special reason. Mention has already been made of the ties of friendship between the Sisters of the Holy Cross and the authorities of the University of the Shahan era, but I had noticed that for some years preceding 1929 the University had not been receiving any appreciable number of the Sisters of the Holy Cross as students. Now, with the beginning of an Eastern Province, there was an opportunity to reestablish the close and friendly re-

[2] Cf. The Summer Session.

lationship of the earlier period. It did not take long for Mother M. Bettina and me to reach an agreement whereby the Sisters of the Holy Cross would take over the old Cain residence, later the Phi Kappa house, on the campus as living quarters for their members while attending the Summer Session. This they continued to do until recently when the residence had to give way to the expansion of the National Shrine of the Immaculate Conception.

My own personal relationship with the Sisters of the Holy Cross became significant in 1934, when the then Sister M. Rose Elizabeth, Superior at Holy Cross Academy, later Provincial Superior and still later Mother General, visited me to discuss the possibility of establishing a junior college primarily for the Sisters in service and for laywomen in government employment. This was to be located at Holy Cross Academy and was to be known as Dunbarton College of the Holy Cross. Then began a most interesting and pleasant educational experience.

It has been a distinct pleasure to give advice and to watch the authorities of the College accept it intelligently, studying it for its true worth and following or abandoning it accordingly. The Junior College received the recognition of the Middle States Association of Colleges and Secondary Schools almost immediately and became a member of the American Association of Junior Colleges. In the summer of 1938, Mother M. Rose Elizabeth brought up the possibility of expanding the Junior College to a complete four year institution of liberal

arts. Many of the students and their parents likewise were eager for this development. There appeared to be a place in Washington for such a four
year college as Mother M. Rose Elizabeth had envisioned, namely, a general college of moderate
cost with a strong basis of liberal arts, but with an
opportunity for the student to equip herself in
some one of several applied arts as well, in order to
enable her to earn a living if she so desired. Accordingly, we got in touch with the Commission on Institutions of Higher Education of the Middle States
Association to learn whether such an expansion at
this time would jeopardize the College's accreditation as a junior college. Mr. Frank Bowles, then
Chairman of the Commission, assured us that it
would not and was most encouraging about Mother
M. Rose Elizabeth's plan for the senior college. Accordingly, in September of 1958 Dunbarton college
became a full-fledged four year institution of liberal
arts. Moreover in the very year in which the College
graduated its first class of four year students, it was
approved by the Middle States Association as a
senior college. In this connection, Mother M. Rose
Elizabeth, according to the then prevailing custom,
had to appear before the members of the Commission on Higher Education of the Middle States
Association and defend her petition for this approval. It was my pleasure to have been a member
of this commission and to have been present to hear
Mother M. Rose Elizabeth present her case very
skillfully before this group of rather formidable
educators. The Association, incidentally, no longer

approves institutions in so short a period, but insists on at least two graduating classes before an application for approval may be made.

I have served as Chairman of the Advisory Board of the College from the very beginning, and, except when illness or some such emergency prevented, which has been very rarely, have always appeared on the stage at the commencement exercise and taken part in the ceremonies. It has also been my privilege to give a number of public lectures there.

From September 1947 until June 1953, I served at the College as lecturer in the Classics and had the pleasure of teaching elementary Greek to a group of about ten young ladies annually. It gave me great amusement to compare the progress of my class with the achievement of the classes in first year Greek conducted by my colleagues at the University. The classes at Dunbarton College did not suffer by the comparison, in whatever manner one might be inclined to explain it. In 1953 it became necessary to give up a most enjoyable task by reason of the increasing labors at the University.

In addition to Mother M. Rose Elizabeth, two Sisters of the Holy Cross stand out prominently in my recollections by reason of their having taken courses and merited the degree of Doctor of Philosophy in our Department of Greek and Latin, and also because of my association with them as administrators of Dunbarton College of the Holy Cross. Sister M. Mildred Dolores obtained her doctorate in Latin under the guidance of Dr. Martin R. P. McGuire and is now President of Dunbarton College of the Holy Cross. Sister M. Monica earned her degree in Greek under direction of the Very Reverend Dr. James M. Campbell and is Head of the Department of Classics at the College.

It has been my lot to evaluate an extremely large number of institutions of higher education for both the Middle States Association of Colleges and Secondary Schools and for the University's Committee on Affiliation. Since perhaps the most important step in these formal evaluations is to appraise the outcomes of an institution's program, that is, to determine how well it achieves its professed objectives, I now almost instinctively think in these terms whenever I speak of a college or a university. It is not my intent to describe in detail the success which Dunbarton College has achieved in attaining its objectives, but one or two features of this success should be mentioned. Any Catholic institution worthy of the name should have a good record in the fostering of religious vocations. Dunbarton College of the Holy Cross has been eminently successful in this. For example, in my daughter's class of thirty-five students, four have persevered in the religious life. It is significant also that these four did not all become Sisters of the Holy Cross, but entered other religious groups as well.

Another achievement of this college in which I have been much interested and which is worth recording is the fact that it has developed a Department of Theology, in which students may concentrate their studies. It has always been a great source of wonderment to me why Catholic institutions of higher education, which place such great importance on training in this field, have not established full-fledged departments of Theology or, if you will, Religious Education, in which students may do major work or concentrate. Surely, a four-year program of college work with its core in theology is most desirable and useful for almost any walk of life, professional or general. Dunbarton College has been the first to recognize this fact and to carry it out. It is to be hoped that other Catholic colleges will follow its example.

The Sisters of the Holy Cross still do me the honor of having me as their guest at Dunbarton College and occasionally of asking me for advice on college problems. I might add that the climax of this relationship was reached when my daughter graduated from the College as the valedictorian of her class, and then entered the Congregation of the Holy Cross, as Sister Teresa Mary.

The Catholic University of Puerto Rico

In 1948, Bishop James Edward McManus of Ponce in Puerto Rico, the southern diocese of the island, who had recently been made Bishop of that see, conceived the idea of establishing a Catholic University of Puerto Rico. It certainly was badly needed. The insular university located at Rio Piedras had all the faults of the average secular institution of higher education without many of the virtues. It was my privilege to have served on an evaluation team of the Middle States Association of Schools and Colleges for the University of Puerto Rico, and I was able to view it closely at first hand. I wish to state clearly that I am viewing that institution strictly as a place for Catholic youth to attend, and the views which I express here are entirely my own personal opinions. Of course, the institution professes to be non-sectarian but like so many colleges and universities of this type it is a teacher willy-nilly of agnosticism and religious indifference. Furthermore, I question seriously whether it is developing in its students any genuine love of learning for its own sake. Also, it is entangled with insular politics. It has always had this misfortune from the beginning, although at the time of its approval by the Middle States Association it had seemed fairly free of this blight. Certainly it was not a good institution for Catholics to attend. Bishop McManus also had almost in his backyard the Presbyterian Polytechnic Institute, which has recently changed its name to the Interamerican University! I need not mention such proselytizing groups as the Seventh Day Adventists and others which were trying to make inroads into the Catholic population. Catholics did have the College of the

Sacred Heart at Santurce, which several years ago received the approval of the Middle States Association of Colleges and Secondary Schools. In fact I evaluated that institution on one occasion for that Association. There were also several other institutions calling themselves colleges but not being really of college grade. Strictly, there was no institution of higher education, good enough to seek the approval of the regional association and conducted under Catholic auspices, which would appeal to the population of Puerto Rico in general and could compete with the insular University and the so-called Interamerican University conducted by the Presbyterians.

Bishop McManus felt this need greatly and determined to establish the Catholic University of Puerto Rico. At first Bishop Davis of San Juan, the northern diocese of the island, joined him in the project, the intention being for each Bishop to promote a branch of the C.U.P.R. in his diocese. A meeting was called at the San Morrow Officers Club in San Juan of all those interested in the idea and able in some way to contribute to carrying it out. Men of importance and wealth from both the northern as well as the southern diocese were invited to attend. Bishop McManus also invited Monsignor Edward Jordan, then Vice Rector of The Catholic University of America, and myself to be on hand. Although I had been in Puerto Rico for a week on a previous visit with the Commission on Higher Education of the Middle States Association, I enjoyed this second visit very much indeed. It was a distinct pleasure to watch Bishop McManus face the many problems that go with founding an institution of higher education and solve them by his wits alone. In the beginning it could be said that he had no funds whatsoever! At this first meeting great interest was manifested by those present. There was even some rivalry between the Southern and Northern Puerto Ricans in pledging funds. Actually, when the time came to collect these monies, they were forthcoming from only a few benefactors in the Ponce Diocese. In the meantime also Bishop Davis, while maintaining an interest in the University, gave up the idea of establishing a branch in his diocese because of the difficulties involved in establishing a Catholic University in the vicinity of the insular University. Thus the Catholic University of Puerto Rico became the responsibility strictly of Bishop McManus and the Diocese of Ponce.

During the first year, the University was housed in the building of the elementary school in Ponce conducted by the Capuchin Fathers, but in the following year the University had its own campus with an all purpose building and a science building under way. It has progressed very rapidly and soundly, and in 1953 received the approval of the Middle States Association of Schools and Colleges. It has a brilliant future in performing the work of the Church in Puerto Rico.

Addresses on Special Occasions

Primarily because of my many years of service in the University's work of affiliation, [1] and perhaps also by reason of my contribution to the development of accreditation chiefly through the Middle States Association of Colleges and Secondary Schools, I have often been called upon for talks on special occasions. Most of these may be placed in three categories: (1) Honors Day Convocations, (2) Institutional Anniversary Celebrations, and (3) Commencement Day Exercises. On these occasions I have always endeavored to prepare my remarks carefully, seeking to take advantage of these opportunities to advance the work of the University. It may not be out of place to present at least portions of one of the latest presentations in each class.

1. *Honors Day Convocations*

On September 24, 1958, I addressed the members of the faculty and the student-body at Dunbarton College of Holy Cross, Washington, D.C., who had gathered to do honor to those students who had achieved highest honors in the studies of the regular curriculum. It reflects my preoccupation with the fear that our Catholic colleges, especially those for women, are entirely too much con-

[1] Cf. Chapter on Affiliation.

cerned with superficialities, with the training of our young people in the amenities of social life rather than in the skillful use of the intellect.

The following quotations will be illustrative:

> The American Catholic college in its day to day existence consists of numerous facets if we were to analyse it in detail. Three phases, however, stand out as the chief elements, which, according as they are meshed together in proper proportions, give us an American Catholic college of excellence. The skill or lack of skill with which this amalgamation is carried out determines the degree of success of any college administration. These three phases are the spiritual, the social, and the intellectual. These three elements are not, of course, sealed off in separate compartments. In fact, it is sometimes difficult to determine where one ends and another begins. More often than not one of them, in order to produce its best effect, must have the cooperation of one of the others or of the other two. By and large, however, these three elements are distinctly discernible, and the wise administrator and even the college leader in the student body, whenever some phase of college life is being planned, will give serious consideration to them, and will lay appropriate stress on each as the particular activity seems to require.

> The great purpose of life in general, including all the activities that contribute to it, for individual, community, and country, is, of course, the spiritual, whether we wish to admit it or not, and whether or not we are conscious of the spiritual effect of any particular activity of our lives. The spiritual is the great over-all purpose to which everything that we experience contributes some-

thing, according as we make an effort to get the
most and the best out of what we do. A college
training is one of the many life experiences which,
if properly received and directed, contributes so
much to man's ultimate purpose in life. But we
must not think of it as being only or even chiefly
concerned with the spiritual. To anticipate slightly
what I wish to discuss in more detail later, the
intellect is very closely akin to the spirit, and is
without question its most powerful ally, but the
training and development of the intellect is the
immediate and primary purpose of any Catholic
college program. This is sometimes lost sight of,
I fear, by some administrators of our Catholic institutions, to the great detriment of the achievement of the spiritual aim itself. I can best illustrate
my point by the story of a text-book published
several years ago, in beginning biology. Assuming
that the statements with respect to biology were
correct, which in many instances were at least
questionable, the statements with reference to our
Creator and His divine plan, some of which might
well have been appropriately inserted, became so
numerous that one critic well said that it was difficult to determine whether the text-book was in
the field of biology or religious education. Surely
the teaching of biology, to say nothing about advancing the understanding of religion, cannot
prosper under such conditions. Such confusion in
the life of a college can be paralleled again and
again. Is a certain social function primarily religious or academic? If it is one or the other, the
costumes worn and the ceremonies will vary
greatly, and any confusion between the two becomes painfully evident to the observant spectator.
An excessive readiness to declare an academic
holiday, or to eliminate classes, ostensibly for the

promotion of piety or religious devotion fails almost surely to achieve its declared religious purpose and seriously obstructs the attainment of the intellectual and immediate aim of the institution. But this is enough to make my point clear, that the spiritual welfare of students is the ultimate aim of all Catholic colleges, which should, of course, be seriously concerned with making their proper contribution to it, but it is not the immediate aim, and any failure to understand this thoroughly will interfere that much with all the aims of the college, whether ultimate or immediate.

A college training is certainly expected to contribute to a student's ability to live in charity with his fellow human beings, to teach him how to be a successful social being, as Aristotle phrased it. This also is important, but of the three basic elements of college life it is the least important. As always, it contributes most to a student's development when kept within its proper sphere and when given its due emphasis and no more.

I have not mentioned the college's responsibility for the proper physical training of its students. On the basis of the benefits which specialists in the field claim for this training, it may well be considered an aspect of the social phase of college life. Examples of over-emphasis here are so numerous in institutions of higher education for men that in many parts of the world educators regard this as a regular feature of American education. To me it is nothing less than shocking to listen to a promising high school athlete being interviewed on radio or television, and to hear him say unashamedly that he chose to enter college "x" rather than college "y", because the authorities of college "x" gave him a more lucrative inducement, or because the director of athletics in that institution could direct him to the best opportunities in the professional phase of some sport. Are our American colleges to be used as proving grounds for prospective professional athletes? And what about the moral and intellectual integrity of those who induce our young people to spend four precious years of their lives for this purpose?

All these are examples of disproportionate emphasis and lack of integration. I hope that you do not get the impression that I am, as it were, playing down the religious and social activities of our Catholic colleges. Far from it. I am playing down their abuse, and I am pleading for a better understanding of their proper place in the college plan, that they may better perform their true functions.

The immediate and chief purpose of the college is the improvement and development of the intellect. You may have noticed that thus far I have not mentioned the word culture or any of its derivatives. Culture and cultural are very much over-worked words in the vocabulary of administrators of Catholic colleges for women. In fact, if we forgot them completely we would be much better off. We would save ourselves the temptation and the embarrassment of acquiring a very superficial veneer of this something which is called culture or cultural, and, which, when brought into contact with the real thing, rubs off quickly and displays the dross which lies underneath.

2. *Institutional Anniversary Celebrations*

At celebrations of college and university anniversaries, I was always troubled by the thought that an institution would become overly self-satisfied, very smug, and thereby cease to exert itself to the fullest in order to push ahead in the never-ending struggle of a college or university to improve itself. Without a chronic dissatisfaction with itself, an educational institution will become static and even deteriorate.

On July 31, 1958, I gave a brief address at the celebration of the tenth anniversary of the founding by Bishop McManus of the Catholic University of Puerto Rico. The following are excerpts from this talk.

It hardly seems possible that it was ten years ago when His Excellency, the Bishop of Ponce, invited the late Monsignor Edward Jordan, then Vice-Rector of The Catholic University of America, and myself to visit Puerto Rico and to join with him in his initial efforts to establish a Catholic University of Puerto Rico. The general idea was indeed attractive to me, since for a great many years I had been serving on the Commission on Institutions of Higher Education of the Middle States Association of Colleges and Secondary Schools, and during that time had visited in an official capacity for that Association both the College of the Sacred Heart at Santurce and the University of Puerto Rico at Rio Piedras. In the work of this Commission I had also heard much of the Presbyterian Polytechnic Institute, recently renamed the Interamerican University. During all this time, while I admired greatly the college work for women offered by the Religious of the Sacred Heart at Santurce, I felt keenly the lack of a strong Catholic University of Puerto Rico for both men and women, which could properly compete with both the insular university and such church related institutions of higher education which might be established by non-Catholic groups. To put it a little differently, I hoped that the people of Puerto Rico could enjoy such educational blessings as we on the continent were enjoying from The Catholic University of America.

On purely academic grounds and out of Christian charity, our Catholic educational institutions should be able to get along on friendly terms with their non-Catholic counterparts, having honest differences of opinion, to be sure, and yet permitting no compromise whatsoever with respect to religious doctrine. It is only when such elements as politics and misinterpretation of divine teachings, especially for selfish purposes, enter upon the scene that bitterness and recriminations arise and so much harm is done to a community and even to an entire country.

Catholics as Catholics, however, can prosper best only insofar as the spiritual, intellectual, and social elements of their lives grow and develop in due proportion and in proper relationship to one another. These three phases of life are influenced tremendously by a Catholic university. Indeed, it is difficult to see how any Catholic people can be truly prosperous and happy without at least one active Catholic university to permeate the very fibre of its structure. For me it is impossible to imagine any Catholic civilization without an active and influential Catholic university. The common belief that man needs to develop his intellect and his body, but that his spirit requires no special nutriment or cultivation is, of course, a very common and a very tragic mistake. This philosophy not uncommonly produces human monstrosities of a most repulsive kind. Moreover, this is the basic philosophy of our so-called non-sectarian and secular institutions of higher educa-

tion. It essentially denies divine grace and everything spiritual by ignoring them, and by forbidding
any serious discussion of the supernatural within
the classrooms. It is pitiful to hear university
students and the parents of these students say
with supreme confidence: "My Mary or Johnnie
can take good care of themselves in such surroundings. They have had a good home training." But
the influence of this atmosphere is much stronger
and more subtle than they realize. There is not
so much danger when one faces clear cut mis-
statements and calumny. With a moderate degree
of academic training one can recognize these and
refute them. But living from day to day in the
midst of complete indifference to the divine and
the spirtual will all too often cause one eventually
to succumb to this same indifference. Before he
realizes it, his faith is extremely weak or entirely
gone. Moreover, if you were to ask him how he
came to suffer this tragedy, he probably would be
at a complete loss to explain it.

Thoughts of this kind were running through
my mind for some years as I came in contact with
the educational institutions of Puerto Rico in my
work with the accrediting agencies, and as I looked
in vain for a Catholic university in this beautiful
island. Accordingly you may well imagine my delight when Bishop McManus made known his
plan ten years ago to establish a Catholic University of Puerto Rico.

We are here today to rejoice over the great
blessing which the Source of all blessings has
granted you in the Catholic University of Puerto
Rico through the instrumentality of Bishop Mc-
Manus. Although a great deal will always remain
to be done, His Excellency has indeed already accomplished much.

The Catholic University of Puerto Rico is an established fact. Its contribution to the educational life of the Island is manifest. You yourselves as individuals are experiencing its manifold blessings. In fact, it would be difficult today to conceive of the Island of Puerto Rico without its Catholic University.

A splendid faculty has been brought together. At this point we must pay our profound respect to the religious communities of men and women who have been cooperating with Bishop McManus in this great work.

An efficient administration has been established for this University. The percentage of good administrators in this institution has always been high. To avoid possible slips of memory, I will not mention them by name, but they include both nuns and priests.

The high and rising cost of conducting the Catholic University of Puerto Rico has thus far been met. I say "thus far" advisedly, because, as I have already intimated, this is a difficult problem indeed. Your Bishop needs all the support in this difficulty that he can get. I am told that the tuition fee here is nine dollars a semester hour of credit or point. This is not only amazing but really shocking, because there must be many developments which the Bishop would like to make in this University for the benefit of all of you, which he cannot possibly consider with such meager financial backing. I know that people cannot give what they do not have. I am only appealing to all of you to support the Catholic University of Puerto Rico with all that you possibly can contribute appropriately. The resulting benefits to you individually and to your people as a whole will be a thousand fold.

3. *Commencement Day Exercises*

Many indeed have been the invitations to give the chief address at the annual commencement day exercises of our Catholic colleges and universities. On each of these occasions I endeavored to give a new and worthwhile presentation. Sometimes I was also honored by being granted a degree *honoris causa.* [2]

The principle, to which I attempted to adhere closely, was never to talk on any topic with which I did not feel especially competent. It is, of course, a great temptation on occasions such as these to discuss some contemporary political problem, either of national or of world significance, and such discussions are usually very well received. This is the kind of commencement address that does *not* put an audience to sleep! If I have any special competence in any field, it is in college and university organization and administration and in the language and literatures of the Greek and Latin

[2] Honorary degrees:
LL.D. Providence College, Providence, R.I., 1939
L.H.D. St. John's U., Brooklyn, N.Y., 1945
Ed.D. St. Vincent's College, Latrobe, Pa., 1947
LL.D. St. Francis College, Loretto, Pa., 1947
LL.D. Notre Dame U., Notre Dame, Ind., 1948
LL.D. Iona College, Iona, N.Y., 1952
Litt.D. St. Michael's College, Winooski, Vt., 1953
Ed. D. Seton Hall University, South Orange, N.J., 1954
LL.D. Assumption College, Worcester, Mass., 1954
LL.D. Dunbarton College of Holy Cross, Washington, D.C., 1959
LL.D. Cardinal Stritch College, Milwaukee, Wis., 1959
Litt.D. Bellarmine College, Louisville, Ky., 1961
Ed.D. Villanova University, Philadelphia, Pa., 1961

Fathers of the Church; I fear that very little can be discovered here which will interest the usual commencement day gatherings.

At any rate, on June 1, 1953, I received the honorary degree [3] of Litt. D. at St. Michael's College in Winooski, Vermont, and gave an address, of which the following are significant excerpts:

FAITH FOR TODAY

Probably nothing that I shall say today will be new to you. However, I venture to present it because I believe it to be the heart and the great unifying force of your entire college training. It represents also the great difference between just a college training and a *Catholic* college training. I believe that as you are about to leave St. Michael's College, you might well meditate upon it. I am sure, knowing the Fathers of St. Edmund as I do, that they have given you a thorough understanding of this.

We believe that it can be truly said that the world, in no period of its history, has had any widely spread fullness of faith, although certain periods in some regions are regarded by historians as exhibiting the signs and the rewards of faith to a higher degree than others. We believe also that our own age exhibits no striking marks of a genuine revival and a really lasting growth of faith; on the contrary, the two world wars and the present cold and hot war are to us clearly the result of a spreading lack of faith.

[3] On this occasion also the Most Reverend Bryan J. McEntegart, then Bishop of Ogdensburg, N.Y., received the honorary degree of LL.D.

We do not wish to spend any great amount of our precious time defining the word "Faith." I believe that the following definition is acceptable to Catholics, but probably it is so to very few Protestants, since, as you will see, I base my definition on the intellect and discount the emotions. "Faith is the acceptance of God's message to mankind, based on His infinite wisdom and truthfulness. It is not a blind, illogical emotion, but is an intellectual act, arrived at only after one has reasonably assured himself that God has delivered a message to man. Faith is perfect and practical only when one adjusts his conduct to the truths of God's message."

We take it for granted that most, if not all of you are willing to believe that an increase and spread of such a faith as this is badly needed in our time, and that thus everything possible should be done to foster its growth and dissemination throughout the world. Surely it is not necessary for me to cite evidences of the decline of such a faith in our land. Corruption in government, character-assassination on the slightest provocation, and a wide-spread disrespect for what we know as fundamentalism in academic circles are only a few of such evidences.

With this understanding, we would like to address ourselves to only a phase or two of this vast subject. The American people are, by and large, tending to lose their faith in Christian doctrine—in large measure, because of their failure to appreciate any historical continuity between the teachings of Christianity today and the doctrines of Christ and His Disciples. In the minds of some a connection may be admitted between the Bible and modern discussions from the pulpit, but comparatively few recognize the steady and unbroken flow of Christian teaching throughout the intervening centuries. Probably the two chief causes of this are: the general decline in interest and the study of the languages in which these teachings are couched, chiefly Greek and Latin, and that special brand of American provincialism that is convinced that nothing worthwhile in the world's civilization ever happened before 1776 and that nothing at all worthy of note has occured outside the confines of the United States of America. In any case, the failure to appreciate this historical continuity may be a serious handicap to a growing faith; certainly it is casting aside a most powerful support for a strong faith.

All through my college and university years, I received a tremendous inspiration out of reading not only the Bible but the voluminous writings of the Fathers of the Church and of the later Medieval and Renaissance authors, and from discovering essential agreement through the ages on the teachings of my faith among all the great Christian leaders of those periods. Much of this teaching was not formally established as officially recognized Christian doctrine at the time when it was written, but there it was set forth by the great teachers of Christianity in diverse parts of the world. The inevitable conclusion for me to draw was that only under the influence of God's grace could such a phenomenon possibly take place. When, in the early second century of our era, the Church at Corinth wrote to the Church at Rome for the solution of some of its difficulties, occasioned by the resulting confusion after the death of St. Paul, and I was able to read the reply of Pope Clement of Rome to his brethren in Corinth, I was truly inspired. In spite of what certain theological and literary critics may say to the contrary, here was a definite recognition of Rome as the first see of the world and of the Pope, the bishop of that see, as the source of true doctrinal guidance. I was confirmed even more in my feeling when I picked up the letter of St. Cyprian of Carthage, who flourished in the middle of the third century, written to defend the unity of the Church and its leadership in Rome. I was inspired too when I read some of the writings of that great Roman citizen, St. Ambrose (340-397), who was the first to set forth clearly to all the people that there was another force in the world besides the Roman Empire which was interested in their welfare, moreover, upon whose authority the Roman emperor might not encroach. It was St. Ambrose, in the fourth century, who first stated unequivocally that principle which has been greatly perverted in modern times, of the separation of Church and State when he said to the Emperor himself: "In questions affecting the faith, it is the Bishops who are judges of the Emperors and not the Emperors who are judges of the Bishops." There was no danger or even fear, in those days, of the Church impinging on the rights of the State, but rather of the State carrying on its pagan role of the sole dominating force in every phase of life, spiritual as well as temporal. Sober reflection will disclose that contemporary conditions in the world have changed little, if at all, in this respect, in spite of the apparent concern of a few groups. Certainly there is no likelihood or danger of the Church authorities ever dreaming of taking over

any of the prerogatives of the State. Immunity of
the Church, however, against encroachments on
the part of civil powers is no fantastic dream,
and like the early Christians we must be eternally
on our guard against it.

The Daughters of St. Paul

It would be a genuine pleasure indeed if I were
able to include in my recollections at least a few
words about every   religious community, both of
men and of women, to which I have in any way been
of assistance in the advancement of its work. Obviously this is impossible. I can speak only of several with which in one way or another I have worked
especially closely. Among these few I feel that I
must speak of the Daughters of St. Paul because of
the unique nature of their work and because of their
very recent acquaintance. In 1957 this group cele-
brated the twenty-fifth anniversary of its establishment in the United States, and it was only late in
1957 that I became acquainted with these Sisters
and even knew of their existence.

Early in January of 1958 I visited Mother Paula
Cordero, the Reverend Mother Provincial of the
Daughters of St. Paul, in her convent located at
50 St. Paul's Avenue, Boston, Massachusetts, for
the purpose of establishing and helping to develop
a secondary school for the training of the postulants
and novices of the community. After completing
their secondary school program, these prospective

nuns were to attend any one of the regularly established institutions of higher education in the area.
I was introduced to them by the Right Reverend
Timothy J. O'Leary,[1] Superintendent of Schools of
the Archdiocese of Boston, with the consent and
approval of His Eminence, Richard Cardinal Cushing, Archbishop of Boston.

It was then that I learned of the very special
work of the Daughters of St. Paul. As Cardinal
Cushing has expressed it: "The special purpose of
the Pious Society of the Daughters of St. Paul con-
sists in this: that the religious work with all their
energies for the glory of God and the salvation of
souls in the spreading of Catholic doctrine with the
apostolate of the editions: press, cinema, radio,
television, and in general with the most expeditious
and fruitful means; that is, the inventions which
human progress furnishes and the necessities and
the conditions of the times require." Mother Paula
then introduced me to the community at work in
the press room, and to the many works already produced and in circulation. I learned of their
promotional activities, not only through the book-
stores conducted by the nuns but also by the actual
door-to-door coverage of the region as they go
around not only diffusing their publications but also
answering the multitudinous questions regarding
the Faith raised by those they meet.

[1] I take this occasion to thank Monsignor O'Leary for the generous cooperation given me, with the consent of His Eminence
Richard Cardinal Cushing, in the University's work of "affiliation"
within the Archdiocese of Boston.

On the very first day of our meeting, we arranged for the publication of my "Latin-English
Dictionary of St. Thomas Aquinas," and only a few
months later, after a very inspiring and interesting
conference with Mother Paula, planned additional
publications of my own and of others. I anticipate a
very fruitful and edifying collaboration with these
industrious and pious women.

The English Translation of
the Works of the Fathers of the Church

Shortly after I arrived at the University, when
it became evident that the reorganized Department
of Greek and Latin would prosper, Bishop Shahan
reported a very interesting conversation which he
had had with His Eminence James Cardinal Gibbons. It seems that they had been discussing the
new arrangement and organization of the Department, and Cardinal Gibbons remarked that he
hoped that some day, after I had trained a sufficient
number of young scholars in the Patristic languages
and literatures, I would plan and carry through a
new series of English translations of these Greek
and Latin works to supplant the existing Pre-Nicene
and Nicene and Post-Nicene Series of translations.
The idea certainly was in order, since the anti-
Catholic bias of these two series is nothing short of
shocking to those who use them. The authors of

some of these volumes, writing in the heat of the
Oxford movement, e.g., the translators of the works
of St. Cyprian and St. Augustine, go far beyond the
province of translators in their interpretations, even
openly attacking fundamental doctrines and beliefs
of the Church. It is true, of course, that these remarks apply especially to the later American editions and adaptations of the original English series.
In any case, new translations were badly needed
also in the light of our better knowledge of Patristic
Greek and Latin, better critical editions, and also
for the sake of contemporary English. Accordingly,
from those earliest days I had always had this important project in mind. I should add that, whenever I have repeated this observation of Cardinal
Gibbons, my listeners have always been quite surprised that the Cardinal had exhibited such a
knowledge of scholarship. Evidently His Eminence
had much more of an intellectual interest in literature than most people realized.

The development of competent young scholars
within the Department of Greek and Latin had
gone on most successfully; there were soon enough
co-workers available to commence work, but the
necessary financial support to launch the project
was still lacking. The University authorities had
been approached on the matter during the rectorship of Bishop McCormick, but the wisdom of going
forward with the work was not evident to them.
The financial consideration as usual was the great
obstacle. As far as I personally was concerned the
idea of the series lay dormant for many years.

A small group at the University later approached the University administration again, not only regarding the publication of a series of English translations of the Fathers but also for the publication of a periodical covering the same field. This petition also was turned down. It seems, however, that Dr. Ludwig Schopp of New York City had been toying with a similar plan. He wrote: [1] "In the summer of 1936 I first conceived the plan of publishing a series of the Fathers in English. In this venture I was encouraged by my old teacher and friend, the great scholar A. Dyroff." The University group and Dr. Schopp soon met, and a series of English translations of the works of the Greek and Latin Fathers, as well as a periodical dealing with their literary problems were planned. I heard of this venture only indirectly. For reasons best known to themselves I was definitely to be excluded. Since I felt that I was extremely busy with publication projects of my own, I suffered no serious grievance over being ignored. In fact, I wished them all possible success in a work which I desired very much to see accomplished but felt at the time that I could not do myself. I supported it on every possible occasion.

Certain members of the group from the University and Dr. Schopp soon came to the parting of the ways. As to the merits on either side of this bitter quarrel, I cannot and would not say. The outcome, however, in a sense was unfortunate in that it resulted in a duplication of effort and expense in

[1] Vol. I, The Fathers of the Church, p. iv.

an important work which needed all the support that it could get financially and otherwise. Several of the University men decided to go their own way and to set up a series of their own. Thus there came into being the series known as "The Ancient Christian Writers," a thorough and careful set of works in every respect, although the practicability of its general plan in relation to its purpose may be questioned.

Meanwhile, in 1947, Dr. Schopp and his group published the first volume of the series known as "The Fathers of the Church," about which Dr. Schopp wrote in the preface: "This series of seventy-two [2] volumes will present outstanding patristic writings and include some works never translated before. The translations, although done by American Catholic scholars, are destined neither for scholars only, nor exclusively for Catholics, but for the entire English speaking world." The first number of the projected periodical appeared under the name of "Traditio" shortly before the break.

In the meantime another development took place in the personnel of the Editorial Board of the series. I was visited in my office at the University by Dr. Schopp and two mutual friends, and received an urgent invitation to join the Editorial Board. I gave it long and careful consideration and

[2] I never had been able to discover from Dr. Schopp himself or anyone else what determined the number of seventy-two volumes. It seems to be quite an arbitrary figure. Some have suggested that it may have a symbolic reason, since 72 is the traditional number of the disciples of Christ.

after a month decided to join the project. There was much in this entire affair, besides the many irons of my own which I had in the fire, to give me pause. Thus Volume I appeared under an Editorial Board composed of the following: Ludwig Schopp, Editorial Director; Rudolph Arbesmann, O.S.A., Fordham University; Roy Joseph Deferrari, The Catholic University of America; Stephen Kuttner, The Catholic University of America; Wilfrid Parsons, S.J., The Catholic University of America; Bernard M. Peebles, St. Johns College, Annapolis, Md.; Anselm Strittmatter, O.S.B., St. Anselm's Priory, Washington, D.C.; and Gerald G. Walsh, S.J., Fordham University.

In 1949, after six volumes of the Series had appeared, repercussions of trouble within the Editorial Board reached my ears. It should be mentioned here that Father Gerald G. Walsh, S.J., had been a loyal supporter of Dr. Schopp in this project. It was largely through Father Walsh's intercession that I finally decided to join Dr. Schopp's group. Father Walsh was very properly greatly alarmed over the unsystematic and unbusinesslike procedure of Dr. Schopp in his conduct of the affairs of the Series and insisted on an immediate reform. If this did not take place, he threatened to withdraw from the work. This, of course, would have been most damaging to the cause, and Dr. Schopp was greatly alarmed. He asked me to visit him and his lawyer in New York, which I did promptly. It happened that Dr. Schopp had had a serious heart attack recently, and this also had added to his anxiety over the Series. Briefly, our meeting amounted to this. Dr. Schopp was very anxious to know if, in the event that Father Walsh withdrew from the Editorial Board, I would still remain on it. As much as I had always admired and respected Father Walsh as a priest, scholar, and gentleman, I did not see any justification in my withdrawing from the Board if he decided to do so. Then Dr. Schopp asked whether, if he should be fatally stricken, I would be willing to take over the responsibility of the scholarly aspects of the Series, provided Mr. Raymond McCourt took over the financial side and Dr. James Tobin the task of putting each volume through press. I agreed to this. A few days later Dr. Schopp called me in my office by telephone and stated that he was coming to Washington the next day with his lawyer to draw up the proper papers which would legalize such a disposition of the Series in the event of his death. Dr. Schopp never kept that appointment. That very afternoon Dr. Arbesmann called me by telephone to inform me that Dr. Schopp had died suddenly.

The entire Editorial Board attended Dr. Schopp's funeral in New York, after which we had a luncheon meeting in a neighboring hotel. At this meeting the Editorial Board unanimously elected me Editorial Director of the Series. I had made it clear that I was by no means eager to take over the editorial responsibilty; furthermore, that if anyone had the slightest disinclination to receive me in that capacity, I would by no means accept it. I should add that we were all happy to find Father Gerald Walsh among us and eager to contribute to the new regime of the Series.

All the records and manuscripts of the Series were turned over to me. Unfortunately, there was little, if anything, worthwhile in the way of records and nothing of the nature of a manuscript that might be regarded as properly organized as a volume in the Series. In fact there was no systematic arrangement of any kind whatsoever. It was difficult to see how the Series could have continued much longer in its existing state of chaos. A completely new plan, or better stated, a plan had to be devised for the entire Series; all assignments had to be rearranged to form appropriate as well as adequate volumes. From the records I received, it was difficult to understand how the number of seventy-two volumes for the Series had been determined. After surveying all the available material, a minimum of one hundred volumes seemed much more realistic. Furthermore, what could possibly have been the purpose of restricting the contributions of the Series to Americans? Certainly anyone with the proper qualifications should be invited to cooperate in this grand work. In my efforts to establish a sound and practical plan, I was assisted greatly by my University assistant, Miss Rita Watrin. Thanks to her help, in a comparatively short time all was in good working order, and any information about the Series could be obtained in a moment's notice. This plan is now being followed and all is going smoothly. The

Series has now reached its forty-third volume, and at the moment we have a backlog of about ten outstanding typescripts awaiting publication.

The Editorial Board, which a few years ago suffered a great loss in the death of Father Gerald Walsh, and very recently that of Father Wilfrid Parsons, is now constituted as follows: Roy Joseph Deferrari, The Catholic University of America, Editorial Director; Rudolph Arbesmann, O.S.A., Fordham University; Stephen Kuttner, The Catholic University of America; Martin R. P. McGuire, The Catholic University of America; Bernard M. Peebles, The Catholic University of America; Robert P. Russell, O.S.A., Villanova University; Anselm Strittmatter, O.S.B., St. Anselm's Priory; and James Edward Tobin, Queens College.

Mention certainly should be made of the Dougherty family of Beeville, Texas, and the great interest in the Series on the part of its members from the very beginning. Judge James R. Dougherty essentially made it possible for the Series to begin. Without his substantial support it could never have been started. He showed a genuine interest in the work subsequently until his death. His widow and his son, Dudley T. Dougherty, have continued his concern for the Series, and the members of the Editorial Board are greatly indebted to them.

The Series has always been a private venture, just as was *Traditio*, the journal established at the same time. After the death of Dr. Schopp, *Traditio* was successfully transferred to Fordham University, where it is having a very successful history. It is to be hoped that in the interest of stability and continuity the Series, The Fathers of the Church, can be similarly transferred to some creditable institution of higher education. My choice of such an institution would, of course, be The Catholic University of America.

It is my pleasure to be able to record that as of May, 1961, the Series has been successfully transferred to The Catholic University of America Press. We all wish to thank Mrs. James R. Dougherty of Beeville, Texas for her indispensible assistance in making this transfer possible. All inquiries relative to these publications should be addressed to the C.U.A. Press. According to present plans I am to continue as editorial director until such time as my successor in the position can be obtained. I have several projects to which I would like to devote the remaining years of my life, and do not feel that I can spare much of my time to this Series.

We are certainly most grateful to Divine Providence for bringing the Series of the "Fathers of the Church" to the Catholic University, and for thus fulfilling the desire of His Eminence James Cardinal Gibbons that a Catholic English version of the writings of the Fathers of the Church be produced at the University. I hope that it is not too much to desire that the Series of the "Ancient Christian Writers" will soon be amalgamated with that of the "Fathers of the Church" under the auspices of The Catholic University of America. This would fulfill the earnest wish of the recent Papal Delegate to the United States, His Eminence Amleto Cardinal Gicognani that there be one American edition of the Fathers of the Church in English.

The United States
Education Mission to Japan

At least two education missions had already been sent to Europe before the Education Mission to Japan had been planned, directly after the close of World War II. On these Catholic education had not been represented, not even on the one sent to Italy, which naturally irritated Catholic educators greatly. Moreover, they were dominated completely by secularistic educators, who were in the habit of thinking of all public education in terms of the secular scheme prevailing in the United States. A group so made up in this case might not have hurt the feelings of Japanese people, since for the previous century or more they had been experiencing a strictly secularized educational system based on that of the Republic of France. But Catholic educators were still smarting under their experience of previous education missions, and when General Douglas MacArthur requested an education mission for Japan and among his suggested members did not name a single Catholic educator, the complaints from Catholic sources, in particular the weekly *America*, were loud and numerous.

It seems that the successful approach to the Department of State for Catholic representation on the Mission was made for the National Catholic Welfare Conference by Monsignor Frederick Hochwalt, although Father Patrick O'Connor, a Columban Father and a representative of the N.C.W.C. in Japan, independently made a direct approach to General Douglas MacArthur on the matter. The latter resulted in General MacArthur cabling the State Department to this effect: "Send two Catholic educators on Mission, President of Georgetown University and President of the University of Notre Dame, or educators of equal calibre." However, by the time this cablegram reached the United States, Monsignor Hochwalt and I had been appointed by the State Department, on the recommendation of the Department of Education of the N.C.W.C. I later asked Father O'Connor whether he had recommended the two university presidents to General MacArthur on the basis of the high repute of their respective football teams, and was answered frankly: "Yes!" (It should be noted that at this time Georgetown University, as well as Notre Dame, was a great power in football!)

On this Mission the Department of State was responsible for all educational matters of the Mission, and the War Department for everything else, e.g., means of travel, accommodations, and the general well-being of the members of the Mission. While it is not my intention here to go into the details, I would like simply to state first of all what the Mission was supposed to accomplish, and then what actually did result from it. I shall also describe some of the more interesting incidents in which I participated.

Some of the ideas set forth in our early conferences are especially worthy of note. Our mission was to bear in mind the two chief points of the peace treaty: (1) Japan must never be permitted to become a menace to the peace of the East; (2) the Japanese should be encouraged to formulate a government of their own toward this end. All the schools in Japan were then running in the usual peace-time manner. [1] The revision of textbooks had been going on for about two months by the Japanese themselves. Here, as in similar circumstances, the Japanese were at a loss as to what to use in place of the old propaganda material. The Japanese as a whole had to learn what the democratic process is which replaces the force, the propaganda, the dictation of a totalitarian state. Our mission would be expected to give advice on such education as was already in operation, also to suggest further developments and improvements. Our group was not to think of going to Japan with any idea of setting up a perfect educational system according to its own thinking. We were to stimulate the Japanese to do something of this kind by themselves. Our work, however was to include all education, from the very beginning through the university. I put in a plea for a careful consideration of the problem of mak-

[1] When we arrived in Japan, however, we learned from first hand observers that in the country and out-lying districts schools were still being conducted in the recent militaristic manner.

ing provision for genuine religious instruction in the public schools according to the choice of the student or his parents. This was not received very enthusiastically but the chairman did write it down for future consideration. It seemed that Christians regularly go to their own schools and not to the public schools, because of the necessity of Emperor-worship in the latter. I also raised the question as to whether or not our job included the private as well as the public schools. I pleaded that strictly there were no private schools in the sense that they had a right to operate entirely as they pleased, completely cut off from all other educational activities. Some of the group demurred at this, but Mr. Gordon Bowles, Department of State representative and our official adviser on matters pertaining to the Far East, was quite enthusiastic in his opinion that private schools should be included in our study. Actually, when the final report was written, no consideration at all was given to private educational institutions and it was only with difficulty that a statement of complete freedom for religious teaching was included. [2] It was also decided that we must do something for the education of Japanese women, which apparently had reached a very low ebb.

The official name of our group was finally settled as "Advisory Group on Japanese Education." As a matter of fact this title was rarely if ever used, but the title given us at the very beginning and

[2] See below.

which entitles this section persisted. We were divided into the following committees, [3] which on arrival
in Japan were to work with corresponding committees made up of Japanese educators, all under
the general supervision of the "Civilian Information on Education Division."

    I. General Administration.
        Stoddard, A. J.— Chairman
        Ely, Kermit
        Givens, Willard Earl
        Hochwalt, Very Reverend Frederick G.
        Norton, Ethelbert B.
        Wanamaker, Pearl.

    II. Psychology and Attitudes
        Freeman, F. W.—Chairman
        Benjamin, Harold
        Hilgard, Ernest R.
        Johnson, Charles S.
        Trow, William Clark
        Woodward, Emily

    III. Curriculum, Language and Philosophy
        Kandel, Isaac L.—Chairman
        Carnovsky, Leon
        Counts, George
        McCloy, Charles H.
        Smith, Lt. Col. Thomas V.
        Reverend Iglehart, a late arrival and last
          minute appointment.

    IV. Teacher, Education and Higher Education
        Diemer, George W.—Chairman
        Deferrari, Roy J.
        Compton, Wilson M.

[3] Bowles, Stewart (of the State Department), and G.P. Stoddard
were members of all committees.

Gildersleeve, Virginia
Horton, Mildred McAfee
Stevens, David H.

Toward the end of our mission, Father Patrick O'Connor called my attention to a very interesting matter. Mrs. McAfee Horton, President of Wellesley College and a member of our group, presented the following letter to Emperor Hirohito. It is ostensibly a letter written by Harry Truman, then President of the United States, to her husband, a very active Protestant missionary.

October 1, 1946

My dear Dr. Horton:

I am happy to know that the Federal Council of Churches of Christ in America will send a deputation to Japan for the purpose of conferring with Japanese Christians.

In my opinion, if Japan is to evolve into a peaceful nation, with an international as against a nationalistic outlook, she must understand and appreciate the religious forces of the world. As General MacArthur so well stated following the surrender of Japan on September 2, 1945:

"The problem basically is theological and involves a spiritual recrudescence and improvement of human character that will synchronize with our almost matchless advance in science, art, literature, and all material and cultural developments of the past 2,000 years. It must be of the spirit, if we are to save the flesh.

Your deputation should in a large measure aid in solving this fundamental problem facing Japan.

Very sincerely yours,
(Signed) HARRY TRUMAN

The Reverend Douglas Horton, D.D.
287 Fourth Avenue
New York 10, New York

I had been conscious of a very strong evangelical Protestant missionary group working in and around our mission. It struck me first on Guam, when Mrs. Horton and Miss Gildersleeve were quite surprised by the fact that ninety per cent of the Guamanians were Catholics and ten per cent Baptists, and resolved to make a special report to the Department of State on the school system there. Whether or not they did so, I do not know. I could not get it out of my head that Mrs. Horton was also thinking of possible Protestant proselytizing there. Then at the last minute Mr. Iglehart, a Japanese missionary of long standing, was added to our mission. He gave little evidence during the remainder of the Mission of being aware of educational problems. Of course, the chief State Department official on our mission was the son of Protestant missionaries, who himself was born and had lived most of his early life in Japan. Also, in Japan we were joined by a Mr. Durgin, who was a freshman at Dartmouth College when I was a senior there. He had spent many years in Japan as a Y.M.C.A. secretary, and, of course, he was very close to this group. It seemed to me that they knew and realized the importance of the contemporary crisis in Japan for the spread of Christianity and they were going to take every advantage of it in the interest of Protestantism.

I talked about this matter to Catholic missionaries and Catholic army chaplains, who seemed well aware of it. However, they were not alarmed. Father Roggendorf, the Dean of Sophia University, typified their attitude very well when he said: "It is very easy to win the Japanese people to Catholicism. When we are pitted against Protestant missionaries, man to man, we have no difficulty. But we do need workers." Fortunately, these have to a large extent been supplied.

It is difficult to gauge to what extent the "Advisory Group on Japanese Education" achieved its aims as I have set them forth above. There was certainly an extensive revision of textbooks. This is evident. How deeply the Advisory Group succeeded in injecting a philosophy of freedom in education is anybody's guess. Clearly the mechanism in education which is responsible for freedom in education here in the United States was not adopted, and I would not say that the Japanese people enjoy it to any great degree as we do in this country. The Advisory Group had been very much impressed by the difficulty of the language problem, and actually recommended the adoption of Romaji, or the use of the Roman alphabet in place of the difficult native Japanese symbols. It was, of course, too much to expect that the Japanese people would break so completely with their past as to abandon their alphabet. As the

Catholic missionaries told us, we were wasting our time when we made this recommendation.

The one thing in which the Apostolic Delegate, Archbishop Paul Morella, and all the Catholic missionaries were interested was a strong recommendation for freedom in the practice and teaching of religion. "If we get that," his Excellency said, "we shall be quite satisfied." Unfortunately, Monsignor Hochwalt was obliged to return to the United States about ten days before the end of our work and the day before we started to put together a complete draft of our report to General McArthur. This left me alone in a group of educators, who, almost to a person, did not favor bringing religion into education. On the very first evening when the group met as a whole to begin the final draft of the report, the Committee on Education in Japan at the Elementary and Secondary level brought in the following statement for approval: "As the first step in that direction, (i.e., toward a new philosophy, new procedure and new structure and form) we recommend the discontinuance of partisan political, or religious teaching in the schools." This, it seemed to me, was poorly phrased and could be dangerous, and I succeeded in getting it emended to read: "As the first step in that direction, we recommend the discontinuance of partisan political or *sectarian* religious teaching in the *public schools*." I was trying desperately for the inclusion somewhere in the report of a statement on the importance of religion in any educational system and did succeed in getting the following into the report of our committee on higher education: "Religion is an important part of study and of life. We approve of having in every institution of higher education freedom for each student to study and practice the religion of his choice." However, Archbishop Marella and the Catholic educators were satisfied with what we had done and felt that it would give them the freedom which they needed to teach Catholicism in Catholic schools.

The most exasperating and effective opponent in this group against any serious consideration of religion in Japanese education was Professor T. V. Smith, then of Chicago University, a member of the United States Army's educational group that worked in Italy and about whose work there I had heard much in the States. One evening at supper I sat next to Professor Smith. As an Army Colonel he had been in charge of running the schools of Italy during the occupation. I wish to record the gist of his remarks for whatever they may be worth. He insisted that his group never eliminated a single statement about religion from the textbooks of the Italian schools, but only improved the very inferior quality of book-making as exhibited in these books. He insisted further that the Church in Italy, from the Holy Father down, was entirely satisfied with their work. "All the kicking came from the N.C. W.C. in Washington and other people stimulated by the N.C.W.C." He was particularly angry at a Monsignor, now a Bishop in the United States, who allegedly spear-headed a movement to oust him and a man named Washburne from their jobs.

One of our trips was to the city of Kyoto and the Imperial University located there. We had several meetings at the University with the Japanese counterpart of our own Committee on Higher Education. We also had several meetings with a very interesting Catholic group consisting of two Catholic chaplains, Colonel Connelly and another chaplain whose name escapes me, the then Monsignor Byrne (later as a Bishop martyred in Korea), and a French-Canadian Dominican, Father Pouliot. They were especially interested in having me propose to the pagan President of Kyoto University, during any one of my meetings with him, that he establish a chair of medieval philosophy in his Imperial University. I was to tell him that I could get the money if he would establish the chair. The priests had a pagan friend who was willing to supply the necessary funds. They agreed that the Catholics of Japan needed a Catholic University of Japan very badly, as the present Sophia University, conducted by the German Jesuits and located in Tokyo, did not serve this purpose. Because they felt that they could not afford such a university for a long time to come, they were trying to do the next best thing: establish a chair of Catholic philosophy in some one or more of the existing non-Catholic universities. Of course, I promised to do all I could. The opportunity came very promptly for me to approach the President of the University of Kyoto on the matter. At first he was hesitant. Then he called his Professor of Philosophy, who happened to be near, into a short consultation, after which he returned to me, shook hands, and promised to set up the chair if the funds were forthcoming. Quite jubilant over the result of my conference, I rushed to the home of Father Pouliot with the good news, but the Professor of Philosophy had arrived there ahead of me, equally as jubilant. He happened to be taking instructions from Father Pouliot to become a Catholic. Several days later Monsignor Hochwalt joined me in Osaka to approach Mr. Torri, a Buddhist man of wealth but interested in the Church, for the necessary funds to complete our arrangements with the President of Kyoto University. Mr. Torri was very willing to do his part. When I returned to the United States, one of the first items which I read in the newspapers was that the Imperial University of Kyoto had established a chair of medieval philosophy and that Father Pouliot, O.P., was the first incumbent.

In relating this incident, mention was made of the late Maryknoller, Bishop Byrne. I met him several times during my stay in Tokyo, usually at Sophia University. One morning he called me from the lobby of the Imperial Hotel and asked to speak with me in my room. I was very happy to receive him. It seemed that there were some Bibles in Japanese at the residence of Archbishop Peter Tatsuo Doi, the Archbishop of Tokyo, which the then Monsignor Byrne wished to have transported to Sophia University where he was conducting religious instructions. At this time, transportation was one of the most difficult problems in war-torn Tokyo. I used my privilege as a member of the

"Advisory Group" to commandeer a car, and we went out to the Archbishop's residence for the Bibles. Moreover, I was eager to meet Archbishop Doi. I found him to be very much what he was said to be: a very saintly man without a great deal of energy. His cathedral had been entirely destroyed by bombing and only a small part of the wall was standing. He was holding services in a room on the first floor of his house, entirely too small for the purpose.

Mention should also be made of my meeting with Bishop Paul Yoshigaro Taguchi of Osaka, whom Colonel Connolly took me to see. On the way we stopped at a bakery and bought some bread to bring to the Bishop. We found him ill in bed with a fever, but he was gracious enough to receive us there. He talked about his American friends, especially Bishop Gerald P. O'Hara, then of Savannah. Most of his churches were destroyed by bombing, and his great problem was how to rebuild them with little or no funds. However, being a man of boundless energy, he has succeeded amazingly well in his rebuilding program. During the war he was drafted, as were all other clergymen of every denomination, and he became an ordinary seaman on an airplane carrier, swabbing the decks and doing all the other menial duties of a gob. The government officials, however, soon found that he was a man of great importance in the Church, and used him as a "front" at public gatherings in the Philippines to give the people of these islands the impression that the Church was behind the militaristic government of Japan. When I returned to the United States, I met a Sister of the Holy Cross who had been in the Philippine Islands at the time and had seen him. It was for this reason that General MacArthur and his staff always looked upon his Excellency with suspicion. I do not wish to cast any aspersions on Bishop Taguchi. In situations such as this it is difficult to evaluate all the circumstances involved and to establish blame.

A few words must be said about Sophia University and its splendid group of priests of the Society of Jesus. During the militaristic regime of Japan and under severe pressures, many Catholics, including some of the native clergy, defected. The superiors of Sophia University very deservedly took great pride in the fact that no one of their native clergy fell away. About half of their institution had been bombed out of existence, but they already had bought much adjoining land and had plans made for a great expansion. This, I am told, has been carried out. I became especially well acquainted with Father Roggendorf, the Dean trained in Oxford, and I shall always cherish this friendship. It was through the kindness of these priests that I was able to telephone my family, about whom I was very much concerned since I had left my wife in very poor health.

On the first day after our arrival in Tokyo, in the evening after supper, Monsignor Hochwalt and I got our permission to visit Archbishop Paul Marella, Apostolic Delegate to the Japanese Empire, whom I had known as a Secretary in the household of then Archbishop Pietro Fumasoni-Biondi, Apostolic Delegate to the United States. We had a government car and driver at our service as did all the members of the group. After some difficulty we located the Archbishop in an old estate which he had hired and which was itself considerably battered up. He had been in his summer home in the mountains when the bombing, which completely destroyed the Apostolic Delegation, took place. He was now living in this wretched house next door. There was no heat in the building except for a small electric heater in one room where we were received. All alone except for a Belgian priest and one or two men servants, he was extremely glad to see us, and we had some difficulty in tearing ourselves away. It was important that we do so early, since the cold was visibly affecting us. On leaving, we had to promise Archbishop Marella that we would visit him once more before we returned to the United States. Monsignor Hochwalt was unable to make this final visit, but I was very anxious and eager to do so. I wished especially to inform him of the results of our efforts to include in our recommendations freedom to teach and practice religion. His Excellency was very much pleased with the total result. On leaving he even walked out to the car, a courtesy which I highly appreciated. He gave me a letter to mail to Archbishop James H. Ryan and spoke about all his friends to whom he wished to be remembered on my return to the United States.

Some time after my return I received the following letter from his Excellency:

Tokyo, April 8, 1946

Apostolic Delegation
12 Shinryudo-Cho
Azabu-Ku   Tokyo, Japan

MY DEAR PROFESSOR:

Please accept my heartfelt thanks for your diligent and successful work here. I was edified by your filial attachment to the Church and your painstaking care that nothing may be done or suggested against our Holy Faith. May God reward you! That famous *correction* has gone through very good. I have now under my eyes the report just published yesterday. . . .

I am sure you found Mrs. Deferrari and your daughter well. Please come again!

Yours very gratefully,
(Signed)   PAUL MARELLA

RECTORS UNDER WHOM
I HAVE SERVED

Bishop Thomas J. Shahan
1909-1927

Under Bishop Shahan I served from 1918 until the end of his administration in 1927. He was a very kindly and sympathetic gentleman, handicapped greatly by the physical defect of almost complete deafness. His rectorship carried the University through a very critical period. The Board of Trustees had not yet learned to consider the University their joint responsibility. On the other hand, Bishop Shahan, a disciple of Cardinal Gibbons, was still under the influence of the formative years of the University, when the institution's existence was due at least at times to the courage and loyalty of Cardinal Gibbons alone, and some of the trustees

were interested in it chiefly with a view to putting
an end to it. Consequently, Bishop Shahan kept the
serious problems of the University, on which he
needed and should have had the support of his
trustees, to himself. He was not ready to take them
into his confidence. As Bishop Shahan once said to
me: "It takes generations to build up institutions,
but they can be destroyed overnight." This thought
seemed to haunt him at times. As subsequent events
have shown, the hostility of some of the members
of the Board of Trustees, which once existed, had
come to an end with the passing of the individuals
concerned, and it was left to Bishop Shahan's successor to bring the Board of Trustees into its right-
ful position in relation to the institution.

Not having the support of the trustees (some
referred to the University facetiously as the University of the Archdiocese of Baltimore), Bishop
Shahan's financial problems were terrific. The annual collection for the benefit of the University,
while indispensable, was comparatively a pittance,
and the University lived truly a hand-to-mouth existence. The procurator of the time told me that on
many occasions he had to borrow funds from the
banks to get enough money to pay current monthly
salaries. Drawing upon endowments and legacies
to meet pressing financial obligations, the forbidden sin of institutional finance, was resorted to because of the extreme urgency of the circumstances.
Yet Bishop Shahan stuck to the task which he
thought most important for the University at the
time, the development of the physical plant. Of

course, he obtained some funds from private sources, as in the case of the Library building, but even such as he received in this manner was always very inadequate for his plans. In such emergencies he resorted to what some critics called "bob-tailed buildings." Bishop Shahan himself frankly said to me that if you have an unfinished building on your campus, you have a very strong talking point for solliciting more funds. Thus the uncompleted buildings multiplied under Bishop Shahan, but who can say that it was not a good thing for the University? They were all indeed badly needed.

I recall that the Association of American Universities had met at least once on the campus of every member institution except on that of The Catholic University of America. The officers of the Association, becoming impatient, openly invited themselves on several occasions, but Bishop Shahan steadfastly refused to acknowledge the very unsubtle approaches until the Library building was well underway. Then he sent the Association of American Universities a very polite invitation to be the guest of the University on the occasion of its forthcoming annual meeting. "Now we have something to show them," he said to me.

Bishop Shahan recognized and appreciated genuine scholarship. He was the chief driving force in the organization and compilation of the Catholic Encyclopedia. He himself told me that he translated the well-known Patrology of O. Bardenhewer on the train when making numerous trips between Washington and New York in this connection. He was, however, destined not to advance the University in productive scholarship but to give it the fundamental buildings so greatly needed. He is often called the scholar among the Rectors, yet he cannot be called a very productive scholar. He published comparatively little but he was an omnivorous reader who retained what he read to a remarkable degree. His bibliographical knowledge of his own field was tremendous. Furthermore, he did enough in the way of scholarship to warrant being made a Fellow of the Medieval Academy of America. Bishop J. H. Ryan followed him in this honor, and I am happy to say that I myself followed them both in this distinction.

Bishop Shahan remains in my mind as the Rector builder. If he had not found his way into the Rectorship, there is no question in my mind but that he would have become a truly great scholar. He cannot be called an organizer, because he allowed the University to stay in the unrealistic European arrangement according to which it was first established—a source of much embarrassment in its dealings with its sister American institutions. It must be said, however, that he approached the possibility of the new organization but for some reason dropped it very suddenly.[1] He did not push the University ahead in a scholarly way, since he did not add any noteworthy scholars to the teaching staff. On the contrary and because he was so pressed for funds for his building projects, he re-

[1] Cf. Reorganization of the University.

sorted to bargaining with members of the staff, endeavoring to keep the teachers that he had at the lowest possible cost and to bring in new teachers with the slightest possible expenditure of funds. True scholars are not attracted to an institution by this method of negotiation. The so-called scale of salaries was fantastic. Of course, there was no scale! Maintaining one's salary was a constant struggle with the Rector on a "catch as catch can" basis! Nor did the University have a regularly organized pension or retirement plan at that time. I remember one of my colleagues rushing to Bishop Shahan one day in a very disturbed state of mind, to determine whether or not he would receive a pension in his old age or, if he became incapacitated after long service for the University, whether he would receive some compensation for the support of himself and his family. He asked His Excellency rather petulantly: "If a lay member of the faculty with a family grows old or becomes otherwise incapacitated, and finds himself, as he must at his low salary, without means of support for his dear ones, what is he going to do about it?" The University did not have a regularly organized pension or retirement plan at the time. Bishop Shahan answered truly sympathetically and with genuine solicitude: "My dear man, the good bishops of the country would take care of him!" The faculty member concerned, who told me about this, thought that the Bishop's reply was highly amusing. As a matter of fact, however, all such cases as arose during my life time, before a regular retirement plan was devised, were very adequately, though not systematically, provided for.

As I have said, Bishop Shahan was a kindly and lovable personality. I will illustrate this again by an incident that took place shortly after I first arrived at the University. He took me with him on a trip to Cleveland where Father John Burns, C.S.C., then Superior of the Holy Cross House of Studies on our campus, had arranged a meeting to establish a so-called Catholic Classical League. The Classical League, non-sectarian, had recently been established by Dean Andrew F. West of Princeton University, and certain Catholics felt that we should have a Classical League of our own. Incidently this was a dismal failure. [2] We were riding in our Pullman sleeper and across the aisle from us was a lady with a baby. With considerable daring, I thought, she arranged the little tot in the sleeper, which she had had made up, and then proceeded apparently without further concern for the baby to the dining car to eat her dinner. The child started to fuss and to carry on as little children will do, and I said some harsh things about a mother who would do a thing like that. But the Bishop chided me and said: "She probably saw a Bishop across the aisle and thought to herself: 'The good Bishop will take care of the baby, if it should need attention!' " The mental picture of Bishop Shahan taking care of a

[2] The reason for this failure was both evident and depressing. No one group was willing to assume the responsibility for carrying on the project, nor was it willing to let anyone else do the work.

young baby was too much for me, and so I endeavored to supply all the care needed to keep the child
quiet until its mother returned.

I also learned on this trip that Bishop Shahan
always travelled with two pocket volumes neatly
bound in leather: his breviary and a complete edition of the works of Vergil. When he wished to read
his breviary, he would take out both volumes, hand
me the Vergil, and say: "Now we will both read our
breviaries!"

Bishop James H. Ryan
1928-1935

Archbishop James Hugh Ryan was a fearless
and forward-looking Rector. Probably the first principle which he enunciated on coming into office was
"no more buildings but more scholars and higher
academic standards throughout the University." He
wished at once to do something about the general
organization of the University. He recognized the
difficulty of the authorities of the University in
meeting and counselling with their fellow American
university administrators. Since I have discussed
the general subject of the reorganization of the University elsewhere,[3] I wish merely to mention it
here to illustrate Bishop Ryan's fearlessness and
foresight and to emphasize that this reorganization
was definitely necessary if our University was truly
to prosper on American soil.

[3] Cf. Reorganization of The Catholic University of America.

Archbishop Ryan faced the problem of making the hierarchy of the country look upon the University as their own responsibility. Actually this was not such a difficult task as it seemed, because the time was opportune to take this step. The period had passed in which Bishop Shahan had been Rector, when members of the hierarchy who were hostile to the University were sufficiently numerous to be a threat to its very existence. These men had passed the way of all flesh, and none had risen to take their places. In fact, the Board of Trustees as a whole had for several years been quite uneasy about the futility of their attending the annual meetings, since Bishop Shahan out of fear for his University never presented the institution's serious problems to them. They thus had little or nothing to do as members of the Board of Trustees. This was reflected in the declining attendance at these meetings. As one member is reported to have said: "We give up several days of our busy time and travel hundreds of miles to hear a very routine report of insignificant details and learn really nothing about the University's serious problems." When Bishop Ryan placed their responsibilties with reference to the University squarely before them, almost to a man they accepted them very willingly, and attendance at the annual meetings improved. This was also reflected in the steady rise in the amount of the annual collection for the University, which began at that time and has continued ever since. To my mind, this marks a very important turning point in the history of the University.

Bishop Ryan found the financial condition of the University in a serious state. This cannot very well be blamed on any individual but rather on the conditions of the time and the fortuitous circumstances surrounding the University. I remember hearing Bishop Ryan say many times: "We must restore the depleted or damaged funds in trust left the University for one kind of endowment or another." I recall also very vividly, when I first came to the University, receiving a letter from my old friend and teacher, Professor Edward Capps, who was then serving on the Board of Trustees of the Rockefeller Foundation. He informed me that the Foundation was ready to donate funds to universities for the improvement of faculty salaries and that probably for the first time in the history of such philanthropies on a large scale non-sectarianism would not be a requirement in the beneficiary. The only requirement was permission for duly appointed persons of the Rockefeller Foundation to examine the financial accounts of the University to ascertain how faithful the University had been in the maintenance of the endowments which it had already received. He assured me that he had no doubt about the University's integrity in this respect, but that this was a requirement for all who would receive the grants. Being very enthusiastic about the matter and feeling certain that we could receive this help, he urged me to take the matter to Bishop Shahan at once and to do everything possible to make him apply. I did so with all the enthusiasm of youth, and Bishop Shahan was greatly interested until I mentioned the one condition. At that point for obvious reasons he became completely indifferent to the proposal. Incidentally, this was a great disappointment to Professor Capps, who through my predecessor, Dr. O'Connor, had come to know Bishop Shahan and to respect the University highly. However, with the cooperation of the Board of Trustees the endowments were restored, and Bishop Ryan proceeded to gather funds systematically for the intellectual and academic expansion of the University.

It is of no great interest here to give the details of Bishop Ryan's plan to gather funds for the University over and above that received from the annual collection. An organization for the purpose was set up, and results in various forms were gathering momentum. Part of the over-all plan was to carry on special drives in one area of the country after another, at different times and, of course, with the permission of the ordinary concerned, until the entire nation had been covered. The first of these drives was actually carried on in the District of Columbia with better success than was anticipated. I recall very well writing and traveling in behalf of this money-raising effort. At just this point, the Rector was transferred to the Archdiocese of Omaha, and nothing more was done. The results of this planning, however, were felt for several years through the special donations and bequests that continued on into the next rectorship. It was very pitiful indeed to see the next Rector drop all the careful and systematic planning for fund-raising that had just been worked out by specialists in this field, and attempt to replace it with such impractical thinking as: "If we could only get every one of the millions of Catholics in the country to give one penny annually, our financial problem would be solved!" Fortunately, this absurdity was never attempted, and no precious time or effort was wasted on it.

Because Bishop Ryan was very much concerned about the improvement of the scholarly standards of the University, he was determined that only the active scholars of the teaching staff would receive promotion. Perhaps he went too far in this. At least two cases come to mind of deplorably poor teachers being promoted to ordinary professorships for their research accomplishments only, and this brought much criticism upon him. I was Chairman of the Committee on Promotions at the time, and I myself received much of this opprobrium. [4]

Bishop Ryan, I always felt, was for the most part greatly misunderstood as a person. He too was very kind, but he made no external show in his display of kindness and consequently often went unnoticed in it. He disliked, much more than is ordinarily the case, to deal with very troublesome problems. He did not, however, lack courage in facing them; when he had a disagreeable duty to perform he rushed at it ruthlessly, almost imprudently, as if in an effort to get the disagreeable matter over with as soon as possible. This was especially evident

[4] Cf. Appointments and Promotions of Members of the Faculty.

in his dealings with the School of Sacred Theology.
He locked horns with this school on the question of
whether or not it was independent of the rest of the
University and was to be governed by an entirely
distinct set of statutes. In fact, this school endeavored to extend this independence even to the details
of examination and course schedules and other routine matters of the University's daily existence,
which often resulted in much confusion. It seemed
to take pleasure in insisting that all things within
its confines be done differently from the corresponding procedures in the rest of the University.
Meanwhile, the Rector had correspondence in his
possession [5] with reference to certain individuals
who were the leading trouble-makers, giving him
the power to remove them completely out of the
University, if so he wished. But he argued: "I want
to beat them on the basis of lawful academic procedures, and do not want to bring in something not
directly connected with the academic problem before us. I will wait until I beat them at their own
game." Unfortunately, when he had beaten them,
he did not proceed promptly to the distasteful matter hidden in his desk. When I asked him why he
was delaying about this, he answered: "For heav-
en's sake, Deferrari, I want to have a little peace for
a while. I am sick of this constant fighting." It was
a pity that he delayed in attending to the skeleton
in the desk. Before long he was compelled by higher
ecclesiastical authority to take care of it and was

[5] This he showed me and permitted me to read.

put in the position almost of condoning it, whereas he was not responsible for it in any way and he was even outraged by it.

Bishop Ryan was a very close and dear friend of mine. I was much closer to him than to any other Rector under whom I have served. Perhaps I was especially attracted to him because he always made me feel at home in his presence. When later I visited him in his episcopal residence in Omaha, his courtesy and friendliness could not have been surpassed by that of any of my many good friends. I never felt in the least ill at ease because he was an archbishop, and he appeared never to be embarrassed by my presence because I was a layman. With it all, I could not possibly have had greater respect and admiration for another member of the hierarchy than I had for him, and I believe that he thought highly of me. I believe also that I was able to see the truly great qualities of the man in spite of the several superficial faults which irritated so many people.

We did, however, disagree on some things. There were two subjects on which we did not seem able to come together in the slightest degree. One was the integration of the races at the University, and the other was "big-time" football. As for the integration of the races, I felt that he was largely influenced by his Vice-Rector Monsignor Edward A. Pace, who in spite of his many great qualities could not rise above his Florida origin in this respect. [6]

[6] Cf. Integration of the Races.

Regarding "big-time" football, Bishop Ryan, it must be remembered, was most anxious to build up his undergraduate College of Arts and Sciences, and he was led astray, as so many other college presidents were, by that athletic will-o'-the-wisp as a quick means of expanding the undergraduate body. His argument ran like this: "The University of Notre Dame has made a most profitable venture out of football. What it has done in South Bend, The Catholic University of America can do in Washington." [7] But "big-time" football and "big-time" athletics in general have been a dismal failure at The Catholic University of America.

Bishop Ryan, from the point of view of formal training, might not be expected to exhibit the qualities of an genuine scholar. However, he did have a natural scholarly instinct which made up to some degree for the gap in his formal training, and he did leave a few scholarly accomplishments, enough to gain for him a Fellowship in the Mediaeval Academy of America.

He was a great academic organizer, which resulted from a remarkable foresight, and this perhaps was his greatest contribution to the growth of the University. It must always be borne in mind that Archbishop Ryan, in the face of most discouraging circumstances, insisted on the reorganization of the University as a whole and the abandonment of the European scheme of things so unsuited to the American scene. At that same time the accrediting

[7] Cf. Athletics.

agencies were coming into being and were beginning to gain the great power which they have today.
The two were almost simultaneous. Thus, the University, as it grew side by side with the accrediting
groups, was approved by them, for it was the good
fortune of the University to have had at their meetings one or two representatives who did it great
credit and who themselves contributed much to the
evolution of the accrediting or evaluating process.
If the University had not been so reorganized and
Bishop Ryan had not sent well selected representatives to these educational meetings, the inevitable
clash between the University and these groups
could well have been at least very damaging to the
University.

Bishop Ryan was also very anxious to change
the existing manner of appointing heads of departments and deans of schools. The European plan of
making these appointments on the basis of the voting of faculty and department members and rarely,
if ever, dissenting from the choices thus expressed,
prevailed completely. He felt strongly, as I do myself, that in this country, where the responsibility
for the success of any academic regime rests so
completely on the rector or president himself, the
rector or president should be entirely free to select
the right persons for these important posts. While it
may be argued that the Rector is privileged to act
contrary to the consultative vote of the departments
or faculties, the fact remains that rarely has any
rector acted directly in opposition to it, and as a
result incompetent heads of departments and deans

of schools have continued in office term after term
to the great annoyance of rectors and to the serious
detriment of the University's good. However, Bishop Ryan was stymied in this attempt.

To me and many others Bishop Ryan was not
only a kindly and gracious gentleman, but one of
the University's most outstanding rectors.

Bishop Joseph M. Corrigan

1936-1942

When Bishop Corrigan came to the University
and I became acquainted with him for the first
time, he elicited my profound sympathy. He was
very unwell, and greatly handicapped physically
and otherwise by his excessive weight. Furthermore, he had had little or no experience with colleges or universities and was quite unacquainted
with the administration of American institutions of
higher education. To my amazement he very naive-
ly said to me one day: "I am surprised to learn that
the degree Doctor of Philosophy (Ph.D) does not
regularly stand for higher studies in the field of
philosophy!" To be sure, he had been Rector of a
theological seminary, but this could hardly be said
to have benefited him greatly for the direction of a
complex university which emphasized training for
and in research. Furthermore, as soon as he put foot
upon the campus, he was beset by a group which

had never been very active in their University duties. They now saw an opportunity to defend themselves against the harassment of the previous administration which had tried in vain to rouse them
into activity. The cry now was: "The University is
given back to the clergy. The laity is out!" Of course,
it was not at all evident that the laity had ever taken
over the institution. Bishop Ryan and Monsignor
Pace had been Rector and Vice-Rector respectively,
and the majority of the Deans had been members of
the clergy. The members of the laity who were to
go out, as far as I could see, numbered only one and
that was I!

The days of transition to the Corrigan administration were a little difficult for me, I must admit.
Some members of the clergy and laity alike scarcely
noticed me or deliberately snubbed me when we
met even face to face. Deferrari was definitely going
out! Some openly offered me sympathy and expressed a feigned admiration for my ability to stand
up so well under the strain!

Bishop Corrigan had clearly been filled up
with all kinds of information, both good and bad,
about me, then the Dean of the Graduate School of
Arts and Sciences. This was more or less to have
been expected. Before Bishop Ryan departed for
Omaha, he had repeatedly urged my friends and
me to accept whoever was appointed Rector with
good grace and to support him in every way, because, as His Excellency put it: "He will need it!"
That was very easy for all of us to do, because we

were all so constituted naturally. Bishop Corrigan, after a short initial period of skepticism, soon recognized this in my friends and in myself, and he grew more and more to appreciate it. In fact, shortly before he died, he told a friend of mine that he had discovered too late that his most loyal supporters were the loyal friends of Archbishop Ryan.

Bishop Corrigan was a man of great natural intellect and general talent, but he had not used these as well as he might have. Apparently, he had become accustomed to doing things in the easy way. Many believed that his inaugural address, which was a long drawn out dissertation on the compatibility of true science and true theology (which hardly any serious scholar ever doubts today), was not written by himself at all. This seemed evident both from the style in which it was couched, closely resembling that of a well-known historian and speaker of the faculty, and from the manner in which it was delivered. Indeed, Bishop Corrigan himself became disgusted with the long drawn-out affair and with the unconcealed heckling of his distinguished audience, and never actually read it all.

In my first conference with Bishop Corrigan, he said: "Deferrari, you know, don't you, that you have many enemies on this campus?" I did not, but it was interesting information at any rate. "Well, I don't want you to be less active than you were under my predecessor; I want you to go on working as you have been doing for the welfare of the

University, but I want you to keep yourself in the background. In other words, I want you to go on moulding the bullets, but I want you to let me fire them!" I am afraid that this was an all too common practice with Bishop Corrigan.

Bishop Corrigan's lack of a keen sense of financial responsibility became notorious. He was not, of course, dishonest in the slightest degree but he did not realize the financial implications of some of the things that he did. For example, as Chairman of the Committee on Scholarships, Fellowships, and Student Aid I was in a constant state of turmoil as to how many scholarships, fellowships, and other forms of aid had been granted by the Rector privately, and to whom. An all too common occurrence was for a Sister teaching in an out-of-way country high school to write to the Rector and tell him of the perfectly marvelous young Catholic boy whom she was teaching, full of potentiality as a great leader for the Church, who wanted to go to the College but had no funds; would the Bishop grant him a complete scholarship. Without any further ado, His Excellency would answer "Yes." He would not think of asking for a transcript of the student's high school record, so as to see if he were really prepared to go to college. He would not even let me know that he had granted such a scholarship! As a result of such procedures, a so-called "Committee on Administration and the Budget" was established to work with Bishop Corrigan in his financial duties and in his many other responsibilities as well.

Bishop Corrigan seemed incapable of diagnosing a problem and solving it objectively. His first and only thought seemed to be of the political aspects of the matter. On becoming Rector of the University, he was most anxious to get something done, but his utter lack of knowledge of the University's problems and of academic matters in general made it difficult for him to start anything. Consequently, he resorted to accepting the suggestions of others without being able to gauge their intrinsic worth. Thus, the University was on the verge of or actually in a crisis at all times, and he himself was in difficulties from which his true friends had to extricate him.[8] I shall present only one example here. I have already described the outstanding College of Arts and Sciences, which Father J. M. Campbell had spent the best years of his life developing. One Saturday afternoon, the well-known Dr. George Derry, formerly President of Marygrove College in Detroit and then President of St. Joseph's College in Portland, Maine, appeared on the campus and gained entrance to Bishop Corrigan's apartment. Before the afternoon was over Dr. Derry had sold himself and his plan for a complete reorganization of the College to Bishop Corrigan, and the Bishop asked me to show him how Dr. Derry's plan was not an improvement over that of the College which we then had. After a struggle we succeeded in persuading him that it was best to let the whole matter drop.

[8] Cf. Organization.

Frankly, it is difficult for me to point to any great advancement made by the University during Bishop Corrigan's rectorship, but several backward steps, or at least decisions of questionable benefit, could be mentioned. At the same time, however, it is to his everlasting credit that he had little patience with any conduct on the part of the clergy or laity, which could in any way be considered detrimental to the good name of the University. While I do not wish to give the impression that there was any great scandal at the University at this time, certain peccadillos did come to light, and Bishop Corrigan dealt with them promptly and vigorously.

Actually, Bishop Corrigan was to be pitied. He was placed in a job for which he had neither natural aptitude, nor the necessary formal training, nor compensating experience. Futhermore, he was seriously ill. In addition to this, by reason of his physical appearance, he was sometimes subjected to ridicule even in high places. I recall well the meeting of the Association of American Universities held in Columbia, Missouri, at the University of Missouri (October 30-31 and November 1, 1939).[*] I had tried to induce him to attend these meetings, as I had all the University Rectors under whom I had served, on the ground that associating with the presidents of the leading universities of the country and discussing common problems with them would be profitable in many ways. He had agreed to attend this one. I later regretted his attendance there very much,

[*] Cf. Graduate School of Arts and Sciences.

chiefly for his own sake. A group of the delegates took great delight in referring to Bishop Corrigan among themselves in a very uncomplimentary manner. Surely he did his very best, however unsatisfactory that may have been at times.

Bishop Patrick J. McCormick
1943-1953

I had known Bishop McCormick from the very first days of my coming to the University. I knew him as Professor of Education, as Dean of the Catholic Sisters College (when it was active in its own peculiar way), as Director of the Summer Session, and both as Vice-Rector and Rector of the University. He opposed bitterly any move to amalgamate the Catholic Sisters College with the University proper. He objected strongly to the admission of women, whether religious or lay, to any of the academic resources of the University not located within the confines of the Sisters College. Yet he was not concerned in the least about expanding or improving the facilities of the Sisters College for the benefit of the Sisters, to say nothing of the laywomen, whom he admitted to the Sisters College or the Summer Session primarily to increase the financial income. He gave no serious consideration to solving the problem of higher education of women under Catholic auspices. Furthermore, he resisted vigorrously Bishop Ryan's reorganization of the University, being one of the group which, headed by Monsignor John A. Ryan, sent the famous letter urging me to put an end to the attempted reform. Yet, when he became Rector, he did not attempt to restore the old organization, which in those hectic days I feared greatly. At least, he deserves credit for this. He maintained the *status quo* rigidly. In fact, some inhabitants of the University campus maintained that Bishop McCormick was appointed Rector for the specific purpose of maintaining the *status quo* during the uncertain period of World War II and the years immediately following. If this be true, he carried out his assignment superbly.

Unfortunately, when one devotes himself to the purpose of maintaining a fixed position over any great length of time, something gives way, and there is regression somewhere in spite of every effort to prevent it. The great regression in the Rectorship of Bishop McCormick was the loss of the accreditation of the School of Engineering and Architecture by the Engineering Council for Professional Development. Fortunately, due chiefly to the energetic work of Bishop McEntegart and a new Dean, this accreditation has been fully restored.

The beginning of the decline of the School of Engineering and Architecture goes back to the Rectorship of Bishop Shahan and was evident to anyone with the slightest understanding of the fundamentals of university administration. It was probably due to one factor much more than to any other, namely, the increasing attraction of the members of the engineering faculty away from research and teaching and from the University in general to personal jobs and independent businesses off campus. Classes were neglected unscrupulously. Departmental administration in most instances was totally ignored. When the inevitable blow came, Bishop McCormick was pitifully helpless and unable to deal with the crisis. Months passed and still nothing positive was being done. [10] Finally, I myself went to Bishop McCormick and submitted a plan of action, which he accepted with real enthusiasm and obvious relief. This resulted eventually under Bishop McEntegart in the complete restoration of the lost accreditation. I should add also that Bishop McCormick acted positively and firmly at last, even though a personal friend of his was involved and was chiefly responsible for the debacle.

In an effort to appraise Bishop McCormick's Rectorship, try as I will, I cannot point to any academic development which was conceived and carried out by him. It was a lustreless and stagnant period in the history of the University. Yet it must be said that he did not interfere with the decisions made by the faculties and deans, and he had high respect for academic freedom in the best sense.

As a person, Bishop McCormick had many friends. He was just, friendly, and courteous. He

[10] Cf. Accreditation.

was an outstanding gentleman. He cherished his priesthood to a truly high degree, and often re ferred to it in his public utterances.

Bishop Bryan J. McEntegart

1953-1957

After the drab Rectorship of Bishop McCormick, we entered upon the dynamic period of Bishop McEntegart's regime. It was a brief Rectorship of only four years, but it marked a period of real awakening. Much was accomplished by way of physical expansion and educational reform. It cannot be said that Bishop McEntegart inherited any important project of any kind that needed to be carried through. It might be said, perhaps, that Bishop McCormick cleared away the obstructions to a reform of the School of Engineering and Architecture, but all positive action for the reestablishment of this School and the actual recovery of its accreditation is one of the academic achievements of Bishop McEntegart. Another academic accomplishment of this period is the guiding of the University through its evaluation by the Middle States Association of Schools and Colleges. [11] The University had never been through such a complete overhauling and examination of both its physical

[11] See Accreditation.

and intellectual resources, and in order to prepare
for it a general self-evaluation had to be conducted
by the University personnel itself. This self-ap-
praisal had to be planned and carried out with
great care, while at the same time remedying and
improving such defects and weaknesses as were
necessarily brought to light. This Bishop McEntegart did to the complete satisfaction of the personnel of the University and the Middle States
Association itself.

The building program had essentially come to
a halt, ever since Archbishop Ryan had decided
that the erection of buildings which had gone on
under Bishop Shahan was sufficient to care for the
needs of the University for some years, and that
emphasis was then to be placed upon the improvement of scholarship. There are, of course, several
exceptions to this generalization. But all in all, the
lack of physical plant by the 1950's had become a
very serious obstacle to the required expansion of
the University. Bishop McEntegart met this problem by carefully surveying the needs and arranging
the physical growth of the institution over several
successive periods in accord with the urgency of
these needs. Moreover, he obtained the wholehearted support of the Board of Trustees for his plan,
and the first fruits are now evident in the completion of the John K. Mullen of Denver Memorial
Library and the erection of Keane Hall, the Physics
building.

Monsignor William J. McDonald

1957

Monsignor McDonald has been on the University's teaching staff for nearly a generation. He has also served under Bishop McEntegart as Vice-Rector. He knows the needs of the University from his long association with it, and he has learned the aggressive approach to the meeting of these needs through his apprenticeship under his predecessor. Certainly the University needs very much the physical plant which Bishop McEntegart has envisioned for it, and we are sure that our present Rector will see this planning through to completion. The University also needs another renascence of scholarship both in the general standards of academic work and in the research activity of the faculty, similar to that which took place under Bishop Ryan. I do not mean to imply that there has been any retrogression in recent years but I am very fearful about the future. In fact I personally am very proud of the accomplishment of the University in this respect during the last thirty years. But every worthy institution of higher education, especially of the unversity kind, needs external vigilance over the standards of its scholarship and the activity of its research potentiality. The University at this moment is in need of a strong stimulus in this respect. I can by no means feel confident that the University is at present receiving this stimulus. Finally, the University authorities in these hard times must not be contented merely with filling vacancies on the teaching staff, but with getting the best available persons for the position. When a vacancy occurs in the top echelon of a department, it is rarely wise merely to push someone from a lower place in the same department to fill the position. Such a situation is one of the rare opportunities for bringing in an outstanding scholar from the outside and thus truly strengthening the faculty.

It is interesting to note that all new Rectors have been interested in strengthening the faculty, thinking that this is a comparatively easy thing to accomplish. But when they discover that people of true university caliber are both difficult to discover and almost impossible to acquire, they have quickly lost their interest. I hope indeed that the present Rector and all future rectors will persist strongly in this phase of their great responsibility.

At this point I am led to remark that it is a great mistake to appoint anyone as Rector or President of an institution of higher education who is not an outstanding scholar in the best sense of the word. Other qualities, such as an ability to raise money and a strong capacity to associate with persons of importance, are also important, but without an appreciation and sense of good scholarship he may easily make decisions of most serious consequence to the institution.

Epilogue

Shortly after my arrival at the University an intriguing question was being debated in the Catholic Press and occasionally by Catholic educators in public addresses which in general could be expressed as "Have We Any Catholic Scholars?" I myself also succumbed to the temptation of treating this topic in Catholic journals. As discussed and treated at that time, it is very doubtful whether any good was accomplished. The question was not defined in detail. Moreover, it was essentially impossible to determine whether scholars of great or less reputation were Catholics or not or whether they were even scholars! All in all the entire discussion was essentially fruitless, and may even have created some animosity among ourselves.

It is a little ironical that just as I was about to retire, this same question, differently stated and better defined, was again a topic of discussion both in press and before general audiences. Today we hear of the general failure of Catholic institutions of higher education to develop genuine scholars of high quality and outstanding intellectual leaders generally. The discussion today is more specific in that it revolves around the nature of the product of our Catholic colleges and universities, and not so much around the question of the religious persuasion of intellectual leaders. Another interesting phase of the present day controversy is the advocacy of the amalgamation of Catholic institutions of higher education, and thus the pooling of resources with resultant more efficient programs of study. For people attracted by the arguments of scientific management, this apparently new phase of the discussion appears very attractive and convincing. I do not wish to go into the details of this controversy, but it would be well to make a few matters clear.

Amalgamation and cooperation are two different things. It is difficult for me to imagine how amalgamation, even if it were feasible, would result in an improvement of conditions. Moreover, as far as colleges are concerned, it is highly desirable that they not become too large and lose the close personal contact between student and faculty members which is so important. It is also a highly desirable asset for Catholic higher education to be able to offer a program of general educaton with different emphases, for example, Benedictine, Jesuit, Holy Cross, St. Edmund, and others. On the other hand, there should be careful apportionment of the professional fields. One school of medicine, dentistry, social work, law, nursing, and others should be sufficient in any diocese. There should be no duplication but well-planned cooperation here. I am very conscious of the fact also that our Catholic colleges of general education might in a few instances be more advantageously placed, but I am definitely opposed to the belief in some quarters that we have too many. When consideration is given to the good which the Catholic general college has done and is doing for both Church and country, I must say: "Let us have more of them!"

It is, of course, always good to have a serious examination of our academic consciences at least occasionally, but on such occasions we must of course be fair with ourselves or we may do ourselves more harm than good. First of all, we are comparing the accomplishments of Catholic higher education with those of higher education under the great variety of all other auspices, which gives an erroneous impression. Secondly, Catholic higher education on the college level is several generations younger than the American college as such. As for graduate studies, these were first undertaken seriously with the founding of The Catholic University of America in 1889. They cannot be said to have been taken very seriously elsewhere under Catholic auspices until 1934. [1] This date marks the publication of the results of the study and evaluation of graduate departments throughout the country by the American Council of Education, and the terrific impact of this publicity on Catholic graduate schools throughout the land. From this time on our

---

[1] See The Graduate School of Arts and Sciences

graduate schools have developed marvelously. The history of the American Catholic college, especially the Catholic college for women, and the history of the American graduate school under Catholic auspices, the time factor being duly considered, are the most brilliant chapters in the story of higher education in the United States. As I look back over the last forty years, I am proud of the contribution which The Catholic University of America has contributed to both these chapters.

As for the existence of any bankruptcy in the production of leaders by the American Catholic educational school system, and in particular of our institutions of higher education, this I do not believe. Here again it is almost impossible to get objective data, or for that matter to get any general agreement as to what are admissible data in an investigation of this kind. Certain more or less superficial evidence is brought forth which appeals to the popular mind, and harmful conclusions may be drawn. It is difficult for me to imagine any good that might come from such discussions.

A thorough study of the accomplishments of Catholic institutions of higher education would be very rewarding. It would, however, take a long time, for it should not be based on general opinion or data collected at random. Furthermore, it should not look for merely sensational evidence, but all evidence including the small everyday matters that all together contribute so much to make the world a better place to live in. Factual evidence is at hand to indicate that, all things considered, we have

nothing whatever of which to be ashamed. It is
good for Catholic educators and especially administrators to be constantly evaluating their achievements, trying always to ascertain how well they
accomplish what they so eloquently set forth in
their catalogues as the aims of their institutions. As
far as leaders and scholars are concerned, we should
all remember that the maintenance of high standards of scholarship in our academic institutions of
all types is the key to the problem, not the promotion of more sports or activities of extroversion.
Moreover, the spirit of anti-intellectualism should be
crushed the moment is raises its ugly head. Only by
an efficient training of the intellect as well as of the
spirit will good scholars and outstanding leaders be
produced. This simple but vital principle is too often
forgotten in the various facets of our educational
life. If we are failing in achieving our purposes (and
this I do not admit at present), we can find the cause
in some defect in our academic standards. All in
any way connected with Catholic education must
constantly bear in mind that when they cut cor-
ners for one of their groups, or give in to pressure
to allow a student to graduate who has not fulfilled
all the requirements for graduation, or for the sake
of tuition fees or favor admit students to a program
of studies which they cannot complete satisfactorily,
or permit students to continue in curricula in spite
of failure upon failure, or carry on any similar un-
worthy academic practice, they are contributing to
the possible bankruptcy of our Catholic educational
effort.

At any rate Catholic educators interested in the appraisal of the success or failure of Catholic higher education should bear in mind that scholarship cannot be legislated. Our growth in Catholic higher education has been an organic one. If we examine Catholic higher education with the proper historical perspective, we have a right to feel reasonably satisfied with our achievement to date, and we can look forward to the future with confidence.

In the twenties almost no priests and comparatively few Catholic laymen were attending non-Catholic graduate schools, and our own enrollment was very small. A revolution has taken place in some thirty years. In this same period, several important scholarly journals under Catholic auspices have appeared and there has been a considerable amount of solid publication. Three or four Catholic university presses are growing steadily. Still other signs of healthy development are at hand. I do not mean to encourage complacency, but I do believe that much more can be accomplished by a well-balanced picture of conditions as they are than by a one-sided portrayal and exaggeration of weaknesses.

In closing I would like to emphasize a final general principle in Catholic higher education. Branches, extensions, and combinations of educational institutions of any kind are at best of temporary value only. It is not good for any single institution or group of institutions to dominate education in any part of the country, to say nothing of the entire country. For example, it is absurd to think of any one institution controlling and directing graduate work over the entire country or over any of its extensive parts. When a religious community or any other group feels that there is a genuine need for an institution of higher education of any particular classification, and that it has the resources to establish and develop it, all other Catholic groups should do all in their power to advance the cause of this institution, without in the slightest degree interfering with its autonomy. The independence and freedom that result from such a policy will promote healthy growth not only of the youthful institutions themselves but also of Catholic education in general. Let us not, perhaps with every good intention, stunt the growth of our institutions of higher education by urging amalgamation, extreme and impracticable cooperation, and other similar will-o'-the-wisps.

Reproducing the Doctoral Dissertation

Through Microfilm

Within the last two years a regulation has been passed permitting candidates for the doctorate at the University to fulfill the requirement of publication by having the dissertation reproduced on microfilm. This was also true for a short period several years ago when I was Secretary General but I succeeded in having it rescinded very quickly.

The constant motivating force behind these demands for the use of microfilm in this connection is the low cost of the process in the face of the ever mounting financial outlay for traditional printing. However, regardless of the low cost of microfilming, it may well be extremely high for what is obtained in return—inferior training, if for no other reason, because of the lack of experience in actually seeing a finished product of scholarship through press, and the complete loss of the scholarly product itself when shunted into microfilm, granting that a high level of scholarship will be maintained when both professor and student know that the final result of their investigation will be relegated to the limbo of microfilm.

The entire problem of the proper publication of doctoral dissertations needs to be reexamined thoroughly with a view to maintaining proper and important publicity for our dissertations, as a proof of our sincerity in the worthwhile nature of scholarship as exhibited in doctoral dissertations. Allowing doctoral dissertations to be treated as perfunctory exercises, as the microfilm process inevitably brings about, should be avoided at all cost. The quality of the training in scholarship sinks to a very low ebb. This has taken place in the universities of other countries, notably Germany, where the publication requirement has been reduced to a mere formality.

The following are suggested means of meeting the problem of publication while maintaining high standards of scholarship:

(1) Certainly all students should be encouraged to publish their dissertations in full, if this is at all possible.

(2) Care should be exercised in assigning topics for investigation, avoiding as much as possible overly extensive projects.

(3) The dissertation might be so planned that it covers only a comparatively small portion of the entire topic, leaving the remainder to be treated by the student after his departure from the University.

(4) Publication *in toto* in professional journals should be urged if feasible.

By these several means and perhaps others the integrity of the doctoral dissertation could be preserved.

Some object to the full publication requirement on the ground that the quality of dissertations, at least in some departments is very poor. The solution here is very simple. The calibre of those departments should be strengthened immediately.

Some members of a university family will argue for or against a certain requirement or procedure on the basis of the usual practice in such matters in other similar institutions. This has been used to promote the use of microfilm at our University. As Dean of the Graduate School of Arts and Sciences I made it clear that such an argument should have very little weight. The solution to any problem must be settled independently by any university on the

basis of what is best for it in its existing surroundings.

Much more could be said on this subject but
this will suffice to alert the proper authorities of our
University to the dangers to academic excellence
involved in the present trend toward the essentially
universal use of microfilm for "publishing" doctoral
dissertations.

APPENDICES

ORGANIZATION CHART FOR THE OFFICE OF THE SECRETARY GENERAL (AND REGISTRAR): 1958

(just before retirement in 1961)

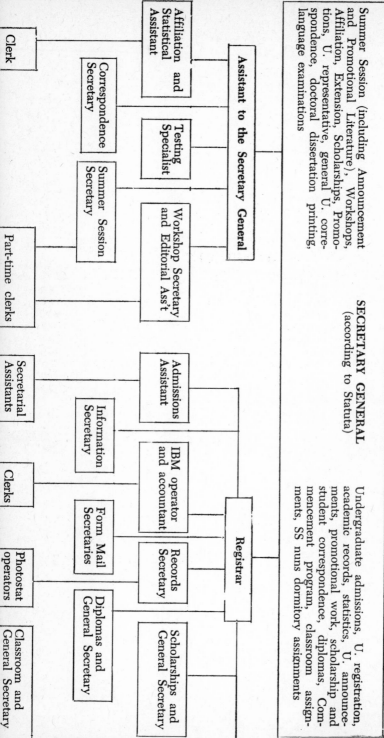

SECRETARY GENERAL
(according to Statuta)

Undergraduate admissions, U. registration, academic records, statistics, U. announcements, promotional work, scholarship and student correspondence, diplomas, Commencement program, classroom assignments, SS nuns dormitory assignments

Summer Session (including Announcement and Promotional Literature), Workshops, Affiliation, Extension, Scholarships, Promotions, U. representative, general U. correspondence, doctoral dissertation printing, language examinations

Assistant to the Secretary General

- Affiliation and Statistical Assistant
  - Clerk
- Correspondence Secretary
- Testing Specialist
- Summer Session Secretary
- Workshop Secretary and Editorial Ass't
  - Part-time clerks

Registrar

- Admissions Assistant
  - Secretarial Assistants
- Information Secretary
- IBM operator and accountant
  - Clerks
- Form Mail Secretaries
- Records Secretary
  - Photostat operators
- Diplomas and General Secretary
- Scholarships and General Secretary
  - Classroom and General Secretary

APPENDIX 2

SUMMER SESSION ENROLLMENTS

Year	Special Students	Regular Students Undergraduate	Graduate	Men	Women	Total
1929	85	350	—	—	350	350
1930	69	755	—	—	755	755
1931	—	580	311	217	674	891
1932	—	515	431	306	725	1031
1933	—	560	502	349	782	1131
1934	39	635	629	373	930	1303
1953	823	385	1566	1100	1674	2774
1954	794	332	1824	1189	1761	2950
1955	722°	890	2187	1275	1802	3077
1956	766°	988	2223	1391	1820	3211
1957	889°	1139	2414	1414	2139	3553
1958	868°	1088	2578	1499	2167	3666
1959	816	1255	2580	1516	2269	3835
1960	1231	158	2023	1685	2386	4071

° Starting with the Summer Session of 1955, special students were classified also as graduate or undergraduate; this figure thus denotes the number of students in the next two columns who were classified as strictly special students: undergraduate non-degree candidates and those graduate students not pursuing courses for graduate credit.

APPENDIX 3

WORKSHOPS HELD AT THE CATHOLIC UNIVERSITY
FROM 1946 THROUGH JUNE OF 1958

1945-1946:   On College Organization and Administration
1946-1947:   On the Philosophy of Catholic Higher Education
On Administration of the Catholic Secondary School
1947-1948:   On Guidance in Catholic Colleges and Universities
On the Curriculum of the Catholic Secondary School
On Mental Health in Nursing: Psychological Approach
On Family Relationships and Marriage
1948-1949:   On Catholic College Integration
On the Teacher in the Catholic Secondary School
On the Coordination of Education and Nursing in Centralized Programs
On Education for Marriage and Family Living
On Creative Writing for Catholic Writers
1949-1950:   On Discipline and Integration in the Catholic College
On Integration of the Catholic Secondary School Curriculum
On Marriage and Family Education and Counseling
On a Dynamic Basic Nursing Curriculum
On Creative Writing for Catholic Writers
On Youth and Group Work
1950-1951:   On the Curriculum of the Catholic College
On the Christian Foundation Program in the Catholic Secondary School
On Marriage Education and Counseling
On the Organization of Hospital Nursing Services
1951-1952:   On Theology, Philosophy, and History as Integrating Disciplines in the Catholic College of Liberal Arts
On Integration in the Catholic Secondary School Curriculum

On Marriage and Family Education and
Counseling
On Special Education of the Exceptional Child
On Art in Catholic Secondary Schools
On the Catholic Curriculum and Basic
Reading Instruction in Elementary Education

1952-1953:   On the Social Sciences in Catholic College
Programs
On Integration at work in the Catholic Secondary
School Curriculum
On Special Education of the Exceptional Child
On Art in Catholic Elementary Schools
On the Art Program in Catholic Secondary Schools
On Philosophy of the Curriculum of Catholic
Elementary Schools
On Music Education
On the Nursing Program in the General College

1953-1954:   On the Problems of Registrars and Admissions
Officers in Higher Education
On English in the Catholic Secondary School
On the Curriculum of the Catholic Elementary
School in Relation to the Home
On Special Education of the Exceptional Child
On the Dynamics of Clinical Instruction in
Nursing Education
On Creative Art
On Music Education in the Secondary School

1954-1955:   On The Problems of Administration in the
American College
On Communication Arts in the Catholic Secondary
School
On the Language Arts in the Catholic Elementary
School
On Individual Differences in Elementary and
Secondary School Children
On Implementation of Clinical Instruction in
Medical and Surgical Nursing
On Art in Christian Education
On Specialized Activities in Music Education

1955-1956:   On the Functions of the Dean of Studies in
Higher Education
On the Teaching of Reading in the Elementary
Schools
On Mental Health and Special Education

On Implementation of the Nursing Curriculum
in the Clinical Fields

On Art as Language

On Musc Activities in the Elementary School

On Military Operating Room Nursing

Institute on Army Health Nursing for Army Nurse
Corps Officers

1956-1957:   On Nursing in the Medical Management of
Mass Casualties

Post-Graduate Workshop on In-Service
Education for Army Nursing Service Personnel

On Art for Christian Living

On College Counseling and Testing

On Music Skills

On Teaching and Implementation of Psychiatric-
Mental Health Nursing

On Speech Correction in Special Education

1957-1958:   On New Trends in Catholic Art Education

On Principles and Problems of Catholic Adult
Education

On Administration in Higher Education in
relation to Self-Evaluation and Accreditation

On Music Teaching Techniques

On the Improvement of Nursing through
Research

On Speech Therapy

1959-1960:   On Quality of College Teaching and Staff

On Religious Education through the Program of
the CCD

On Psychological Counseling in High School
and College

On Teaching Foreign Languages in the Modern
World

On Music Teaching Methods and Techniques

On Epidemiology in Nursing

APPENDIX 4

PUBLICATIONS OF ROY J. DEFERRARI

I. Books

The morphology of the verb in Lucian. Princeton diss. 1915. Published as *Lucian's Atticism: The Morphology of the Verb.* Princeton, 1916. ix, 85p.

Selections from Roman Historians. Boston 1916. With L. R. Dean.

A First Latin Book for Catholic Schools. Washington 1921. Also 1923.

Editor: *Catholic University Patristic Studies,* 1922-60.

The Letters of St. Basil. 4 vols. London and New York. 1926-31.

Concordance of Prudentius. Cambridge, Mass. 1931. With J. M. Campbell.

Editor *Catholic University Studies in Mediaeval and Renaissance Latin.* 1932-60.

A Concordance of Ovid. Washington 1939. With Sister M. Inviolata Barry and M.R.P. McGuire.

A Concordance of Lucian. Washington, D.C. 1940. With Sister Maria Walburg and Sister Ann Stanislaus.

Editor: *Classical Studies of the Catholic University of America.* 1939-1960.

Editor: *Vital Problems of Catholic Education in the United States.* Washington, D.C.: CUA Press, 1939.

Editor: *Essays on Catholic Education in the United States.* Washington, D.C.: CUA Press, 1942.

A Concordance of Statius. Washington, D.C. 1942. With Sister Clement, C.C.U.I.

Editor: *The Catholic High School Literature Series.* 4 vols. New York: Sadlier, 1941-1946. With Sister M. Theresa Brentano and Brother Edward P. Sheekey.

Marian Latin Series for High Schools. 4 vols. Milwaukee: Bruce, 1946. With Sister Francis Joseph. 1947-1953.

Editor: *College Organization and Administration.* Washington, D.C.: CUA Press, 1947.

Translator, "St. Augustine's On Faith in Things Unseen," Vol. III, *The Fathers of the Church.* New York: Circa, 1947. With Sister M. Francis McDonald, O.P.

A Latin-English Lexicon of St. Thomas Aquinas. Washington,

D.C.: CUA Press, 1949-1953. With Sister Inviolata Barry, C.D.P.

Editor: *Philosophy of Catholic Higher Education.* Washington, D.C.: CUA Press, 1948.

Editor: *Guidance in Catholic Colleges and Universities.* Washington, D.C.: CUA Press, 1949.

Editor: *Integration in Catholic Colleges and Universities.* Washington, D.C.: CUA Press, 1950.

Editor: *Discipline and Integration in the Catholic College.* Washington, D.C.: CUA Press, 1951.

Editor: *The Organization and Administration of the Minor Seminary.* Washington, D.C.: CUA Press, 1951.

Hugh of St. Victor, *De Sacramentis.* Translation and commentary. Cambridge, Mass.: Mediaeval Academy of America, 1951.

Editor: *The Curriculum of the Catholic College.* Washington, D.C.: CUA Press, 1952.

Editor: *Early Christian Biographies.* Vol. XV *Fathers of the Church.* Translator of "Life of St. Cyprian by Pontius." With Sister M. Magdeleine, O.S.F. New York: Fathers of the Church, 1952.

Editor: *St. Augustine: Treatises on Various Subjects.* Vol. XVI, New York: Fathers of the Church, Vol. XIX, 1953.

Editor: *Theology, Philosophy and History as Integrating Disciplines in the Catholic College.* Washington, D.C.: CUA Press, 1953.

Editor: *Latin and English Syllabi in the Minor Seminary.* Washington, D.C.: CUA Press, 1953.

Translator, *Eusebius Pamphili, Ecclesiastical History,* Vol. I. New York: Fathers of the Church, Vol. XIX, 1953.

Translator, *Funeral Orations by Saint Gregory Nazianzene and St. Ambrose,* Vol. XXII, New York: Fathers of the Church, 1953.

Editor: *Latin and Religion Syllabi in the Minor Seminary.* Washington, D.C.: CUA Press, 1954.

Editor: *The Social Sciences in Catholic College Programs.* Washington, D.C.: CUA Press, 1954.

Editor: *Curriculum of the Minor Seminary: Religion, Greek, and Remedial Reading.* Washington, D.C.: CUA Press, 1955.

Complete Index of the Summa Theologica of St. Thomas Aquinas. Washington, D.C.: CUA Press, 400 pp., 1956.

Translator and Commentator. *Eusebius Pamphili,* Vol. II. New York: Fathers of the Church, 1955. Vol. XII, 325 pp.

Editor: *Curriculum of the Minor Seminary: Social Studies,*

Greek, and the General Curriculum, Washington, D.C.: CUA Press, 1956. iv, 81 pp.

Editor: *The Problems of Administration in the American College*. Washington, D.C.: CUA Press, 1956. vii, 191 pp.

Editor: *Functions of the Dean of Studies in Higher Education*. Washington, D.C.: CUA Press, 1957.

A *Latin-English Dictionary of St. Thomas Aquinas*. Boston: St. Paul Editions, 1960, 1115 pp.

II. Articles

On the date and order of delivery of St. Augustine's Tractates on the Gospel and the Epistle of St. John. *CP* 12 (1917) 191-4.

The Classics and the Greek writers of the early Church; St. Basil. *CJ* 13 (1917-8) 579-91.

Terence, *Phormio* 502-3. *CW* 11 (1917-8) 151.

The tradition of the study of Latin in modern education. *CER* 17 (1919) 279-86.

A Catholic classical conference. *Ib.* 18 (1920) 111-2; *CW* 13 (1919-20) 143.

The inductive and direct methods of teaching Latin. *CER* 18 (1920) 469-74.

The proposed classical investigation by the American Classical League. *Ib.* 19 (1921) 453-7.

The Classics in education. *Ib.* 20 (1922) 385-90.

Classical section. *Ib.* 428-31; 496-500; 551-6; 606-10.

Latin in the grades. *Ib.* 217-24.

St. Ambrose and Cicero. *PQ* 1 (1922) 1-2.

St. Augustine's method of composing and delivering sermons. *AJP* 43 (1922) 97-123.

Classical section. *CER* 21 (1923) 49-53; 108-12; 172-7; 239-43; 301-6; 371-6; 431-6; 494-8; 559-64; 513-8.

Classical section. *Ib.* 22 (1924) 44-8; 112-7; 171-6; 237-42; 298-304; 367-72; 425-8; 495-9; 557-61.

Classical investigation. General report *Ib.* 23 (1925) 269-74; 357-64.

Classical section. *Ib.* 43-8; 107-12; 174-9; 225-30; 233-8; 294-8; 299-303; 365-9; 430-4; 554-8; 626-31.

Classical section *Ib.* 24 (1926) 42-6; 106-10; 173-8; 231-300; 365-70; 418-22; 487-91; 549-53.

Early ecclesiastical literature and its importance to classical scholars. *Ib.* 521-8. Classical section. *Ib.* 25 (1927) 38-42; 107-11; 172-7; 363-7.

Early ecclesiastical literature and its relation to the literature of classical and mediaeval times. *PQ.* (1927) 102-10.

Introduction to F. M. Kirsch: *The Classics,* etc. Milwaukee 1928.

A study of patristic and mediaeval Latin, and its significance for schools and colleges. *CER* 26 (1928) 12-30, 88-97.

St. Augustine's *City of God*: its plan and development. *AJP* 50 (1930) 109-37.

The United States Education Mission to Japan. *C.U. Bulletin* 14 (1946) 2.

The Challenge to Catholic Colleges and their Graduates. *JRI* (October 1946) Vol. XVIII, 2. P. 162.

Workshop on College and Organization and Administration. *Higher Education,* 15, (1947) Vol. III, 14:9.

Adult Education—A Challenge to Catholic Educators. *C.U. Bulletin* 16:5 (March, 1949) pp. 6-9.

Sociology in the Program of the Catholic General College. *American Sociological Review* (June 1952), pp. 89-102.

The Nun and Research. *Benedictine Review* (Summer 1952), pp. 11-15.

Philosophy and Theology and the College Curriculum. *N.C.E.A. Bulletin.* (Nov., 1952), pp. 7-15.

The Catholic College. *The Small College Annual* (1955), pp. 8-9.

The Catholic University and the Affiliation of Sister Formation Institutions, *Sister Formation Bulletin* (March 1955), pp. 4-5

A Consideration of Some Phases of Social Work Education Today, *Proceedings of the 41st Meeting of the National Conference of Catholic Charities* (1955).

Why the Catholic University of America. *C. U. Bulletin* (1956).

GENERAL INDEX

A

Academic Senate, 13.
Accrediting agencies, 10, 252 ff., 280 ff.
Addresses on Special Occasions, 356 ff.
Adelphi College, 147.
Adult Education, 218, 221 ff.
Advisory Board, School of Social Work, 36.
Advisory Committee on the School of Engineering and Architecture, 277 ff.
Aeronautical Engineering, 274 ff.
Affiliation, 10, 193 ff.
Albert Hall, 21
Alter, Karl, 30 n.
American Association of Collegiate Registrars, 48.
American Association of Schools of Social Work, 270 f.
American Association of University Professors, 309 ff.
American Book Company, 213.
American Classical League, 402 f.
American college, 27
American Council of Learned Societies, 115.
American Council on Education, 215, 220, 258.
American League of Nursing Education, 138 ff.
American Library Association, 102, ff. 157 ff., 187
American University, 286.
Ancient Christian Writers, 388 ff.
Arbesmann, Rudolph, 376.
Architectural Engineering, 274 ff.
Architecture, Department of, 28.
Armistice of 1918, 9.
Army Air Corps, 22, 24.
Art, Division of, 160 ff.
Arts and Sciences, College of, 29, 31, 37, 39 n., 80 ff., 285.
Arts and Sciences, Graduate School of, 29, 89 ff., 100 ff., 285 ff.
Association of American Colleges, 258 ff.
Association of American Universities, 10, 31, 99 ff., 123, 254, 256, 399 f., 417 f.
Association of Collegiate Schools of Nursing 125 ff., 136, 139.
Association of Deans and Directors of Summer Sessions, 53 n., 215.
Association Guillaume Bude, 156.
Association of Professional Schools of Social Work, 36.
Assumption College, Worcester, Mass., 36, n.
Athletics, 301 ff.

B

Baltimore Urban League, 288.
Baptists, 387 ff.
Bardenheuer, O., Patrology, 399 b.
Barwick, Arthur R., 312.
Beckmann, Archbishop, 181 ff.
Behrendt, Leo, 170 ff.

Belgian government, 19.
Bellarmine College, Louisville, Ky., 365 n.
Benedictine Heights College, 60.
Bergman, Arthur J., 305 ff.
Bernadini, Monsignor, 142 ff.
Biberstein, Frank A., 276.
Bishop, Wm., 101 f., 182 ff.
Bisletti, Cardinal, 142 ff.
Bolling, George M., 25, 147.
Borden, Charles Fox, 51, 81, 323.
Boston, Archdiocese of, 9.
Bowles, Frank, 349.
Bowles, Gordan, 384 ff.
Boyce, Malton, 170.
Brady Hall, 70.
Brady, Leo, 164.
Brawner, Frances, 230.
Brother Amandus Leo, 279 ff.
Browne, Henry J., 315 n.
Bruce Publishing Company, 213.
Bulletins, for secondary and higher education, 195 ff.
Burke, John J., 270.
Burns, John, 346 f., 402 f.
Busch, Joseph F., 231 ff.
Butin, Romanus, 23, 25, 282 n., 292.
Byrne, bishop martyred in Korea, 391 ff.
Byzantine History, 19.

C

Cain, Harvey, 249.
Caldwell Hall, 21.
Callan, Josephine, 165.
Cambridge University, 225.
Campbell, James M., 37, 73, 83 ff., 121, 152 ff., 273 f., 323,
    351, 416.
Canon Law, 28, 30.
Capps, Edward, 21, 290 f., 309 ff., 405 f.
Cardinal Stritch College, 365 n.
Carey, Thomas Fabian, 162 ff.
Carrigan, Thomas, 89.
Carroll, Thomas S., 40 n.
Catholic Classical League, 346 ff.
Catholic Committee of the South, 61 ff.
Catholic Education Press, 210 ff.
Catholic Encyclopedia, 399 f.
Catholic Hospital Association, 138 ff.
Catholic Scholars, 425 ff.
Catholic Scholarships for Negroes, Inc., 289 ff.
Catholic School System, American, 11.
Catholic Secondary Schools, 268 ff.
Catholic Summer School of America, 66 ff.
Catholic University of America, Faculty of, 9, 10; Branches, 66; 125 ff.,
    255 and passim.
Catholic University of America Press, 210 ff., passim.
Catholic University of Puerto Rico, 353 ff.
Chicago Area Branch, 61 f.
Christian Brothers, 201.
Church, 11.

Gregorian Chant, 166 ff.
Griffin, J., 20.
Guamanians, 387 ff.

284, 293, 299, 303 f., 311, 316 f., 326 ff., 334, 395 ff., 400,
403 ff., 419, 422.
Ryan, John A., 97 ff., 234, 343.

S

Sacred Congregation of Seminaries and Universities, 65, 97.
Sacred Sciences, Schools of, 28.
Sacred Theology, 28, 30; School of, 141 ff.; Faculty of, 143 ff.
Sadlier Corporation, 213.
Saint Anthony's High School, 333.
Saint Augustine, 292, 373.
Saint Basil, 292 f.
Saint Benedict, College of, St. Joseph, Minnesota, 232.
Saint Benedict's Convent, St. Joseph, Minnesota, 231.
Saint Catherine, College of, 320 ff.
Saint Cyprian, 373
Saint Francis College, Loretto, 365 n.
Saint Gertrude's School of Arts and Crafts, 130.
Saint John's University, Brooklyn, 365 n.
Saint Louis University, 46, 138, 328.
Saint Michael's College, Winooski, Vt., 365 n.
Saint Thomas Aquinas, 294, 336.
Saint Vincent's College, Latrobe, 365 n.
Salve Regina Building, 161 f.
San Morrow Officers Club, San Juan, 354.
Saville, Thorndike, 272 ff.
Sciences, School of, 95.
Schneider, Joseph, 25, 50, 180 ff., 187.
Scholarships, Fellowships, and Student Aid, 248 ff.
Schopp, Ludwig, 375, ff. and note.
Schrembs, Archbishop, 171 f.
Schwitalla, Alphonse, 136 ff.
Scullen, Anthony, 276 f.
Secondary School Department of Middle States Association, 265 ff.
Secondary school system, 10, 266.
Secretary General, 10, 40 ff., Office of, 435.
Sellew, Gladys, 133.
Semitic Languages and Literatures, 25, 33; Library, 156.
Senior Colleges, Catholic, 10.
Seton Hall University, 365 n.
Seventh Day Adventists, 353.
Shahan, Thomas J., 21, 23, 24, 25, 75 f., 80, 117, 143, 149, 152 ff.
178 ff., 241, 299 ff., 303 ff., 311, 346 ff, 397 ff., 419 f.
Shanahan, Professor, 143.
Sheen, Fulton J., 67.
Shields, Thomas E., 50, 51, 69 ff., 190 ff., 230, 346.
Shimer, William A., 317 ff.
Siena College, 60, 62.
Sigma Xi, 317 ff.
Sister M. Agnesine, 170 f.
Sister Albania Burns, 78, 341.
Sister Aloysius Molloy, 119 ff.
Sister Angela Elizabeth Keenan, 344.
Sister M. Angelica, 346.
Sister Bernice Beck, 131 f.
Sister Catherine Dorothea, 238.
Sister Formation Conference, 71, 202, 338.
Sister Mary Frederick, 238.
Sister M. Inez Hilger, 231.

DAUGHTERS OF ST. PAUL

In Massachusetts
    50 St. Paul's Ave.
    Jamaica Plain
    BOSTON 30, MASS.
    315 Washington Street
    BOSTON 8, MASS.
    381 Dorchester Street
    SO. BOSTON 27, MASS.
    325 Main Street
    FITCHBURG, MASS.

In New York
    78 Fort Place
    STATEN ISLAND 1, N.Y.
    39 Erie Street
    BUFFALO 2, N.Y.

In Ohio
    141 West Rayen Ave.
    YOUNGSTOWN 3, OHIO

In Texas
    114 East Main Plaza
    SAN ANTONIO 5, TEXAS

In California
    827 Fifth Ave.
    SAN DIEGO 1, CALIF.

In Louisiana
    86 Bolton Ave.
    ALEXANDRIA, LA.

In Florida
    2700 Biscayne Blvd.
    MIAMI 37, FLORIDA

In Canada
    33 W. Notre Dame
    MONTREAL, CANADA
    1063 St. Clair Ave. West
    TORONTO, ONTARIO, CANADA

In England
    29 Beauchamp Place
    LONDON, S.W. 3, ENGLAND

In India
    Water Field Road—Extension
    PLOT N. 143—BANDRA

In Philippine Islands
    No. 326 Lipa City
    PHILIPPINE ISLANDS

In Australia
    58 Abbotsford Road
    HOMEBUSH N.S.W., AUSTRALIA